Group Homes and Community Integration of Developmentally Disabled People

Micro-Institutionalisation?

Group Homes and Community Integration of Developmentally Disabled People

Micro-Institutionalisation?

Janice C Sinson

Jessica Kingsley Publishers
London and Philadelphia

First published in the United Kingdom in 1993 by
Jessica Kingsley Publishers Ltd
116 Pentonville Road
London N1 9JB

Copyright © Janice C Sinson 1993

British Library Cataloguing in Publication Data
Sinson, Janice C.
  Group Homes and Community Integration of Developmentally Disabled People:
  Micro-institutionalisation
  I. Title
  362.2

ISBN 1 85302 125 3

1003492695

Printed and Bound in Great Britain by
Bookcraft Ltd., Avon

Contents

Acknowledgements

Grateful thanks are due to:

Dr Peter Davies, former head of the erstwhile Department of Psychology, University of Bradford (now relocated in the University of Leeds), and the technical and secretarial staff for facilitating much of the research contained in this book.

Professor Robert Naylor, Department of Pharmacology, University of Bradford, who inherited the author and provided a base from which to continue the research.

The Mental Health Foundation who funded and published the research into attitudes during the years 1984–8 to whom I am grateful not only for their financial contribution but also for their invaluable advice.

Sister X, Mrs F and Henrietta Reynolds who helped me to gain insights into their working worlds and with infinite patience accepted the constant questions and probing. As important was the help of their residents, who with such good humour shared their lives with me and my tape recorder.

The staff and residents of the ten group homes who so willingly gave the help and access necessary for all the assessment procedures.

Dr Denis Cook who facilitated the most enjoyable part of the research.

A particular debt of gratitude is due to Dr Peter Davies and Dr Norman Wetherick for their meticulous onerous and dutiful reading of the draft. The text is almost certainly the better for their amendments and possibly the worse for those that I tenaciously refused to take on board!

Dr H C Gunzburg, whose work has been a constant inspiration to those of us who struggled over the decades to find a way through the maze of 'mental deficiency', and a powerful influence in achieving reform. I have been particularly grateful for his personal encouragement and support.

Prolegomenon

The author has spent some 20 years in the field of learning disabilities. Initially 12 of these years were spent working for a local MENCAP and applying the new found theories of normalisation to the assessment and education of pre-school children. The salutary effect of a previous three months teaching nursery rhymes to teenagers in an inner city Junior Training Centre left her with an overwhelming desire to seek out the theories of normalisation and apply them from birth. The attempt appeared to be reasonably successful (Sinson 1973, 1975).

Despite the advancing knowledge and acceptance of the abilities of learning disabled children in the educational field, when concurrently the local MENCAP opened one of the first private adult community group homes in the country, they were accused by the local authority of wanting to create their 'own private lunatic asylum'.

Some of these MENCAP pre-schoolers went straight into mainstream education. However, some parents opted for provisions within the special education sector, usually in the old type schools for children with moderate learning disabilities. After up to five years of intensive pre-school training in the unit they were well able to hold their own in these environments. If one stays in a locality long enough, inevitably such babies become adults. Many of these same MENCAP babies are now confident and assured adolescents and young adults. Having benefited from the new and improved educational facilities, their eventual placement in the local mental subnormality hospital is no longer the only dreaded option for elderly parents. They look forward to the new independence they and their children will gain when the young adult moves on to a local community group home.

The author became curious to see the lifestyle of this new, confident generation and how normalisation theories had worked out in the community group homes. She decided to make a comparative evaluation of ten geographically disparate local authority group homes, away from the immediate locality, using an evaluative assessment tool which indicated to what extent a group home for people with severe and profound learning disabilities contributed to their social and personal development.

It was also possible to investigate whether managerial strategies helped the residents to maintain a level of reasonable independence compatible with normalisation theories. A separate assessment was made of two establishments in the non-statutory sector.

Unusually, the reader is presented with the conclusions at this stage, and invited to examine the supporting evidence contained in the following chapters. If the reader is to be the jury, then it is important to remember that the concern of the prosecutor is not to secure a conviction but to see that a correct result is obtained.

It was hoped that the investigation would find that the consequences of relocating people with learning disabilities into small community group homes could not be as detrimental as the consequences of large-scale institutionalisation. The evidence contained in many chapters indicates that in some respects, such as social life, relocated people may be worse off than they were in their larger institutions. This is also supported by the direct statements from relocated residents both in independent community housing and group homes. There is also clear evidence that in some cases residents achieve a far greater independence than was ever envisaged.

Chapter 1 contains the somewhat disturbing results of a national inquiry into community attitudes to mental handicap. Chapters 4 and 5 indicate that in the majority of group homes there may be very little difference between life in a large institution and life in a community group home. The author has defined this finding as '*micro-institutionalisation*'. The reader is asked to examine the ambiguity of the evidence presented in Chapters 6 and 7 with respect to normalisation theories and individual community relocation.

For the defence, Chapters 8, 9 and 10 show that given certain circumstances, exceptional results can be achieved in an institutional setting.

And there, temporarily, the case rests.

Part One

Approaches to Living

CHAPTER 1

Community Attitudes to Mental Handicap

At the time of this research the term 'mental handicap' was in common use and that of 'developmental disability' would not have been understood by the general population.

Many people are aware of the political, historical and legislative aspects of community care and acquainted with current literature which enthusiastically demonstrates the benefits of community care and the success of relocation projects from the point of view of both professionals and developmentally disabled adults. This chapter will present a perspective somewhat sparsely covered in the literature – the attitudes of the local community who may well one day be neighbours and unwilling participants in such community relocation schemes. The facts are drawn from two research projects covering the years 1984–8 funded by the Mental Health Foundation (Sinson 1985b, 1990) and a later study of 12 group home/hostels which included the two institutions discussed in the town and village (Sinson 1990). The people speak for themselves, the author merely transcribed their words from audiotape to print. Each quotation is typical of the majority view expressed. As such people are rarely featured in the ongoing debate their views go mainly unremarked and any literature search shows them to be, as yet, a neglected research area.

The implementation of the 1981 Education Act caused much thought to be given by professionals and parents to the integration of children with special needs into mainstream education. During an earlier research project investigating ways of integrating young Down's children from her own inner city unit into local mainstream playgroup, nursery and school provisions, Sinson and Wetherick (1980, 1981ab, 1982, 1986; Sinson 1985b, 1986) found that this new professional concern for the young child with learning disabilities in the integrated community had not filtered down to the parents whose own children would become classmates of the Down's children. In fact it became clear that most ordinary parents were unaware of these new liberal policies, and had negative feelings to many aspects of integration, particularly in rural areas. It appeared that rural parents had little or no experience of mental handicap and would strongly resist integration even at playgroup level.

The initial reaction of a group of rural Yorkshire mothers of pre-school children to the request that a local three-year-old Down's child should come into their homes with her mother to be videoed playing with their own children, ranged from fearful refusal to open hostility. To quote some parents' responses: 'It's not what it does to her now – but we have to think of the effect it may have on her in later life,'...'I wouldn't want one in my house – think of the mess,'...'My husband doesn't want our Mandy to risk it – catching it.' These responses were to an amiable Down's child from their own village. Due to such overt hostility it proved impossible to continue with the project in the rural area and because of this it was decided to investigate the apparently differing attitudes towards mental handicap of urban and rural mothers in Yorkshire.

Such open hostility had not been found in the industrial urban area of Yorkshire where the project was also being videoed. There was an easy interchange of children between the local playgroup and the MENCAP unit concerned. The playgroup leader brought down small groups of the playgroup children to be videoed playing with the MENCAP children and a local child from the MENCAP unit attended the playgroup two mornings a week. Parents willingly gave permission for their children to participate in the project and also welcomed the MENCAP children into their own homes to be videoed playing with their own children as part of the research.

With the help of the Mental Health Foundation it was possible to investigate the differing attitudes to mental handicap by mothers of pre-school children in these two urban and rural districts. The investigation was also able to explore the effect of integrating adult mentally handicapped people into a local community and to what extent external agencies (such as the church, the media etc) influence attitude change towards developmentally disabled people. The umbrella term 'developmental disability' is unhelpful in this context in that it embraces a full range of disabilities, from partially sighted to profound mental and physical handicap. Both communities had a local institution which catered mainly for adults with severe learning difficulties and fairly obvious clinical syndromes, many of whom were to be seen shopping and walking in the vicinity.

The Study Design
The Village
The village consisted of extended families who had lived and worked in the area for several generations, plus newcomers who had moved into a newly built private housing estate serving light industrial and engineering developments on the outskirts of the village. Social groups A–E

lived in the area which was served by a playgroup in the village hall, a first school, a church and two shops. There was no GP's surgery or clinic in the village. A hostel/group home for mentally handicapped adults was on the outskirts, close to the shopping centre in the next village. The bus stop connecting the village to this shopping centre was outside the hostel and also used daily by the hostel residents to travel to and from the local adult training centre in the nearby town.

The Town

The urban industrial area was surprisingly similar, also with extended families and up to three generations having attended the local Church of England first school in the area. The playgroup was in the church hall and on the edge of the area was a large Victorian ungated mental subnormality hospital.

This hospital had adapted two villas as independent training units for 12 residents who were part of the hospital community relocation programme. There was a similar mix of old cottages, council houses and a newly built private housing estate. Social groups A–E lived in the area which was served by a first school within walking distance. The area was also fringed with light industrial developments and engineering works. A shopping centre and health centre were within walking distance for most of the residents. Patients from the local mental subnormality hospital walked unaccompanied throughout the area and had access to all local services as did residents of the training villas and three people already relocated in a council house in the locality.

The People

A hundred mothers of pre-school children attending their local playgroups were interviewed, 50 from each area.

By chance, no doubt due to similar environmental opportunities, they were well matched for age, social class, religion and number of children. Thirty-two of the rural group and 35 of the urban group were born into the Church of England with 14 people in each area no longer attending church. Eight people in the rural area and seven in the urban area were Roman Catholics.

Extended interviews were recorded with the two playgroup leaders and also two mothers of pre-school Down's children in the rural area, to establish the effect of the local community attitudes on such families. These responses were not included in the main study.

The Method

Similar letters were given to all mothers by the two playgroup leaders asking if they would meet the author for a short time to talk about their attitudes to mentally handicapped children. Everyone was given the choice of being seen at home or at playgroup at a time of their choice and the letter contained a form to be signed and returned to playgroup. All the town mothers returned the forms and were happy to be seen by the investigator, the majority preferring to be seen at home. Only two of the village mothers returned their form and the rest had to be approached again and interviewed at the playgroup held in the village hall where there was a private room for these interviews. A minority of village mothers in outlying hamlets were seen at home.

Each mother was interviewed by the author for 10–15 minutes with the option of talking for longer if they wished. Permission was obtained to tape record the interview, which enabled the interviewer to code the answers on a pre-prepared sheet and keep note taking to a minimum. Mothers were told that the information would be categorised and used anonymously in the writeup and then the tapes destroyed. They all agreed to verbatim quotes being used on an anonymous basis and many mothers from both town and village offered to see the interviewer again if further information was required.

The Interview

Mothers were encouraged to discuss topics related to mental handicap in the following order:

The media – in an attempt to assess the effect of the media on people's attitudes to mental handicap mothers were asked if they could remember any programme on television about mental handicap or with people with learning disabilities in it. Currently a child with Down's syndrome was appearing in the popular 'soap' *Crossroads*. Similar questions were asked about radio, films, books, magazines, newspapers and colour supplements. A separate question was asked about a current case widely debated in the media where a father was awaiting trial for the murder of his Down's baby. Mothers were asked whether they thought he should be punished if found guilty.

Amniocentesis – leading on from the murder trial mothers were asked if they knew what amniocentesis was, whether they thought it should be available on demand, and whether they would have amniocentesis and a subsequent termination in the light of the results.

Adoption and fostering – mothers were asked if they thought Down's children should be available for adoption or fostering; if they would consider such an option either currently or if their sister died in childbirth leaving a Down's baby. Would they have such a baby fostered or adopted.

Experience of mental handicap – mothers were asked if they had any experience of mental handicap before they were 18 or in adult life and what effect the local institution had on their lives and that of the community. They were asked to categorise these as positive or negative experiences.

Religion – information was gathered on all aspects of religion, family churchgoing as both children and adults and also what their parents thought about mental handicap. These questions were asked after the question of amniocentesis as it was felt that if mothers did not know they were to be asked about their religion this would not influence their responses to termination.

The 1981 Education Act – the implications of the Act were explained to mothers who were then asked how they would feel if they arrived to collect their child (always named) from first school at the end of the first day to find that they had been sharing their desk with a Down's child. If the parent had persistently used the term mongol in the interview, the term mongol was used rather than Down's child. Mothers were asked to rate themselves on a scale of 1 to 5 as to how they would feel both *socially* and *educationally* – this division was made when it became clear that many mothers saw two distinct problems. The scale ranged from 1, where they would encourage the situation through to 5 where they would remove their child from school.

Attitudes to mental handicap – mothers were also asked to rate themselves on a similar scale of 1 to 5 denoting their own feeling towards mentally handicapped people, and in particular Down's syndrome. Ranging from 1 where they would not mind living with such a person through to 5 where they believed that all such babies should terminated before or at birth. The ratings for this scale were taken from the original statements of the rural mothers who originally refused to have a Down's child in the house. An additional scale of 1 to 5 was used to denote the interviewer's perception of the mothers' positive or negative feelings. This was used to counteract a not infrequent situation where a person had given consistently negative answers but rated herself totally accepting of mental handicap or when after the interview was completed, a mother would say 'Of course if I actually had one – I'd smother it at birth'.

Using data from the analysis of both the coded questionnaires and the open-ended interview tapes it was possible to establish the respondents' perceptions of mental handicap and to evaluate the effect of environment, familiarity and experience on their current attitudes.

The Results
The Media
The result of the effect of television was surprising in view of the considerable television coverage of many aspects of mental handicap during the previous year. Particularly disturbing were the 22 per cent of

people in the village who admitted turning off any programme about mental handicap – many others in the town and village would avoid watching such programmes in a family situation. Typical comments were:

> 'We don't tend to watch that sort of thing as my husband doesn't like it.'

> 'Having three normal children, the thought of watching abnormal children on TV is upsetting – that's why we don't bother watching on TV'.

> 'My husband says he doesn't like to watch them – he says they're not entertaining – they're not really – it's life. In the evenings it preys on your mind a lot more – it's not so bad in the afternoons'.

> 'My husband's very sensitive and he does get emotionally involved watching things on TV – so we don't watch programmes about learning disabilities because they upset my husband'.

So many wives blamed their absent husbands it became clear that they must have been speaking for themselves!

Only 27 per cent in both town and village could remember any programme they had seen in the previous year about mental handicap, with 21 per cent remembering the presenters rather than the programme content. This left 73 per cent in both town and village who had no recollection of any programme relating in any way to mental handicap in the previous year.

The Independent Broadcasting Authority's (IBA) viewing figures indicated that 40 per cent of Yorkshire viewers watched *Crossroads* each week. Only 2 per cent in this study spontaneously remembered Nina, the Down's child whose appearance was organised by MENCAP in collaboration with Central TV. After prompting, 20 per cent of the town parents had watched *Crossroads* at sometime – and after further prompting remembered Nina. Forty-two per cent of the village parents had watched *Crossroads* but again needed further prompting to remember the appearance of a Down's child. Nobody in either town or village had heard about the booklet produced by Central TV to go with the series nor would they have been interested to see it. A point made by most parents was that the early evening viewing time of *Crossroads* clashed with meal and bedtime routines of young children and hungry husbands. Many families said their parents and grandparents watched. It would appear that if MENCAP and Central TV had hoped to target families with children of a similar age as Nina – they actually excluded this age group by the timing of the programme.

Wober (head of research at IBA) points out that 'there are a number of studies which suggest that TV is a medium in which people tend to be involved at a relatively shallow level. This means, on the one hand, that there are higher ratings for enjoyment than impact, for the large majority of programmes: and correspondingly not much is learned' (personal communication 1985).

Only 12 per cent of people in both town and village remembered seeing or hearing anything about mental handicap in any other form of media coverage. These turned out to be people with a vested interest in the subject either by the nature of their work or family ties.

More revealing was the effect of the Louise Brown case where her father was currently waiting trial for murder. This topic was only featured in national news programmes on TV with no subsequent feature programmes. IBA's viewing figure for their Yorkshire sample indicated that the case was rated second in 'knowledge of the facts' and 'interest in the case' – to the miners' strike which was rated first in Yorkshire in that particular week. Several months later 96 per cent of both town and village mothers remembered the entire case and were able to discuss it in a surprising amount of knowledgeable detail. It would appear that news programmes, unlike others, are closely watched and also retain their impact.

Twenty-six per cent of mothers, equally divided between town and village felt the father should *not* be punished when he came to trial if he were found guilty of murdering his Down's child, as they would have done the same.

Typical comments were:

'I think they killed that child to put it out of a life of misery'.

'Not as severely as if he'd murdered a normal child'.

'I feel when I see them there should be something you can do – no he shouldn't be punished'.

Several mothers said that if they had given birth to such a baby at home they would have smothered it. However the recorded proportion who felt the father should *not* be punished should be higher as many people were ambivalent and decided he should be punished only after some very revealing comments such as :

'No – that's hard to say, me being an ex-policewoman – well I suppose he should.' (another ex-policewoman in the town gave a similar answer).

'He should be punished for covering it up – but not for doing it. It must be an awful shock having a mongol baby, and I can understand the woman doing it – if she'd had it and was depressed'.

'I don't think he should go to prison or anything – I don't really – well yes – I suppose you don't murder children – but until you've had one – you don't really know what he felt like'.

In marked contrast to these views were the minority of mothers who felt the father should be punished and were quite clear in their own minds that 'no-one has the right to take another life', invariably using those words.

Amniocentesis

The technique was explained to those mothers who were unaware such a test existed. Thirty-two per cent of village mothers had never heard of amniocentesis compared to 4 per cent of town mothers. Equally divided between town and village, 68 per cent would terminate a Down's child if such a test proved positive. Of the 32 per cent who would not terminate 9 were Roman Catholic out of a total of 15 such mothers. Eighty-eight per cent thought that amniocentesis should be available on demand, including all but 1 of the 15 Roman Catholic mothers. When asked about watching TV the majority of mothers referred to their husbands' wishes, but when considering termination of a Down's child no mothers suggested they would consult their husband before choosing to do this. In neither case were they asked about their husband by the interviewer.

Adoption and Fostering

These questions revealed attitudes to mental handicap in more depth than was expected as they gave mothers a chance to explore their own feelings in non-threatening imaginary situations. A number of mothers in both town and village said clearly and succinctly what the majority hinted at but were too inhibited to say. One example as to why a mother could not contemplate bringing up a Down's child sums up all the answers.

> 'My children are totally me – they're 100 per cent me – they're healthy, fit, and have all their bits and pieces – and its the reflection on yourself that hurts more than anything I think – its a mother's pride. The children are the pride and joy of my life and they have to be perfect. If at the time of birth there was something wrong – I couldn't accept that – you have to do what you think is right.'

There were also significant differences in attitudes to adoption and fostering between the town and village mothers. Three times more village mothers than town mothers thought Down's children should not be adopted or fostered. Twenty per cent of town mothers could contemplate adopting a Down's child against only 4 per cent of village mothers. All the mothers in both town and village seemed to feel that to give birth to a Down's child was an unacceptable 'reflection on (or of) yourself', that they could not comfortably talk about.

Experience of Mental Handicap

Early Experience up to 18 Years

The majority of mothers had little early experience of mental handicap. Of those that had, there was no numerical difference between the town and village mothers. Fourteen per cent of village mothers and 36 per cent of town mothers had experiences of mental handicap which they expressed as positive memories. Eight per cent of village and 14 per cent of town mothers had either unpleasant or embarrassing memories but these were usually influenced by their parents or other adults. The village was near a seaside holiday camp where most village children had their first experience of mental handicap.

Experience of Mental Handicap, 18 to Present Day

This question excluded any contacts with the local institution which was dealt with in a separate question. Forty-eight per cent of village mothers and 38 per cent of town mothers had no experience of mental handicap during these years and of these, 34 per cent of village mothers and 16 per cent of town mothers also had no childhood experience. There was little difference between the town and village mothers in terms of current experience. Fifty-two per cent of village mothers and 62 per cent of town mothers had some experience but it was difficult to accept their own ratings as to whether these were positive or negative experiences. Many of the contacts were limited to seeing friends or family with handicapped children or adults every two or three years. It appeared that mothers had tended to stop visiting such families. This response was typical of most.

> 'A friend of mine had one – she was the most beautiful baby you ever saw – but I felt ashamed to take my daughter to see my friend afterwards. My daughter was a year younger than it – and she could d do more than it could do at two to three years old. It was so heartbreaking – I didn't know what to say – and I wouldn't tell her what mine was doing because I knew hers couldn't do the things. I felt terrible. I felt so guilty I had a perfect child and I was embarrassed and sorry for them because they were such nice people. It was a peculiar feeling.'

Contact with Local Institution

The answers to this question provided the key to the difference in attitude between the town and village mothers. There was substantial difference between the two areas in terms of contact with the local institution with 88 per cent of town mothers having contact compared to 22 per cent of the village mothers. This indicated that 78 per cent of the village mothers had no contact with the mentally handicapped adults who were part of their community compared to only 12 per cent of town mothers.

The Village

Although over three-quarters of the village mothers claimed to have
neither knowledge of nor contact with the residents of the local group
home/hostel, it became clear from the answers to the questions that the
residents used both the local shopping centre and bus service with the
rest of the surrounding villages. Subsequent LOCO analysis of the hostel
(see Chapter 4) demonstrated that they went to at least one village pub,
used the local bus daily, walked through the shopping centre to the bus
and also visited the doctor's surgery. Not surprisingly, the 22 per cent
of village mothers who had contact with them confirmed this:

> 'Yes – they go shopping. You find they talk to you – so you talk to them.'

> 'When I worked at the pub quite a lot of them came in the early evening.
> They lived just round the corner. They seemed all right, they would all
> talk to you.'

> 'When I go to the shops there's a lot there. I have a dog and they come
> and talk to the dog. I tie the dog up by the door and when I come out
> they're talking to it.'

The only place where mentally handicapped people were not seen was
the village church – or any local church attended by the village mothers.

A possible explanation of the 28 per cent of mothers who claimed to
have no contact with the residents of the hostel was given in reply to the
same question by the village mother of the three-year-old Down's child.

> 'I saw them going to the training centre over the back there – they used
> to get off the bus – a lot them. I'd see them when they got off the bus. I
> was afraid of them. I was ignorant – I didn't know – because they have
> deep voices and they shout a lot. I thought that if you encouraged them
> they would do something. I would cross over the road many a time if
> I thought they were going to come near me. Absolute ignorance when
> you think about it. I'd avoid them whenever I could. I never spoke to
> anybody about it really. It was something within me – a fear came up.
> The ones that shouted frightened me.'

After 20 years of this frightening daily experience in the village, this
mother had a Down's baby herself. It may well be that many other village
mothers experienced similar feelings which they too did not discuss with
their friends.

The Town

Of the 88 per cent of town mothers having contact with the local
institution, 22 per cent had reported unpleasant experiences causing
negative attitudes to mentally handicapped people at earlier times in
their life. Only 2 per cent of these people now considered they had
negative experiences with the local institution with which they had
considerable contact. Twelve per cent of mothers reported negative

contacts, and as can be seen from their answers, these are not unreasonable reactions. It was surprising that more mothers did not define their experiences as negative. The responses from these town mothers gave some indication how attitude change to mental handicap can take place in one generation. It also became apparent from the answers that the church, playgroup, Sunday school, Church of England first school, Church Young Wives group, Mothers Union and the local mental subnormality hospital were inextricably linked, accounting for the high proportion of mothers having close contact with mentally handicapped adults through the church. These links can be traced throughout the mother's answers as can the development of the new attitudes that they are passing on to their children:

'We've been here years. Seventeen years ago you didn't use to see anyone – but now you do.'

'When I lived here as a child they used to walk through and we called them loonies – now I always say to my children – "you shouldn't laugh".'

'You do see more of them – you see them walking down, you see them at the shops. I don't feel anything because it's just normal.'

'They're out in the community these last 15 years more than they were 30 years ago. So you do see them about a lot more. I'm teaching my children – I hope – that they're not to be afraid of – not to be laughed at – not to be abused.'

Many mothers who had originally been frightened by or of mentally handicapped people wanted their own children to grow up without this fear:

'We're anxious that they won't grow up having this fear. We're keen on them to see that the handicapped people are around and you can't just push them out of sight.'

'It's good for the children to see them and then they're not afraid when they get older.'

'We see them every day and I always talk to them – it doesn't bother me now though – living here. I would like the kids to grow up not with the fear I had.'

'We see them every day – there's one particular one – John, all the children know him. I think its good for them because it's not going to be a shock for them if they suddenly meet some handicapped people – they're not frightened of them. We went up to the summer fair they have (at the hospital) and I think if you took a child that had never seen any handicapped people they'd be really frightened... Most people know at least one of the patients that come from there by name. I think myself I'd have been frightened as child.'

The hospital summer fair is also opened by the local May Queen chosen at the Sunday school. The church Young Wives Group take their annual pantomime up to the hospital as do the local dancing school.

> 'My children did a show – and I wasn't worried about them going up there and doing a show. To begin with I was a bit worried about them doing it. My oldest child – because she's older – thought about it and said 'I don't want to go'– they came up to her in the street. Then I did the pantomime and it was fine – went down great. I related this to the children and then they weren't bothered.'

Many of the mothers who were born in the area and grew up with the hospital and its patients seem to have adopted a surprisingly protective attitude to them.

> 'I've got used to it – I'm not bothered about it. Occasionally what I assume are the more difficult patients do get out – and you get the orderlies rushing round here in white coats saying "Have you seen a chap looking like so-and-so – he's eating somebody's flowers" but everybody round here – from what I can tell – seem to take it as part and parcel of this community. Even the teenagers stay and talk to them.'

> 'We have a lady who comes round – she wants my little boy to be her little boy. I actually gave her a photograph. She used to say "Can I take the baby for a walk?" poor soul – I was worried before I got to know her. We used to talk regularly at the gate. When she first called she actually had her hands on the pram – that frightened me. She explained they won't allow her to have babies in hospital and she said "I want this baby." I said "You can't because she's my baby." I brought her into the garden to see the baby and gave her a photograph. I think with having the hospital here everyone shows a bit of responsibility.'

> 'We have one boy in particular who exposes himself and plays with himself. He's allowed to wander out in all weathers and at all times – I do get cross about that. They turn his trousers back to front. It's not that he's doing it – that doesn't bother me – it's the fact that they allow him out.'

> 'It's been throwing it down and he's still out.'

The few mothers who reported unpleasant and difficult incidents which they construed as negative experiences did so with an ambivalence and choice of words that were unexpectedly protective and often their attitude appeared to be far from hostile and negative.

> 'We've had quite a lot of trouble. We've had patients walking into the house – we do have to keep the front door locked. One had eaten everything in sight in our garden. We found a man upstairs sitting on the bed reading a magazine. It bothers me, especially with the children. I don't like the children playing in the drive. I keep them in the back... The ones that live close to the hospital you never see them shouting and calling the patients names. The times we've rung up we've been met

with a negative attitude and my husband's had to go up and get a nurse to come and get a patient. They're so short staffed. I feel it's terribly wrong and something should be done about it. I feel they've not enough staff. It's not fair.'

'I just hope they only let the ones out who are responsible – I do wish they wouldn't let that one out who exposes himself now and again.'

'There was an incident and we got very worried by this. He was touching you and coming up to the children. I was very wary. He used to follow us. It used to worry us especially when she was a baby – but there again I was a new mum and I was worried. I've seen him since but now it doesn't worry me.'

Many mothers reported similar incidents but seemed to regard them in a positive way.

'I was sitting here one Sunday evening – about 6 o'clock. My husband was out and suddenly I saw this little man walking up the pathway and he just carried on coming into the house. The children were terrified. He had a pound note and he held it out to me and said 'cigarettes' So I said 'No – I'm sorry – we don't have any – we don't sell any here'. So I just turned him round and said 'Back you go' and he went out of the door. I'd have been terrified of that before I moved here.'

'They'll pinch your shoelaces off your garden gate if you tie your gate up – and then sell them to other people. John used to scare me – sometimes he used to come in the back garden and peer through the kitchen window. Now he doesn't bother me.'

Most mothers seemed to be aware of the difficulties patients had in communicating.

'You can see what difficulties they have – if they want to ask you something they can't express themselves. They do come to the door but it doesn't bother me.'

'They stand outside the school gate and the children talk to them – and outside the club. If you're new to the area you might bother – but not if you live here.'

The hospital had started its relocation programme and moved three patients out into a house on the local council estate who were supported by a keyworker living in an adjacent street. Many of the young local mothers were involved in helping the residents adjust to life outside the hospital.

'A lot of voluntary workers from the Church come and help. We've a lot of people who are churchgoers in the Hospital League of Friends and particularly the Mothers Union, they all help out. I think the mentally handicapped have become more accepted.'

'They're no trouble – no bother. The lady sits in her garden just the same as anyone else.'

'I don't think people know how to react to them. They should ask them in and let the old ladies make them a cup of coffee. They should make them go in. I think that would change a lot of attitudes if people met them. I don't think people bother too much about it here – it's a fact of life – the hospital.'

These were the views of the young churchgoing mothers. There also existed a vociferous lobby of older residents campaigning to put the patients back in their villas, preferably behind securely locked doors.

The Church

The Town

It appeared that several mentally handicapped patients also went to church just like everybody else.

'They like to sing – you can't hear anyone else when they're singing. The congregation find the place for them. They turn round and you know they want to know which page it's on – and you find them the page and they sing away in a different tune and nobody takes any notice – they can't read so they just la along and make their own words up. Nobody takes any notice. You get the odd child who sniggers when they first go in – but once they're used to it they don't. The patients are very staunch – they go morning and night. I sometimes wonder if they know what they're actually there for. If anyone complained I would just turn round and say "Well find a church that suits you". Two were confirmed recently – they were quite old.'

The playgroup leader who also ran the Sunday school gave a very clear picture of the place of the church in the community which was also reflected in the answers of the majority of mothers.

'A fair few playgroup mothers go to Young Wives. Somebody in the church Sunday school is chosen as May Queen – she opens the hospital garden party usually. The Young Wives take the pantomime up to the hospital when they've done it in the church hall because they love to watch it up there. More than a third of them lived here as children and went to the church school. I went there, my mum went and my grandfather and my great-grandfather. Our children went there. There are two schools our children go to here, the church school and the other one. There's always been competition between the two. When the 11 plus examination came in – the church school – although its old and small got a good reputation. The 11 plus results were high and it's only a one class intake. Every year they take 30 new children. The new private estate wasn't there when I went to school – but once they built it everyone wanted to go to the church school. A lot of them were local people who started off in a terrace house and then moved to new houses

– specially as their parents still lived in the area. They created a demand far greater than the school could cope with – then the vicar stepped in and they also brought into the system a church middle and high school – so as to go to the Church of England Senior School. If there was a choice between a child whose family were practising Christians and went to the church…you would get told no. Most of the people who come to me (the playgroup is in the church hall) do go to the church. Our vicar goes down to school every Wednesday and takes the morning assembly. Someone from the church runs the men's society…They have a darts and dominoes night and they go round places too. Most of their children go to the church school. I think you find that most people who are doing something are more than likely part of the church. A lot of this churchgoing is to get your children into the Church of England Middle School as our First school children are given preference. I would assume the children have to be baptised to go to school. I did the Sunday school up to this year. Most of my children in playgroup come to Sunday school as well. In most villages the centre of the village is the Church. I know they say the pub is the centre of the village – and a lot of the time it is – but I do think the church has a big pull. The hospital vicar comes and works at our church – he takes over when our vicar goes on holiday – when he retired from the hospital he still wanted to keep his hand in.'

Such a circuitous route to community integration was hardly envisaged in the various legislative measures implemented over the past five decades where the role of the church is barely mentioned.

The Village

There was very little mention of the church in the village mothers' answers, but several of them had part-time jobs in the local pub and it appeared that the pub played a larger part in village life than the eight-hundred-year-old church. The darts, pool and domino teams all operated from the pub. In view of the total lack of reference to the church it was necessary to approach the husband of one of the village mothers who had been church warden the previous year. He confirmed that the church seemed to play only a small part in village life and even the vicar lived in the next village and was responsible for both churches. There was no Mothers Union and the Young Wives group was not confined to churchgoers and met in local homes. Only one or two families with young children attended the Sunday morning church service which was held at 9 am to enable the vicar to get to his own village service at 10.30. Seventy-five per cent of the congregation were senior citizens. There was no church school in the village and the first school was highly thought of by all village mothers regardless of their social class or educational status.

There had been talk of closing the centuries old church and amalgamating the two congregations in the new church in the next village where the vicar lived. It seemed that all the social, educational and spiritual needs of the young village mothers and their children could be met without reference to their local church. Somewhat surprised by the contrast between town and village and in view of the fact that the proposed new amalgamation of congregations would geographically favour the group home/hostel, the interviewer attempted to find out whether their absence was a feature of hostel or church strategy. The vicar was unavailable to comment but his wife indicated that the local people liked nice quiet services and her husband could not subject his congregation to any possible disturbance. It seemed it would not be appropriate for the hostel residents to attend church services but the vicar did occasionally visit the hostel.

Educational Integration

Social Integration

The idea of social integration of Down's children during the first years at school was accepted by 82 per cent of mothers with little difference between town and village. Mothers defined social integration as playing in the playground, going swimming and other non-educational activities. Only eight town mothers did not want this type of integration and three of those were involved in the teaching profession. The town mothers stressed the benefits to their children – a fact not considered at all by the village mothers.

'It wouldn't bother me, I think its a good thing. J would grow up with more understanding.'

'I think it would help her accept in later life.'

'It would be nice to mix in the playground with withdrawal classes for learning.'

Those village mothers who were not prepared to accept social integration in the first class at school took a far more emotive view than the equivalent negative town mothers.

'It would be disgusting.'

'I think they should be put down at birth.'

'They'll pick up bad habits.'

Social integration was only rejected by 18 per cent of all the mothers, equally divided by social class.

Educational Integration

Educational integration was far less popular than social integration. Sixty-eight per cent of village mothers did not want educational integration even in the first class, nor did 48 per cent of the town mothers. All these mothers would have considered removing their child from the school had there been a Down's child sitting close to their child in class. One perceptive village mother spoke for all the mothers:

'If it's your child that's handicapped you want the best for it, but if it's your child that's not handicapped you obviously want the best for her too.'

In social class AB five out of six village mothers and five out of nine town mothers did not want educational integration. Seven out of nine mothers involved in teaching would not accept educational integration at first school for their own children. Their comments appeared to be both rational and informed as seen in these examples.

'You'll have the real problems of a slow learner keeping others behind – I see it from the teacher's point of view. I have slow learners and at the other end children who are very bright. I have trouble finding my bright ones something to do while I cope with my slow ones. In a traditional teaching situation… I think there will be problems.'

'It's already very difficult for a teacher to teach all the things she wants and I personally see it as an extra strain on the teacher. I don't think anybody would benefit – to have that mongol child – with that one teacher in that classroom all day. I personally think that all the children would suffer.'

'Obviously a child like that does need special help – I should have thought. I would be very wary as the parent of a handicapped child – they wouldn't get the special help they need… It depends how much damage it was doing to my child. If I thought she was being held back, I would consider it.' (Taking her own child away from school.)

The other mothers in both town and village that could not accept educational integration fell into three distinct groups, those who were concerned about the teachers' ability to cope, those who were convinced their children would be 'held back' and the many village mothers who had friends in the nearby town where there had been some attempt at integration – of which these are two typical responses:

'My niece goes to school in B and there's a mentally retarded girl in her class. I'm not sure if it's an experiment – and they refer to her as 'the naughty girl'. She has tantrums and screaming fits and many of the teachers can't cope with it – they've never been trained to cope with it. My niece refers to her as 'the naughty girl' which I think is a terrible shame. She should perhaps be in a special school – but her parents would probably disagree. I think a mentally handicapped child needs a lot more attention.'

'There's a child in his class who's badly brain damaged. John comes home and says she does silly things – she scribbled all over the board – she didn't know which was the girls' toilet and which was the boys'.

Both town and village mothers were equally concerned with the teachers' ability to cope with such a situation and all expressed similar doubts.

'She'd want more attention than the rest of them and it would put a strain on the teacher. No – I'm not happy about it – no.'

'You only have one teacher – they learn them at one rate – I'd hate to think my child was held back because of a mongol child.'

'Her education would suffer if the teacher had to give the Down's child a lot of attention. I feel strongly about that.'

'A mongol child doesn't understand – they'd be messing up trays – I couldn't accept them sitting next to her.'

Many parents in both town and village felt the whole situation would be distasteful and unacceptable.

One of the overt ways this difference in attitude between town and village mothers manifested itself was in the effect on mothers of pre-school Down's children in both areas. In the town, local Down's children had been to playgroup, church and Sunday school. Whatever problems the parents of these Down's children experienced were not related to neighbourhood or family acceptance. This was also demonstrated by the enthusiasm of a hundred town parents of pre-school children who had willingly allowed Down's children from the author's MENCAP unit to be videoed in their own homes, playing with their own children, and had also allowed their children to be videoed at MENCAP in a similar exercise.

As such a different situation existed in the village it was decided to interview the two mothers of pre-school Down's children who lived in the village and who did not feel able to take their children to the local playgroup, church or Sunday school and establish whether the prevailing hostility had any effect on their lives. One young mother had a two year old Down's boy and a baby girl and was obviously happy with both children. Her account of visiting the village toddler group showed a less confident approach than would have been expected from her assured manner at home.

'No – I didn't tell the playgroup leader he was a Down's baby. No – I didn't tell the other mothers – they just kept looking at him – and someone told them one week when I wasn't there. There are some people that turn away from him.'

This mother only went a few times to the group and now no longer attends. When the interviewer questioned the playgroup leader she insisted that there had never been any Down's or other handicapped children in either toddler or playgroup. When the Down's child mother was asked about her own family, of whom three generations live in the village, it was a similar story.

'There are some people that turn away from him – there's one in my family that does it. She'll say 'hello' to me without even looking at him or anything. She'll walk away – and that's my own grandmother. She just doesn't want owt to do with him. She's cut herself off from all of us now – she doesn't want anything to do with any of us.'

The second mother was in her forties and had two older children and two younger ones by her second marriage. She and her husband were Jehovah's Witnesses and accepted their three-year-old Down's son as a welcome addition to their family. They were very involved with house-to-house preaching in the locality and she took both her children with her and also to church meetings in the nearby town. Her initial feelings to mental handicap are given on page 20 and in the light of her own experience she appreciated the feelings people in the village might have about her son during her preaching sessions.

'I would explain he was a Down's, and they were amazed. I think they think that they'll be really grotesque and unable to communicate or associate with normal people. Going round on our house-to-house work he goes in his buggy – we meet people. Some have had another look and said "Isn't he gorgeous". I think if you can meet them – young or old – it breaks down the barrier.'

Neither mother would accept the prospect of educational integration in the village school although the three-year-old had been offered a place in a nearby first school. Both had arranged for their sons to go to the special school in the nearby town at three years old. The younger mother justified her decision on educational grounds: 'He won't get treated right by the teachers and he won't get the education he needs to bring him on'.

The older mother had no social life in the village and spent most of her time in the nearby town with her church, where her son already went to the special school. When asked why she had not accepted the place offered in a village school she replied: 'He'd be better – he'd have normal children to associate with – he'd be better in that sense'. Nevertheless she felt she'd be happier with him at a special school in the town where her church and social life were. These two cases not only illustrate the difference in attitude to mental handicap in the town and the village, but also the failure of any influence by outside agencies on the parents of both handicapped and non-handicapped children.

Further Investigation into Attitude Change

In the light of the Yorkshire results and with the help of the Mental Health Foundation, a national study was mounted to see if similar attitudes would be replicated in geographically disparate urban and rural areas. If so, an attempt would be made to apply action research techniques to a proportion of the sample to see if it would be possible to modify proven negative attitudes to mental handicap.

The Association of Health Centre and Practice Managers agreed to participate in the project and circulated their 650 members with a questionnaire designed by the author to give geographical information about their practice area and local statutory and voluntary provisions for mentally handicapped people. It also elicited the willingness of the practice to co-operate in the main study by the display of a poster in the waiting room and the selection by age, sex and social class of ten people from the waiting room to complete a questionnaire during the week the poster was displayed. A full statistical treatment of the various complexities of the design and results can be found in Sinson (1990).

The practice managers returned 156 questionnaires (25 per cent was an acceptable response in the light of the more usual 2 per cent uptake experienced by medical magazine editors and journalists) indicating that 19 per cent of urban and 20 per cent of rural practices would not be prepared to take part in any further research. From those that were willing, 50 urban and 50 rural practices were twinned to provide comparable geographic and demographic data to that found in the Yorkshire study.

The People

Eight hundred people were selected on the basis of age, sex and social class to conform as far as possible to the distribution expected in the general population. Sixty-six per cent of the sample were Church of England, 14 per cent Non-conformist, 9 per cent Roman Catholic and 4 per cent subscribed to no religion. The health centre provided 720 responses and a further 37 Scottish people, 10 English adults and 33 students were selected to balance the sample.

The Method

The 50 urban and 50 rural Health Centres and surgeries (representing practices in every area health region in England, Wales and Scotland) were sent a pack containing a poster and five male and five female questionnaires with full instructions for their use to ensure a representative sample of the general population. The questionnaires were similar to those given to the Yorkshire sample but were filled in by the respondents without interviews. Extra questions related to the poster, knowledge of local voluntary organisations and whether the respondent would be prepared to talk to the author about the completed questionnaire at a later date. Two super imposed posters were selected from those supplied by MENCAP for the project. Both had recently appeared in London Underground stations. The poster was displayed in the public area of the waiting room during the week the questionnaires were completed.

Seven urban and 21 rural practices refused to display the poster, GP's being concerned that the public would be distressed by having their attention drawn to mental handicap, and consequently withdrew from the investigation. The remaining 72 participating practices returned their 720 completed questionnaires for analysis. Of these, 536 people unequally distributed over disparate geographical areas were prepared to talk to the interviewer.

Analysis of the Postal Questionnaire

The media – yet again only 16 per cent of the total sample could remember any media coverage on mental handicap in the past six months, of these 9 per cent also recalled newspaper, 2 per cent film or video, and 1 per cent radio coverage. There were no significant geographical, male/female or age differences in these results. Again, these people were those with a vested interest in mental handicap.

Attitudes to mental handicap – in this analysis 67 per cent of the total sample believed that the father who killed his Down's baby did not have the right to take his baby's life. The remaining 33 per cent had no doubts about the ethics of killing a newborn Down's child, seeing this as 'mercy killing' and an extension of amniocentesis. The views of the Yorkshire group on amniocentesis were replicated nationally with 64 per cent of males and 63 per cent of females prepared to terminate a pregnancy after a positive amniocentesis equally distributed in urban and rural areas. Of these a higher proportion of Catholics were opposed to termination than in the Yorkshire sample, possibly reflecting the older age range of the sample. Less than half the sample were aware of the technique of amniocentesis or its availability and there was little evidence of the younger age groups showing increased knowledge.

Experience of mental handicap – the national results broadly replicated the Yorkshire sample with 39 per cent having no contact with mental handicap at any time in their lives. Of the total sample 38 per cent had some contact before they were 18 and half of the national sample had contact during their adult life. Twenty-eight per cent were still in close contact with mentally handicapped people. Statistical analysis showed some association between positive experience of mental handicap and a positive attitude to educational integration. However in the proportion of the sample with no experience of mental handicap three-quarters of social group D/E were against educational integration compared to 63 per cent of the other social classes. There were no other male/female, urban/rural or geographical differences.

Educational integration – the questionnaire was designed so that the first question on integration would elicit a general response and 61 per cent responded positively in favour of integration. An intermediate question as to whether the respondent would like his or her own child to sit next to a Down's child in school obliged people to consider the implications of integration and was answered positively by 64 per cent of the re-spondents. The original question about integration was then repeated with a highly significant change in response in all ages and social classes, only 48 per cent of the sample were now in favour of educational integration. Of the 24 teachers in the sample 18 would not accept any form of integration while the remaining 6 would only accept social integration in school. Of the total sample 73 per cent wanted mentally handicapped children to be educated in special units on the same school site with 47 per cent preferring separate special schools. The numerical discrepancy was caused by a percentage of people opting for special units for the majority but separate schools for severely disabled children such as those with cerebral palsy. A regional difference was the Scottish preference for separate special schools. This was based on the histori-cally differing policies of Scotland and England. Scottish educational integration had been common between 1930 and 1950. Many people had had direct experience of mentally handicapped classmates and were concerned at the treatment meeted out to them by their peers. There were vivid memories of such children having their heads held down lava-tories flushed by their classmates and similar practices.

MENCAP poster – only 58 per cent of people reported noticing the poster although it was displayed in a prominent position in every waiting room and was dramatic enough to result in 28 practices withdrawing from the study. A small percentage of the sample added comments on the poster of which 16 per cent were favourable and 21 per cent forcefully negative. In the light of these results the poster was placed for a week on the daily notice board of the sub-group of students in the investigation. Only 25 per cent reported noticing it although they consulted the board daily.

Action Research

When used as a process action research involves: systematically collect-ing research data about a system relative to some objective goal of that system: feeding these data back into the system: taking action by altering selected variables within the system based on both the data and hypothesis: evaluating the results of actions by collecting more data...These actions typically entail manipulating some variable in the system that is under the control of the action researcher. Later a second static picture is taken of the system to examine the effects of action taken. (definition from Harre and Lamb 1983)

In the action research stage of the project 31 per cent of the sample drawn from Scotland and most area health regions in England and Wales were interviewed by the author. Before the interviews the 254 people were sent a specially prepared information pack derived from literature supplied by both MENCAP and the Down's Syndrome Association (DSA), a simple crossword and acrostic for younger members of the family. a personal letter from the interviewer offered the opportunity for people to meet local handicapped children and adults with their families with the address and phone number of their local DSA contact as supplied by the association. These 254 people were visited in their homes or on practice premises and audiotaped interviews were carried out in which the original questionnaire was repeated and seven additional questions asked. The interviews took place between six months and a year after the respondent had completed the first postal questionnaire.

Responses
The analysis of the audiotaped interviews showed that only 3 per cent of people changed their original responses in stage two of the study and when questioned these changes were for positive reasons i.e. since doing the original questionnaire they had either met a handicapped person or noticed their local MENCAP for the first time. Even under stringent questioning nobody changed any of their original responses but appeared to enjoy discussing their opinions. The effect of the information pack was negligible in that although 50 had read the literature, only 27 per cent remembered anything about it when questioned. In comparison 51 per cent of the same sample had read and remembered a recent AIDS leaflet. Nobody had any wish to meet any families with handicapped children or adults nor were any contact made with the DSA as a result of their literature.

Part of the interview time was spent explaining the currently prevailing policy of relocating previously hospitalised mentally handicapped people within the community. Of the total sample 68 per cent were prepared to live next door to such people but there was a significant difference in response between the north and the south of the country. Following the rise in house prices in the south of England far fewer people were willing to live next door to such people and considered the proximity of mentally handicapped people would lower the market value of their property. There were also isolated reports in the northern urban conurbations of houses acquired for community relocation of hospital patients leading to the immediate sale of several other houses in the same street. One of these was in a well-researched relocation project which made no mention of this problem in the ensuing publications!

Overview

The initial investigation had started out to see if there was any real difference between the attitudes to mental handicap of mothers of pre-school children living in two particular urban and rural areas of Yorkshire. Superficial enquiries had indicated that the two groups held very different attitudes and statistical analysis of the responses proved that the initial impressions of hostility had been well founded. Over half the village mothers demonstrated consistently negative attitudes to all aspects of mental handicap compared with less than a quarter of town mothers (full statistical data can be found in Sinson 1985b). An interesting feature of the total social class distribution was the large proportion of social groups AB who could not accept the integration of mentally handicapped individuals either in schools with their own children or as neighbours in their own community. In view of the results, the surprising factor was the similarity of the two groups of mothers who were chosen at random from the playgroup population. This similarity indicated that the difference in attitude between town and village was dependent on external influences in each neighbourhood. A more subtle problem is to define which influences – and why?

There was evidence that the media had little influence on either group. Both areas had an institution that encouraged residents to wander freely about the locality. However, in view of the lack of contact demonstrated in the village, it would appear that it is not sufficient for living units to be geographically sited in a community unless the professionals involved make some direct attempt to educate and involve the local community. In view of the comments and complaints of the town mothers, who were basically sympathetic and protective towards the residents, it would also seem necessary for all hospital residents to be part of an ongoing social competence programme. This would ensure that those people moving freely in the community remained suitably dressed and continuously aware of acceptable social behaviour. If such goodwill is to be maintained they must not become a source of embarrassment to the community.

Both areas had a church, thriving in the town but barely surviving in the village, and initially this seemed to be the key to the differences. It was however a key of some complexity and in many ways unrelated to straight forward Christian worship. The social structure of the town was intimately related to the social life of the church whose young congregation wished their children to benefit from being educated at the church first, middle and high schools. This contrasted with the village where the majority of the diminishing congregation were senior citizens who probably had much in common with the town lobby of older residents campaigning to put the patients back in their villas.

When it came to the problem of integrating mentally handicapped children into their local school, although social integration was acceptable to the majority of town and village mothers, the majority were firmly opposed to educational integration. In the light of their acceptance of most aspects of handicap within the community it was particularly disturbing to find that the town mothers differed little from the village mothers in this aspect. It might be assumed that this opposition derives from ignorance and that when mainstream education becomes a reality for mentally handicapped children, people's attitudes will change. That this is clearly not the case can be seen from the comments of those village mothers who had experience of mainstreaming.

A feature of the active social life of the many groups within the town church was that it gave people close positive links with the hospital. These links have been found to exist in other areas as can be seen in later chapters. Such links are not the sole prerogative of religious belief and could in fact be formed by any non-religious group with a similar propinquity and community spirit. However, in this situation they resulted in a change of attitude from negative to positive within the community, and a wish to ensure the next generation accepted these positive attitudes to learning disabilities. It would have been helpful if the hospital had capitalised on this good will and their professional staff had made some attempt to educate the local children. Both the Sunday school and church first school would have been sympathetic to such an approach. Further enquiries as to the lack of information in local surgeries and waiting rooms elicited the information that the mandatory post graduate training for general practitioners in the Yorkshire area did not include any input in learning disabilities. It was also clear that little or no attempt had been made to advise or inform parents of non-handicapped children about the existence and extent of the 1981 Education Act .

The Yorkshire study had shown clear urban/rural differences with an urban effect associated with the proximity of church and hospital which was not found anywhere in the national study. This was therefore assumed to be unique to that chance propinquity of institutions in a particular time and place. However, a further study described in later chapters indicated that the church offered important social opportunities for some residents. In the most successful private group home (Greystones) the village church also provided outside employment.

Although the national study was designed to allow analysis in terms of age, sex, social class, urban/rural, north/south and religious differences there was little general evidence of any of these differences in the final results, except for the two regional differences which were based on well-founded social, educational and economic factors.

As in the Yorkshire study, the effects of any type of media coverage of mental handicap were negligible and the action research part of the national study replicated these findings. There was clear evidence in the audiotaped interviews that, as in Yorkshire, the majority of viewers would usually avoid watching TV programmes concerning mental handicap in a family viewing situation. Many of the sample who noticed the MENCAP poster had their attention drawn to it by the questionnaire. There was however clear evidence that a higher proportion of rural people were initially aware of the MENCAP poster. In 39 geographically disparate health centres visited during this stage of the study, although information about many community facilities was displayed, MENCAP and DSA were not among them. Stockdale and Farr (1987) when showing posters produced by charities dealing with the handicapped, found that posters which tried to inspire pity were not as successful in attracting funds as posters that portrayed the handicapped in a more positive light as did the Down's Society posters. These received a much more positive response than MENCAP posters even though the nature of the handicap was similar.

The attempt in the national study to target people by attracting their attention to various facets of handicap, utilising information provided by both MENCAP and DSA could be seen to be a total failure. The 50 per cent of the sample who actually read the information only did so because of the impending interview, and the 27 per cent demonstrating any recall of the facts were yet again those with some involvement in handicap due to family or work circumstances. There was evidence from the audiotaped interviews that much media coverage of mental handicap is designed to elicit pity (often with a view to fundraising) and had served to re-inforce outdated stereotypes rather than increase society's awareness of the considerable abilities of some mentally handicapped people. A telling example of this was the BBC 1 QED programme *The Foolish Wise Ones* which presented highly gifted autistic adults and children in a positive light and on equal terms with their peers. This was the only media coverage mentioned by name in the national study and remembered up to a year later by 7 per cent of the sample. The programme also had the second highest QED audience rating of 8 million viewers and the highest audience index of 90 per cent.

In the light of these somewhat discouraging and politically emotive findings, a recent British literature search was even more dispiriting.

Current researchers would appear to have shied away from this particular aspect of community relocation and present brief and conflicting findings buried deep within their studies of successful relocation publications. Alaszewski and Ong (1990) in their Liverpool study have reservations about the present role of the community in relocation of people with learning disabilities and suggest that for such projects to be successful they must find better ways of involving the community: 'Surprisingly, there are few studies of the ways in which the informal sector can be mobilised'. They cite Shearer (1986) who described a survey of 35 adults with mental handicap living independently in Avon and found 'that isolation and loneliness remain a major problem' and that 'to live in the community is not automatically to be a part of it'. McConkey's (1987) lively and accessible Irish trilogy which takes all the mystery out of research methodology, giving ready-made packages and guidelines for holding public meetings and in other ways educating local communities on the relocation of developmentally disabled people, tends to use and replicate earlier MENCAP findings to good effect. However the negative aspects of the problem are barely touched upon.

Accepting the dearth of British literature, possibly the most realistic appraisal of community responses to the integration of people with learning difficulties can be found in a study of 43 group homes in Boston, USA (Seltzer 1984). The small homes of up to six relocated hospital patients had been in operation for two or three years. About half of them had encountered opposition from their local community regardless of the ages or levels of disability of the residents or whether local people had been involved in setting up the project. Homes which had initially established themselves with a 'high profile' programme of public meetings, use of media and open houses were significantly more likely to have encountered opposition. A frequent finding (replicated in the author's British national study) was the fear that adjoining property would decrease in value.

It seemed clear from the results of both the Yorkshire and national investigation that many opportunities for educating the public were being lost through lack of foresight and basic general research into the practicalities of the problem. There is evidence that specialist media programmes go unremarked by the members of the public who demonstrate consistently negative views towards mental handicap. Likewise public meetings and attempts to educate the target communities merely serve to reinforce these negative views. It is to be hoped that more thought will be given to the plight of ordinary citizens caught up in the wake of liberal policies for which they are totally unprepared. Like the developmentally disabled – they too must be prepared for community integration.

CHAPTER 2

Historical and Legislative Origins of Residential Community Care in England

Readers may prefer to omit or return to this chapter, the function of which is to acquaint the general reader with the origins of community care. The general reader may also prefer to read it at a later stage for further clarification of the more interesting parts of the text!

Historical Background to Community Care

In 1793, Pinel, Physician Superintendent of the Bicetre Hospital in Paris, removed the chains from his patients and taught his colleagues to look upon insanity as a disease rather than a manifestation of demonaical possession affecting only the wicked. In doing so he enabled French humanitarian psychiatrists to start a series of reforms which spread throughout Europe, substituting the concept of disease for the contemporary theory of demonaical and supernatural possession of the insane. Itard's (1798) study of the wild boy of Aveyron initiated the first practical scientific study of both medical and psychological aspects of learning disabilities in Europe. By 1828 his pupil Seguin had established the trainability of these so called 'idiots' in a school founded for them in Paris. By 1840 the news of this humanitarian movement had crossed the channel and the need for provision for English idiots was recognised by the philanthropist Andrew Reed, who expressed the view that the training and care of such people was a suitable cause for 19th-century patronage. Due to his efforts the first English asylum for idiots was founded at Park house, Highgate which became a charitable institution under the patronage of Queen Victoria and the Prince Consort. This rapidly expanding institution opened a further charitable annex in Colchester in 1849 to train the inmates in simple mechanical skills.

The Victorians, with their strong moral codes and paternalistic views embraced the idea of asylums for vulnerable sections of society. Particularly as they served the dual purpose of caring for such people while isolating them from the rest of society in palatial purpose-built buildings which were sited well away from the rest of the community. This alienated, segregated world of mental subnormality merely served to increase the fear and re-inforce the prevalent myths that had grown up around such people, perpetuated even in the newly industrialised society. A tribute to the structural quality of these edifices is the fact that in 1991 many of the developmentally disabled residents awaiting relocation in the community still inhabit the same buildings.

The British Royal Commission of 1904 made the first attempt to determine the incidence of mental handicap and the possibility of providing some form of community care, being appointed 'to consider the existing methods of dealing with imbeciles, feeble minded or defective persons not certified under the Lunacy Laws'. (In view of the changing nomenclatures used to describe people with learning difficulties over the years, the contemporary usage of the period will be adhered to.) In 1908 the Commission recommended the creation of a system which would enable mentally defective people to be trained by some friendly authority and their relatives supported by help with the necessary constant supervision where possible. Failing this, mentally deficient people were to be detained and treated in a similar way to Wards of State. The investigation reported an incidence in the general population of 4.6 per thousand who were likely to need special educational or institutional care, however, due to the methodology used it is difficult to determine the true incidence of mental subnormality from this estimate. A more accurate estimate was provided by Lewis (1929) for the Departmental (Wood) Committee, who found 8.7 persons per thousand to be mentally defective with the categories idiot, imbecile and feeble-minded being roughly in the ratio 5: 20: 75.

The 1913 Mental Deficiency Act acting on information supplied by the 1908 Royal Commission established a network of large 'colonies' for mental defectives who were said to need institutional care. The Act also attempted to support those families who preferred to keep their relatives within the local community by requiring their local authorities to provide daily occupation and supervision, which was the genesis of our present day Adult Training Centres. The National Health Service Act (1948) reinforced the concept of the mentally handicapped as being diseased by changing the name of the colonies to hospitals. By 1954 a Royal Commission was appointed to enquire into all aspects of existing legislation governing the certification, care and supervision of mentally ill and mentally defective people. It recommended in 1957, that treatment and care for these patients should become similar to that provided for patients who need treatment and care for physical diseases. Compulsory powers should only be used in the interests of the patient's own welfare or the protection of others. The 1957 Royal Commission is widely held to be the earliest reference to community care. In fact, its recommendations were little different to preceding inquiries and legislation.

What was different was the determined and rapid implementation of new mechanisms to affect such a transition, which resulted in the 1959 Mental Health Act. At the same time the Lunacy and Mental Treatment Acts of 1890–1930 and the Mental Deficiency Acts of 1913–38 were repealed.

Yet again the 1959 Act introduced new, less specific, terminology and definitions of both mental illness and mental defect. The term 'mental disorder' was introduced to cover every kind of disease and deficit of the mind. As Penrose (1972) points out: 'The result is somewhat confusing for 'disorder' suggests (and is used to designate) acute illness and insanity rather than intellectual defect.' The emphasis was on freeing mentally handicapped people from legal detention in hospitals and encouraging 'local authority services' to provide day and residential care for people who did not now need hospital treatment. Residential care took the form of accommodation provided in residential homes and hostels. However as the Wagner Report (1988) points out:

> In practice the large hospitals continued to be the main providers of accommodation outside the family home. Local authorities developed some facilities in the community and appointed Mental Welfare Officers to make routine visits to the family homes. a few residential homes, or hostels, appeared here and there. There was, however, no wholesale move from hospital care to community care. (p.128)

The 1960s were characterised by a series of media investigations into staff misconduct and poor conditions in the long stay hospitals, while the number of mentally handicapped people admitted to these self same institutions actually went on increasing. By 1969, 56,000 mentally handicapped people were living in hospital. There was a general feeling voiced by Lee (1969) on behalf of MENCAP that 'the government had not only failed to promote community care, but had not even ensured minimum standards in the hospital system'. Against this background of discontent with a declared aim of accelerating 'the shift in emphasis from care in hospital to care in the community' the 1971 White Paper *Better Services for the Mentally Handicapped* was published.

Legislative Background to Community Care

Historically the approach to people with mental handicap has been twinned with a variety of restrictive legislative procedures designed to protect them from an insensitive and often fearful public. This view was finally challenged by the 1971 White Paper which committed people with mental handicap to a new policy of community care by stating that 'mentally handicapped children and adults should not be segregated unnecessarily from other people of similar age nor from the general life of the community' (DHSS 1971).

Over the past two decades, dogged by financial restraints, political policy has moved painfully slowly towards implementing such ideology. Now into the third decade there is still no cohesive or unified policy of community care for developmentally disabled adults although the 1990 NHS and Community Care Act is expected to be fully implemented in 1993 (NHS and Community Care Act 1990). As yet there is no overall national strategy of either deinstitutionalisation or community integration for the considerable number of people still in hospitals, hostels and large group homes who are caught up in the wake of these liberal policies. A review of both legislation and research in the field since 1971 serves to highlight the administrative disorganisation, fragmentation and ad hoc programmes adopted during this lengthy procedural delay.

Better Services for the Mentally Handicapped outlined the policy that services for developmentally disabled people should follow to achieve specified targets over the next 15 to 20 years which would shift the balance from hospital to community care. In principle this should have been achieved with the ease with which the 1970 Education Act withdrew the responsibility for the education of mentally handicapped children from the Ministry of Health and gave it to the local education authorities (DES 1970). The Warnock Report estimated that by April 1971 24,000 children in junior training centres and special care units, 8000 in a hundred hospitals and an uncertain number at home or in private institutions had ceased to be treated as mentally deficient and became entitled to special educational provision on similar lines to their peers who already attended the 16 types of special school catering for the specific needs of the blind, deaf, physically disabled etc (Warnock 1978).

Nationally, teacher training courses were set up to train newly specialised and well-qualified teachers in special education until such time as the training of teachers in special education could be integrated into the ordinary initial teacher training. Combined with these were conversion courses for diploma holders already in posts in junior training centres and two postgraduate teaching courses giving a PGCE in special education, which were overwhelmed with applicants holding degrees as diverse as psychology, physical education, maths, music and speech therapy. A financial incentive for teachers considering training in this new field was the special education allowance on top of the initial starting salary. Four hundred new schools were formed and 42 per cent of the 1974–5 and 33 per cent of the 1975–6 special school building programme budget was devoted to Educationally Subnormal (ESN) places. Within a very short time the special education field had a large body of well-trained professionals to implement the new provisions. Within ten years the 1981 Education Act had opened the way for the integration of children with special needs into their local community mainstream educational provisions to be educated alongside their brothers and sisters if their parents so wished.

The progress of this new generation has been punctuated by a series of political and philosophical publications initiated by interested parties in both government and independent sectors but the period was also characterised by the lack of practical implementation of these developing strategies. By 1975 Barbara Castle, Secretary of State for Social Services, publicly conceded that financial restraints had contributed to the lack of progress and established the National Development Group for the Mentally Handicapped (NDG), chaired by Professor Peter Mittler, to advise ministers on the development and implementation of policy. A consultative document followed in 1976 which yet again affirmed the government's commitment to moving resources from institutional to community care (DHSS 1976). Simultaneously joint finance was introduced to provide new funding for collaborative projects between the health and social services. The 1976 sterling crisis effectively imposed budgetary restraints ensuring that regardless of the prevailing philosophy of community integration, the reality was tenuous. By 1978 the NDG reported to the Secretary of State that they 'were not satisfied that enough people are being discharged to local authority services' and that 'more attention needs to be given to people in hospital that could make use of community services, and who deserve a greater share of community resources than they have so far received'. They also noted that the discharge rate was still only reducing the hospital population by less than 2 per cent a year and that 1300 new admissions to mental subnormality hospitals were still being recorded annually. With some asperity the report challenged the current provision by suggesting: 'we think the time has now come for a specific commitment by each RHA, AHA and hospital to reduce the number of hospital residents and for local authorities to enter into a planned commitment to provide services for those who no longer require hospital services' (NDG 1978). Historically twinned with these publications was the influential Jay Report (1979) and the 1980 DHSS progress report on mental handicap which concluded that almost a decade after the publication of *Better Services* very few people had in fact been moved out of institutions and community provision remained far from adequate.

The Jay Report still remains the foundation for current models of care, unequivocally advancing the philosophical standpoint that mentally handicapped people had similar rights to the rest of the community to live as normal a lifestyle as possible in the least restrictive environment and to be fully supported by the relevant services. The report also outlined the environmental expectations that mentally handicapped people should have from good residential care 'where personal competence and personal identity were continually strengthened' and insisted that residents should not be merely passive users of the services provided in the new community settings. The 'Home Life' code of practice stated the view that residents 'should be involved as much as possible in making decisions concerning the way in which a home is run'.

The next decade from 1980 to 1990 was characterised by a series of DHSS reports and consultative documents restating the original message of *Better Lives* and attempting to find financial means to accelerate the implementation of community care while trying to move responsibility and resources from health to local authorities and from large institutions to small homely units (DHSS 1981a, 1983, 1984b, 1987). A detailed policy analysis of this period can be found in Booth *et al* (1990).

Two decades later there are only a few well-documented pilot projects, mainly initiated with central funding of 15 million over four years during the mid 1980s to demonstrate the practical applications of these policies. The Audit Commission (1989) assessed the community care services of 50 local authorities and highlighted some major problem areas. It appeared that 60 per cent of the combined local and health authority budget was still locked up in hospital provision to be released only as and when the residents were relocated in the community. Sixty per cent of local authorities had not yet been able to reach agreement on financial and practical arrangements for such relocation and half of the 50 authorities assessed had not yet relocated any residents into the community. Such lack of initiative has conspired to ensure that the currently available network of group homes and hostels have remained the main relocation option, thus reinforcing attitudes of institutionalisation.

Critical responses to the official documents were provided throughout the decade by independent agencies such as the Independent Development Council, the National Development Team, MENCAP, People First and the King's Fund Centre. *An Ordinary Life* (King's Fund Centre 1980) is the most influential independent working paper of the two decades and pursues a vision of community care containing the principles on which most of the effective pilot research projects have been based. The report stated that the goal was to see people with learning difficulties 'in the mainstream of life, living in ordinary houses, in ordinary streets, with the same range of choices as any citizen, and mixing as equals with the other, and mostly not handicapped members of their own community'.

For the grassroots multidisciplinary force with whom the practical implementation of community care policy rests, the key publication over the past two decades has been the Wagner Report which was an independent review of residential care commissioned in December 1985 by the Secretary of State for Health and Social Services to assess 'what changes, if any, are required to enable the residential care sector to respond effectively to changing social needs: and to make recommendations accordingly' (Wagner 1988). Titled *Residential Care: A Positive Choice* the report expands the policies enshrined in the Jay Report, viewing residential provision as being a positive experience in which 'the needs and wishes of the user must be paramount' The report indicated that it was written not only for politicians, policy makers and practitioners in the field of residential care, but addressed to a far wider audience 'for the quality of residential services affects, directly or indirectly, almost the whole population'. Accordingly it canvassed a wide range of views from service users which are detailed in the second part of the inquiry *Residential Care: The Research Reviewed* (Wagner 1988). The committee noted with regret that they 'failed effectively to reach people with mental handicap and mental illness' but nevertheless managed to take extensive evidence from both carers and service providers in both these fields.

The Wagner Report pointed the way to a new vision of residential care for mentally handicapped people which would only be achieved by a set of clear aims, shared philosophies and common values running throughout all provisions to be implemented and adhered to consistently by all staff in their daily work. Effective leadership by senior members of staff with both basic and advanced staff training was particularly stressed. One of the clearly stated principles was that 'Living in a residential establishment should be a positive experience enjoying a better quality of life than the resident could enjoy in any other setting'. Also recognising (as did the Jay Report) that this can only be achieved by 'access to the full range of community support services.'

Privacy of the individual was regarded as basic to the implementation of community residential care and 'a room of one's own where one may live as one pleases' was stressed as both a matter of principle and design. To this end it was suggested that the current group home and hostel system, replacing hospital provision, with its 'buildings-based service' was inflexible and incorporated many features of hospital life in both architecture and organisation. The report was critical of the day-rooms, long corridors and out of bounds kitchens staffed by separate domestic and catering staff, all duplicating familiar hospital regimes, but there was also an ambivalence about the existing new hostel provision of single rooms:

> Providing individual space it was assumed, would lead to people expressing their individuality. This, as Gunzburg points out, (Gunzburg 1982) may not be enough. Private space is not the same as 'a personalised space which has been moulded, furnished and adorned

to spell laughter and fun'. If no thought is given 'to loneliness, to anxiousness and lack of human closeness' then that prized single room all too easily becomes an 'isolating cell'. (Wagner 1988, pp.135–6)

The recommendation for people with mental handicap stated unequivocally that: 'Education and training for young people with mental handicap should aim at enabling them to live with minimum support in ordinary housing' – hedged with the caveat that this population is among the most vulnerable in society and as such, their alternative environment has to be 'proven and apt'. The DES would seem to have facilitated this philosophy by the rapid advance in special educational provision over the two decades. The following chapters should go some way to indicating the successes and failures of this approach to community integration.

Into the third decade after *Better Services*, the advent of the NHS and Community Care Act (1990), due to be fully implemented by 1993, has led to a considerable shift in the ground rules. From 1993 local authorities will assume full responsibility for co-ordinating community care provision for people with learning difficulties. From 1990 hospital closures have been halted with no further closures being approved unless proven alternative services are in place. Due to current economic stringencies some authorities are currently undecided whether to halt all relocation plans until 1993, whereas some are rapidly resettling as many residents as possible before the Act is fully implemented.

We also have a new generation of young confident developmentally disabled adults, some of whom have been educated alongside their peers in mainstream educational settings, many of whom have graduated to specialised courses in colleges of further education from their special schools, now poised to leave home to enter this brave new world of community integration which is so far singularly unprepared for their arrival. Alongside them are an older generation of less fortunate institutionalised adults in long stay mental subnormality hospitals and a population of ever ageing developmentally disabled adults who are currently living in hostels and large group homes. There are now estimated to be between one and one and a half million people with mental handicaps in the UK, 30,000 of whom (in England) are still living in NHS institutions.

Contemporary Residential Provisions Within the Community.

As policies of reform have strengthened, the provision of residential accommodation within the community has suffered the same nomenclatural confusion as the ever changing terminology for people with severe and profound mental handicap.

However, bricks and mortar remain immutable and in political and financial terms they have to be used in their existing forms – regardless of euphemistic name changes. Large purpose-built hostels are a feature of the existing pattern of residential services and although the residential numbers are now reduced, the environmental pattern of living for the residents has changed little over the years.

The Wagner Report (1988) lists the five categories of residential provision for adults with mental handicap as being hostels, group homes, ordinary housing, residential accommodation for people with 'special needs' and private and voluntary homes. It then confuses the situation by stating: 'This is an artificial distinction and there is considerable overlap between categories... The recent history of projects for people with profound handicaps and challenging behaviour involves the use of ordinary housing. And "group homes" are usually "ordinary houses" too'.

Hostels

Hostels are the main providers of residential care for people with mental handicap. The Social Services Short Committee Report (1985) was critical of existing hostels, concluding that their 'institutional feel' made them 'a pale reflection of hospital wards, transplanted almost intact to the community'. This seems a far cry from the original 1971 White Paper concept which offered the term 'home' rather than 'hostel' because it was thought to convey the homeliness of a domestic family environment. Each fully staffed home was to provide a permanent place for up to 25 residents, each with their own single room. This immediately became the accepted architectural model for such residential care.

There has always been some ambivalence about the aims and objectives of such 'hostel/homes' which has increased as social policy became more community orientated. Are they now, as originally envisaged, to provide permanent homes or to be domestic training grounds to promote yet further independence and gently ease the residents into even smaller units in the wider community? Current practice often results in such living units attempting to provide a permanent fully staffed institutionalised home for some residents, an ineffective independent-living training for a few selected residents, and somewhat inhospitable short-term respite care for others. The study of 12 such institutions in later chapters explores this problem.

Group Homes

Group homes are generally accepted to be living units of indeterminate size that provide permanent accommodation for smaller groups of people with learning disabilities who require some staffing input according to their needs and abilities. Some have permanent arrangements for staff to sleep on the premises each night, others require a more relaxed daily supervision by 'keyworkers', some have a judicious mixture of both types of care. Some group homes have evolved from the training-units within larger hostels and are regarded as their satellites looking to familiar care staff for continuing support. As Wagner (1988) indicates 'In their traditional form, group homes provided early examples of small-scale domestic living for groups of fairly able people who needed only domiciliary support'. By definition these residents could hardly be drawn from a population of hospital residents with profound or severe learning difficulties.

A more realistic contemporary definition of group homes is provided by Gunzburg (1990)

> GROUP HOMES: in this context the term refers to 'hostels', 'half-way houses', 'family group homes' etc. usually catering for groups of adults in excess of the size of a family unit, and with full staffing during the day and mostly during the night as well. These group homes may include special training facilities for a small proportion of residents, but the majority do not receive full or even part time training on the premises. To some extent there is a risk that the size, constitution and management of Group Homes will make them liable to become displaced hospital ward units of institutions. (p.3)

Ordinary Housing

Ordinary housing would appear to be a purely architectural definition. Staffed and unstaffed group homes, co-residences where people with severe and profound learning disabilities share residence with co-tenants drawn from the local community, satellite houses attached to larger hostels and small scale research projects, all avail themselves of ordinary houses.

Residential Accommodation for Adults with Special Needs

This terminology would appear to have its origins in the 1971 White Paper's assumption (supported by the 1978 NDG Report) that people with severe and profound multiple disabilities would still need specialist hospital service and treatment from the NHS. It became a useful service definition for funding pilot research schemes to establish the relocation needs of this particular group of long-term hospital residents. The 1984b DHSS Study Team Report, although expressing a preference for such residents to be relocated in ordinary housing which could be 'rented or bought and adapted to meet the needs of those with restricted mobility' also saw the need for small purpose-built residential units run by local health authorities.

The Independent and Voluntary Sectors

The Warnock Report is ambivalent about the involvement of the private and voluntary sectors in residential provision for the mentally handicapped adult population and limits discussion to the less favourable aspects of such provision by citing the Social Services Committee Report (1985) as viewing the sheltered therapeutic communities like Steiner villages as selective and segregationist and by citing the Independent Development Council's (1984) view that 'voluntary homes may be high quality, flexible and innovative but are not necessarily so, and in private homes, the level and quality of services is based on the profit motive rather than on considerations of need' – they would seem to be taking an unnecessarily dismissive view in the light of current government provisions.

In the same year as the Wagner Report a more reassuring view was presented by Renshaw *et al.* (1988) in their detailed study of the Department of Health's Care in the Community demonstration programme. The Personal Social Services Research Unit, University of Kent (PSSRU) was commissioned to monitor and evaluate the 28 pilot projects aimed at moving people from hospital into the community. Eleven projects were set up for 350 people with learning difficulties of which 4 schemes were either totally run by the voluntary sector or the residential provision was by the voluntary sector.

Much of the pioneering work in community care for adults with learning difficulties has been achieved by the various charitable organisations. Alternative therapeutic communities set up by Steiner and L'Arche accepted relocation of young adults from institutional care many years before such relocation became public policy.

In 1954 the first Steiner Village Community in England was formed, although Konig originally founded the Camphill Movement for the care of mentally handicapped children and adults in Scotland in 1939. By the 1971 publication of 'Better Services' the Steiner movement already provided places in their five therapeutic community villages for 280 adults, mainly with severe learning disabilities, who lived alongside their co-workers in small family homes training to work in their self-sufficient communities. Their philosophy was far from insular as Roth (1972) pointed out in their journal: 'For many, the village is a place of learning in order to be independent and to work, to mature and to adjust socially – but then, after a longer or shorter time villagers may experience the need to pass on to different conditions: hostels, outer employment, even "digs"'.

Both Robinson (1988) and Williams (1988) develop valid and interesting arguments around communities such as L'Arche and Steiner which to some extent challenge the currently fashionable doctrine of 'normalisation'. Robinson suggests that our society 'provides a very unwelcome environment for anyone with mental handicaps' and that if the option of exercising alternative choices were available to them some of this minority population would prefer an alternative lifestyle, than that offered by our attempts to institute 'maximum feasible normalisation'. Although our concept of normalisation would see this as segregation contrary to the hoped for integrated community care policies, 'it will be a segregation necessary to produce a counter lifestyle which may offer a better quality of life to some people, rather than a segregation to hide mentally handicapped people away' (Robinson 1988).

Williamson (1988), by regarding people with learning disabilities as an oppressed minority develops a parallel argument suggesting that 'one important strand in the struggle against oppression is the formation of autonomous groups'. She outlines three strategies usually pursued by such minority groups and their application to adults with learning disabilities. Strategy one is for 'integration into the world as it is', which implies that the individual has to change to fit into society, rather than society changing to fit the needs of the individual. This strategy has obvious and inherent difficulties for a population that can never fully adapt due to 'their own incapabilities'. Strategy two is 'withdrawal from society into a separate culture' represented by such therapeutic communities as Steiner and L'Arche which stress 'the positive attributes which they, as an oppressed group, share against the negative attributes of the outside world'. The drawback to this strategy is that it 'does not require of society that it confronts its own prejudices'. Strategy three requires the individual 'to enter the world and change it' which is recognised to present a Herculean task for this particular oppressed inarticulate minority group.

A political factor not to be overlooked is that individuals accepting relocation in the independent and voluntary sectors currently attract benefits from central government. This removes much of the financial burden from their local authorities.

CHAPTER 3

Assessment and Normalisation

As shown in Chapter 2, over the past 20 years attitudes to developmentally disabled people have changed as the traditional 'medical model' of care, which saw mental handicap as an incurable medical problem, has been gradually supplanted by a multi-disciplinary developmental approach. This more recent approach, pioneered simultaneously in 1969 by Nirje in Scandanavia and Wolfensberger in America is characterised by a normalisation model which takes 'an optimistic view of the modifiability of behaviour, and usually does not invest the differentness of the retarded person with strong negative value. Even if severely retarded, he is perceived capable of growth, development and learning' (Wolfensberger 1976). Deinstitutionalisation, normalisation, community care and mainstreaming have been the enthusiastic slogans of this new age.

Rose-Ackerman (1982) highlights the oversimplicity of this approach when it comes to translating these slogans into policies which have to accommodate conflict. Inevitably, in such wide-ranging reforms, conflicts of moral and financial interest arise which are not helped by the reluctance of the general public to share the enthusiasm of a small group of professionals who are acting on behalf of a very small percentage (currently estimated at 2 per cent) of the general population. Chapter 2 illustrated that when reform is finally achieved the community may not yet be ready to implement it and in many cases provides a hostile and unwelcoming environment. Clarke and Clarke (1987) conclude that; 'Currently under the rubric of "normalisation", quite unrealistic goals are being set. Over-optimism may be as dangerous as the pessimism of the past'.

Wolfensberger first derived the theory of normalisation from sociological concepts of deviance. Traditionally mentally handicapped people had been perceived as deviant by virtue of their innate characteristics and clinical syndromes. In the days when standardised measures of intelligence were both fashionable and obligatory, professionals could be reasonably precise about such definitions. The American Association of Mental Deficiency (AAMD) defined mental retardation as 'substantially subaverage general intellectual functioning which originates during the development period and is associated with impairment in one or more of the following: (1) maturation, (2)learning, and (3)social adjustment' (Heber, 1959) Subaverage was indicated by an IQ of at least two standard deviations below the mean which was currently assumed to include all people with IQ70 and below. Severe retardation was defined as an IQ between 20 and 35 and profound retardation below IQ20. 'Intellectual function' was defined in terms of responses to objective tests, 'developmental period' was accepted as childhood to 16 years, with 'learning ability' being defined as the acquisition of achievements during these years. 'Social adjustment' was defined as the ability of adults to maintain themselves in community living, employment and conformity to accepted social standards. Such definitions appeared internationally acceptable.

More recently, in *A Search For Definitions* (1991), the British Psychological Society (BPS) recognised the ambiguity of the current confused terminology in England, Scotland and Wales and the lack of any standardised operational criteria to define learning disabilities. Recent legislation has provided us with an umbrella category of 'mental impairment and severe mental impairment' to describe people who are 'liable to detention as a result of a particular combination of loosely defined intellectual, social and behavioral characteristics'. There are two separate categories differing only in severity with respect to 'development of mind', 'impairment of intelligence' and 'impairment of social functioning'. The report stresses that for the profession on whom it falls to assess such individuals 'there are no operational criteria provided to guide decisions concerning severity, which can be classified as either "incomplete or arrested" or "significant or severe" when applied to intellectual or social functioning. Adults classified as "severe" are exempt from their personal community charge if provided with a certificate by their general practitioner (GP) who is the doctor responsible for primary care in the community. However the various legislatory acts give little guidance to GPs other than advising them to seek information and guidance from colleagues in other professions, or from carers'.

The BPS express their concern about the usage of identical terminology for quite different legal purposes. As there could be potential confusion over the meaning 'of the term severe mental impairment depending on to which Act reference is being made, it is important to be clear whether one is referring to mental health or local government legislation when using the term'. 'We are greatly concerned over the implications for the person so classified for one legal purpose having restrictions placed upon them in other areas of social and legal functioning e.g. the exercise of rights in relation to marriage, sexual relationships, making a will and voting'. The BPS suggest that 'close monitoring of these potentially devaluing effects be carried out'.

The guidelines issued by the BPS regarding the definition of mental impairment and severe mental impairment reflect the earlier AAMD recommendations that the IQ cut offs remain IQ55–69 for mental impairment and IQ54 and below for severe mental impairment. They suggest that these should only be quoted 'in the context of psychometric analysis and a sound technical knowledge of the uses and limits of assessment methods' which should only be undertaken by skilled professionals. However, they recognise a catch 22 situation by admitting that 'Unfortunately there does not currently exist a precise psychometric solution to these criteria'. They note the existence of a 'selection of assessment strategies that offer descriptive statements, of which some are amenable to statistical manipulation'. However the four scales listed as illustrative examples in their advisory document bear little standardised relationship to each other and often sample slightly different areas of performance.

The BPS would appear to advise a return to the presently unfashionable strategy of using psychometric analysis to map general intellectual functioning within the mentally impaired adult population in terms of the normal distribution and suggest the use of the WAIS-R (Wechsler Adult Intelligence Scale – R) to achieve an operational definition of significant impairment (IQ55–69) and severe impairment (IQ54 and below) for people of 16 years and over, with the proviso that for 'certain minority groups, culture-fair tests might be used to supplement the WAIS-R'.

Normalisation

Wolfensberger adopted the sociological perspective that suggested that once an individual was thus labelled as deviant by current methods of psychometric analysis he conformed to a group stereotype in the eyes of society and so experienced loss of status and social value while acquiring the ensuing social stigma. One of the tenets of the normalisation principle was the emphasis on breaking down large institutionalised groups and relocating retarded people into either individual or very small living units within the community; and by doing so reducing their contacts with other retarded people. Being within the community they could then be perceived by society as individuals involved in activities that stressed their positive image and highlighted their abilities rather than their disabilities. A drawback to this assumption is the inevitable labelling of such individuals as a consequence of their inability to function independently and normally in mainstream society. Mesibov (1990) illustrating some of the problems which oversimplistic interpretations of the theoretical basis of normalisation have led to, points out that 'for developmentally disabled people a major problem is the inescapable fact that normalisation represents a goal that is in most cases unobtainable' and by 'establishing a goal that many of them will not achieve we are doing them a disservice'.

In England, the influence of the theoretical basis of transatlantic and Scandinavian normalisation theories, combined with the humanitarian swing away from institutional values for people with mental handicap, led inevitably to a pragmatic approach to normality. There was a genuine wish to see the relocated patients in normal community settings alongside their peers and reinstated with all the civil rights previously denied to them. Wolfensberger had later subsequently redefined the term 'normalisation' into the concept of 'Social Role Valorisation' (1983) in an attempt to reduce the international misunderstanding of the original concept. By 1989 he was propounding a new and simpler definition that 'normalisation implies, as much as possible, the use of culturally valued means in order to enable, establish and/or maintain valued social roles for people'. (Wolfensburger and Tullman 1989). Oversimplistic international definitions of normalisation had led to the interpretation that mentally handicapped *people* were to be 'normalised' rather than their environment and services. Simultaneously Nirje offered a spirited defence of the normalisation principle, outlining both current international misconceptions and Wolfensberger's own deviation from both his original principle and Nirje's own Scandinavian concept. This critique of some of the more frequent misconceptions of the normalisation principle (Perrin and Nirje 1989) clearly states that 'physical placement in the community does not necessarily represent integration or normalisation'.

However, the early pragmatic approach to normalisation can be seen to have influenced political policy in England where the influential 1979 Jay Report stated clearly and categorically that 'mentally handicapped people have a right to enjoy normal patterns of life within the community' (para 89a) Patients relocated into the community were to be provided with residential accommodation in 'ordinary houses, suitably adapted for those with additional physical disabilities' (para 135). The report was particularly critical of the institutional regime and architecture of the newly built group homes. a decade later the Wagner Report with similar pragmatism supported the findings of the 1985 Social Services Committee Report that the ordinary house was 'the living arrangement most likely to provide high quality care' and that sheltered village-type communities were 'selective and segregationist'. Research findings in later chapters show that this emphasis on reducing contacts between handicapped people can lead to even greater alienation than was ever experienced in the institutional setting.

There has always been a pattern in our culture for like-minded people to form social subgroups because of common skills, interests or needs. Political, sporting, professional and social groups often contain some of the closest friendships in people's lives. In a similar way supportive groups for adults of like sexual orientation, one-parent families, people with clinical problems such as the blind and the deaf are regarded with sympathy and often receive local authority funding or premises to facilitate their continuance. A telling example of this type of supportive network in relation to mental handicap was found in a MENCAP group for parents of pre-school Down's children which the author ran for 12 years. Many of the children went on to mainstream educational provision, while others opted for special education. Regardless of social background many of these parents and their children made lasting and supportive friendships due to their common interest which continued long past the pre-school stage of the Down's child. Booth *et al.* (1990) make a particular study of the disruption of such family and friendship networks in community relocation schemes of previously hospitalised adults, pointing out that these informal groups are very often the only community friendships of relocated people. The author's research in this book confirms this finding.

In a climate of financial restraints there has been of necessity a lack of diversity in community provisions in England and a pattern of relocating people into urban community settings adjacent to major services has become the norm. However, the inference that such settings provide enriched environments with a subsequently enriched lifestyle has started to be questioned by recent evaluative research of pilot relocation projects as shown in later chapters. It is an interesting fact that the voluntary societies with a longer experience of relocation problems, and often catering for particular clinical groups of developmentally disabled people, have an extended history of successfully providing enriched lifestyles in rural self-sufficient working communities such as can be found in L'Arche, Steiner and the Home Farm Trust. Such communities value each person equally and in the high staff/villager ratio provided there is no shortage of willing so-called 'normal' people who also find living in these communities and sharing their lives with developmentally disabled people a valued option for themselves and their children. Given a choice, it may well be that many relocated people would prefer to live in caring communities where work, friendship and recreation were guaranteed. From such a base they could explore the pressures of the 'normalised' urban world at their leisure. Chapter 9 presents the case of 12 middle-aged long-term institutionalised patients from a mental subnormality hospital who moved with their ward sister into a private home she started for them in a remote rural hamlet. They regard their secluded farmhouse as their home for life and far from being isolated from the community most of them have found jobs within the surrounding villages. These particular people would appear to have an enriched quality of life not found in the diversity of urban community settings presented in later chapters of this evaluation.

Assessment for 'Normalisation'

Although much of Wolfensberger's work has been misrepresented, it had the merit of focusing international attention on the *services* necessary to support developmentally disabled people in the community. He was anxious to ensure that newly developing services took account of the theoretical basis of normalisation. To this end he devised a 'human service accounting tool' (Wolfensberger 1972, p.223) to teach people how to implement community services. Many local authorities in the UK have adopted this method of assessment with networked national workshops on PASS and PASSING being run by the Campaign Community and Mental Handicap Education and Research Association (CMHERA) who introduced and developed PASS and PASSING training in this country.

Programme Analysis of Service Systems (PASS) Programme Analysis of Service Systems of Normalisation Goals (PASSING)
These two evaluative tools elaborate the practical implications of normalisation in fine detail to assess how closely existing and newly developing services approximate to the principle of normalisation. They challenge authorities setting up new community services for severely and profoundly disabled people to assess their provisions against the best possible provision imaginable and one that would be valued by the rest of society, rather than to adapt their own norm for currently existing services. One of the drawbacks of this assessment process is that it is aimed not at individuals but at the quality of services delivered to them. This enables many PASS and PASSING evaluations to be carried out on services and settings without any personal knowledge of the participating developmentally disabled adults.

The scoring of a PASS evaluation emphasises the need for developmentally disabled people to adopt a similar value system to their 'normal' peers. It is assumed that increased contact will effect this change. Consequently 'deviant contact' measurement is given the lowest rating when 'the deviant clients are placed to a major degree in social groupings which are comprised of deviant individuals' and the highest rating when services 'go to great lengths to avoid client contact with deviant groups'

(Wolfensberger and Glenn, 1973, p.17). This would seem to hold an implicit message for developmentally disabled individuals that directly challenges their self-esteem and far from offering the socially valued role that Wolfensberger suggests, merely reinforces the notion that their non-disabled peers are considerably more desirable. Mesibov (1990) points out that as 'the effects of normalisation on the self-concepts of handicapped people have not been fully explored, it seems likely that they have been quite detrimental'.

Normalisation theory hinges on Wolfensberger's belief that the professionals implementing the services would appear to be the guardians of 'normality' and thus able to specify standards of behaviour to which people with mental handicap must conform. Their attempt to 'normalise' people through the provision of relevant services may well involve a certain amount of coercion. 'Normalising measures can be *offered* in some circumstances, and *imposed* in others' (Wolfensberger 1972, p.28, original italics). Examples of this in a PASS evaluation are the downgrading of a bathroom if it has special gripbars or other departures from domestic design and the fact that a person with mental handicap should not wear a visible hearing aid even if this is the only clinical correction available.

As services based on PASS evaluations have developed in the UK it has become apparent that they are not fully based on the needs of the developmentally disabled individuals they were designed to serve. Evaluative research on pilot studies of community integration has shown that the majority of relocated residents live isolated lives in segregated settings, physically within the community – but without becoming part of it. It seems that they have difficulty in establishing contact with their 'normal' peers in either occupational or socially valued roles when relocated in the larger community. As shown in Chapters 4 and 5, *micro-institutionalisation* is now becoming a feature of the daily life in many group homes. To add insult to injury an analysis of 52 PASS evaluated services (Williams 1988) showed that none of the authorities involved had reached the level of 'minimal acceptance' as defined by Wolfensberger.

Twenty years on from the original conception the theoretical basis of normalisation has been shown to be more effective than the practical implementation. Many professionals now feel the original goals are unobtainable and do not pay enough attention to the individual needs of developmentally disabled people. The philosophical basis of Wolfensberger's theory insists 'the most explicit and highest goal of normalisation must be the creation, support and defence of valued social roles for people who are at risk of social devaluation' (Wolfensberger 1972). In a time of increasing unemployment developmentally disabled people are not able to maintain their social status in the community through vocational roles. However it would have been hoped that the successful implementation of the theory would have led to social integration in the wider community in the form of social relationships and friendships through leisure activities. A review of the research findings over the last decade relating to the leisure activities, friendships and social participation of people with learning difficulties shows that this is far from being the case (Garvey and Kroese 1991).

The rapidity of the political impetus that propelled institutionalised adults into the community in the UK left little time to implement well thought out tried and tested schemes. Currently there is a growing feeling that there is little evaluative help from normalisation theory or PASS practicalities as to whether the service provided, however good, is producing an enhanced quality of life for the individuals concerned. We would appear to have completed the full circle as the gradual practical implementation of normalisation theories has merely served to show that developmentally disabled people are different. They demonstrate these differences by functioning at below average social and intellectual levels regardless of enhanced environmental placements, and sadly will rarely achieve the capacity to appreciate the abstract concepts that would allow them to profit fully from normalisation theory.

Assessment for Community Integration

If the current residents of hospitals, group homes and small living units in the community are to benefit from their relocation, we must be in a position to train them, assess their individual personal progress within their domestic environment, and also their progress into the wider neighbourhood. We need to assess the quality of the material provisions in their home and how effectively they use them. A similar assessment must be made of the geographical provisions within the new neighbourhood and the use the relocated residents make of these new facilities. The study of the ten group homes in Chapters 4 and 5, shows we are in danger of assuming that merely by relocating people into a pleasant environment some osmotic process will occur to imbue them with an enhanced quality of life.

Starting with Tizard in the early 1950s there has been much research evidence that training programmes are successful in teaching new skills to adults with mental handicap and result in effective transfer of training of various motor and perceptual skills. More recently the work of researchers such as Clarke and Clarke, Gold, and the Medical Research Council team headed by O'Connor and Hermalin have given us greater insight into the abilities of developmentally disabled people. There is however less evidence that social skills taught in isolation can become new living skills incorporated into everyday life. It would appear that unless people with learning disabilities consistently practice any learned skill in context, after a short passage of time these skills are dropped from their repertoire. A once fashionable philosophy was that in Piagetian terms, adults with mental handicap failed to reach Piaget's developmental stage of abstract (formal operational) thought usually reached by adolescence in the general population (Woodward, 1961). The adolescent then no longer needs concrete material but has acquired a capacity for abstract thought and can reason by hypothesis using an inductive method to derive generalisations from a number of previous actions. It would appear that the mentally handicapped adult cannot retain memories of these previous actions and consequently needs concrete information in the correct setting to enable him to carry out and successfully complete relevant life skills.

However outmoded this philosophy now seems, it would appear to have a direct connection with the failure of current social policies aimed at integrating developmentally disabled people into a realistic community setting. Sinson (1990) indicated that this failure may well be due to social training programmes being carried out either in day centres, or only for selected individuals in separate small units attached to the group home or hospital but isolated from the main living environment. Consequently such training becomes a somewhat artificial exercise when unrelated to a resident's everyday life. There was also evidence that developmental work in social and life skill training was being hindered by inappropriate geographical locations of group homes, misdirected administrative practices and neglect of simple domestic learning situations.

The original aim of the study of ten group homes described in Chapters 4 and 5 was to see if a unified assessment technique could give useful comparative evaluations of several group homes using different training programmes and various managerial strategies. By the use of a unified system it was hoped to see how the different managements enabled the residents to capitalise on their domestic and neighbourhood environmental facilities. The Learning Opportunities Co-ordination (LOCO) (Gunzburg and Gunzburg, 1987) assessment was chosen as it appears to be a unique tool capable of assessing the total environment (i.e. both domestic and geographic) and its relevance to the continuing social and intellectual development of adults with developmental disabilities. The LOCO assessment also allows for comparative data between different living units in geographically disparate areas, and also between living units and their own attached training units under the same management. LOCO can indicate whether such units are either *capitalising on* or *compensating for* their environmental surroundings.

Learning Opportunities Co-ordination Assessment (LOCO)

LOCO is a specialised assessment tool indicating to what extent a living unit whether group home, hospital or individual community housing for people with handicaps is able to contribute significantly to their social and personal development so enabling them to maintain a reasonable level of personal independence. The LOCO was primarily designed as a diagrammatic check list and analysis approach and is similar in construction and circular appearance to the well-established Programme Assessment Charts (P-A-C) scale (Gunzburg, 1977). The two left quadrants form the LO (learning opportunity) scores and the two right quadrants the CO (co-ordination) scores. The chart draws attention to any material or administrative obstacles which need to be considered to avoid artificial ceilings being placed on the developmental progress of any developmentally disabled adult in their own particular domestic and geographical environment.

The LOCO scale lists 100 scored items. Of these, 48 LO items refer to learning opportunities depending on environmental, domestic and material provisions. a further 48 CO items refer to management practices and their efficacy in utilising these learning opportunities. This utilisation is achieved by coordinating training and education programmes which encourage the frequent use of realistic social skills in the correct context both in the living unit and in the surrounding neighbourhood. A further 4 items termed Basic Training Conditions (BTC) record purely management practices relating to aims, goals and record keeping.

LO Items

The 48 learning opportunity items are subdivided into two groups of 24. Twelve of the first group refer to the quantity and quality of furnishings and provisions found within the living unit and are essential to normal everyday living. The second group of 12 items refer to additional provisions of the same type offering further opportunities within the home for expanding the residents' social competence above the minimum level and also involving some element of personal choice.

The first 12 LO items of the second group indicate to what extent essential physical and environmental opportunities usually deemed necessary for everyday living (such as shops, public transport, leisure facilities etc) are available in the immediate neighbourhood. The second group of 12 items indicate additional similar neighbourhood facilities and learning opportunities in the locality.

CO Items

The 48 CO items indicate whether managerial practices permit the use of those environmental provisions which have already been scored (in the LO section) as available in both the living unit and the surrounding neighbourhood. A residents' score also indicates how much use is made by the residents of these opportunities and whether any internal rules or regulations interfere with their subsequent social development.

These 48 CO items mirror the LO items on the opposite side of the chart. The first CO group indicates management practices relating to the home living unit, while the second CO group shows whether residents do actually use their living skills within the living unit. The third CO item group indicates the managerial approach to the use of the facilities in the surrounding neighbourhood. The fourth set of CO items chart whether the residents are actually encouraged and helped to make full independent use of these available facilities in the surrounding neighbourhood and so live a reasonably independent life using these carefully taught skills in a realistic context.

LOCO Score

As the LOCO consists of 100 items it is possible to arrive at a *general LOCO score* drawn from the total of positive scores obtained on each item. However the general score is often less indicative of the prevailing situation than the analysis of the sub-scores. For this reason the three main groups of scores should be studied separately. The LOCO score is therefore not a 'value judgement' but an indication of the learning opportunities available in any normal environment and the number of environmental and managerial obstacles present in a particular environment which may inhibit the development of genuine living skills in the residents. The LOCO also highlights the environmental deprivation often encountered in living units for adults with developmental disabilities which are either not found or compensated for, in the same environment by their more able peers.

Progress Assessment Charts (P-A-C)

The P-A-C system was initially designed to provide a method of identifying, assessing and charting progress in the life skills necessary to enable individuals with various degrees of learning disabilities to adjust to the demands of their particular environment. This comprehensive system enables a unified assessment to start at a pre-school age and by use of the relevant developmental forms build up a diagrammatic profile of an individual's social and personal development through adulthood. The various P-A-C's are appropriate for all ages and levels of development each flowing easily into the next developmental stage.

The P-A-C method consists of six comprehensive forms complemented by a Progress Evaluation Index (PEI) also designed to be completed at six monthly intervals. The PEI indicates standardised average attainment levels of the relevant age groups and enables a condensed record to be kept over several years and the comparison of an individual with the average personal and social functioning of a similar age group. A comprehensive manual accompanies each level of P-A-C to enable clearly defined scoring criteria to be maintained for each skill. This is of benefit to an individual transferring between similar educational establishments or resource centres.

The method is particularly appropriate for people transferring from school to residential accommodation where pupils could be asked to bring a completed P-A-C from their previous school which would enable the group home and the adult training centre or resource centre to decide whether to continue the current P-A-C or extend the student's potential by moving to a more demanding schedule.

A unique feature of the P-A-C assessment is the Personal Assessment Scale which also appears in diagrammatic form along side the main skills chart and highlights facets relating to the actual 'person' rather than his knowledge of social skills. The object of this assessment is to sample community tolerance to the individual and is highly relevant to community integration. If the group home resident were to blend unobtrusively into the local community then the community would not be put into a situation of having to make allowances for their social inadequacy. The areas sampled in this section are independence, adaptation, temperament, sexual attitude, communicativeness, truthfulness, honesty, responsiveness, peers attitudes, social relationships, co-operation, dominance and occupational attitudes. Although this is of necessity a subjective assessment by members of staff, all residential staff live closely with all the residents so a fair consensus of opinion is obtained.

The Scottish control group homes were drawn from an area, where fortuitously, due to departmental reorganisation in 1984 the residential hostels and adult training centres came under unified management. On examination a 'rag bag' of ad hoc assessment programmes and packages were found to be in use in all the different institutions and the new departmental team identified a need for both a common language and a more scientific assessment approach to enable communication between all related units in the region. The management opted for a behavioral approach utilising assessment, goal planning, training packages and evaluation. Pilot schemes were run for four months using four different packages with the P-A-C emerging as the most successful programme to provide a common unified language across the region, i.e. where competence in one town would equate to competence in another.

Overview

Relocation literature is typified by the lack of a common assessment language. Each new pilot study or report of substantial successes in residential projects tends to use a different assessment tool often designed by the various local professionals to evaluate the effectiveness of their particular work.

This makes comparative social progress or community integration impossible to evaluate and one is left wondering how social integration in Wales equates to social integration in Yorkshire. Both areas have produced successful and well-researched relocation schemes (Booth *et al.* 1990; Felce and Toogood 1988), but the diversity of assessment criteria detracts from their didactic value. Throughout the formative years of developmentally disabled people we assess them by a variety of standardised criteria which apply equally to both normal and disabled children. By such means as Mary Sheridan (Stycar) developmental assessments, standardised psychometric tests, reading and number tests, weight and height charts, a variety of professionals focus their individual assessment skills to design remedial programmes for the developing child. This holistic approach which often utilises a specifically designed environment seems to fail the still developing adult.

The following chapters will demonstrate, that by using a unified assessment method it is possible to indicate comparative successes and failures of personal development and community integration in a variety of different and contrasting environments. In both private and public sectors the use of a common assessment language serves to highlight exciting new developments that allow developmentally disabled people to attain the highest level of independent functioning and also to illustrate the environmental poverty of their less fortunate peers.

Part Two

Patterns of Living
The Public Sector

CHAPTER 4

Micro-Institutionalisation
The Examination

Introduction

There is much historical research evidence indicating that educational and social skills training programmes are successful in teaching new skills to adult mentally handicapped people and people with less severe disabilities. However, as demonstrated in later chapters there is less evidence that these new skills eventually become living skills successfully incorporated into everyday life unless constant ongoing training is available. This may well be due to the fact that training programmes are often carried out in separate training units attached to a group home. These training units are often detached from the main living environment and frequently cater only for selected individuals. More usually they are used on a daily or even hourly basis, with most social skills training delegated to the Adult Day Training Centre (ATC) which often belies its name and merely functions as an occupation or social centre. Social and domestic skills training then becomes a somewhat artificial exercise often totally unrelated to the daily living experience of the person concerned.

Many group homes regard themselves as providers of a particular type of homely hotel service which ensures that their residents have a secure and sheltered life. They do not see their role as being concerned with individual personal development and consequently do not provide their residents with any opportunities for such development. In many group homes there is also evidence that individual developmental work is often hindered by inappropriate geographical locations, misdirected administrative practices and neglect of simple domestic learning situations.

To look at these problems in more detail the LOCO assessment scale (see Chapter 3) was utilised in an attempt to examine which environmental and managerial factors affected the social and personal development of the 212 permanent residents living in ten group homes. The purpose of the LOCO assessment was to pinpoint such environmental and managerial weaknesses that would interfere with the success of subsequent developmental intervention programmes and the progress of the residents. The investigation explored the hypothesis that many group homes were neither capitalising on, nor compensating for, their environmental surroundings and that a systematised unified assessment procedure such as LOCO, implemented at both the group home and any attached training unit could effectively identify such problems. It was also hoped that the investigation would offer evidence to show that if the residents were taught more life skills in context, they would have a better chance of long-term survival in the new integrated community placements offered by government legislation or a more independent existence in their current group home.

The Group Homes

The ten group homes selected were in geographically disparate areas and thought to be broadly representative of current British practice. The sample included urban and rural areas with both a 'new town' and a hospital location. An additional selection criterion was that each group home should be a fully staffed residential unit housing at least 16 adults, even if some had progressed to various independent permutations such as integral internal flats, training flats or houses within the grounds. In accordance with social services recommendations the residents whose lifestyles were examined in the study had their own single bedrooms, with the exception of two or three residents in two training units. This chapter can only give a brief subjective outline of the salient features of each group home although they were all subject to the same stringent LOCO assessment where even the distances walked by residents to the various local facilities were measured by a mechanical device.

Fortuitously, further examination of the ten participating group homes indicated that they fell into two separate groups. Five units were unified by the use of a common individual assessment tool (the P-A-C, see Chapter 3) for each resident and were systematically following this programme of education and training in both group homes and ATCs. The other five group homes were characterised by a more casual approach and utilised various differing training programmes separately in group homes and ATCs. This quite unexpected finding of 'unified' and 'casual' groups, not anticipated in the original design, enabled additional comparisons to be made to see whether there were any differences between the two groups. Using the LOCO assessment, it was possible to establish differences in the utilisation of learning opportunities for the residents and any managerial practices which affected these in the two groups.

The Five 'Unified' Group Homes

As described in Chapter 3, a large Scottish region had chosen a unified system of assessment which provided a common parlance and easy communication between all the related units in the region. The management had opted for a behavioral approach utilising assessment, goal planning, training packages and evaluation. Pilot schemes were run for two to three months using four different systems. By common consent of staff and management the P-A-C programme emerged as the most successful, providing a unified common language across the region where competence in one town would be exactly equivalent to competence in a neighbouring town. Having chosen such a system, the region embarked on a comprehensive long-term programme of staff training in P-A-C methodology. All other assessment procedures were temporarily halted in the region until the staff were fully trained. The region bought in services from the Health Board to implement this P-A-C training programme which was offered to every staff member in residential and day care services for the adult population with learning disabilities – ranging from domestic staff to unit managers. In theory this would provide standard, valid and reliable goal-directed assessment and provision throughout the region.

Sadly, one of the drawbacks of the common philosophy of provision was a uniformity of architectural design in all five group homes which incorporated many of the less happy institutional features in the large communal open-plan areas including a lounge and dining space culminating in a long kitchen counter. This counter formed an effective barrier to the large kitchen with its heavy-duty machinery designed for institutional-type preparation of meals, to which the residents did not have free access.

Braeside was situated by the main road on the outskirts of a small town with an adequate range of shops, services and public transport within easy walking distance. The purpose-built, single-storey group home for 22 permanent residents, 15 males and 7 females (7 of whom had been relocated from hospital) and additionally catered for 20 regular visitors in two respite care beds. There were three wings, two male and one female and it would appear that once the initial separation had been made, the residents were resistant to change and remained in single-sex wings by choice. The author had only the staff's point of view on this decision! A particularly successful design feature was the integral training flat for three residents which was separated from the main building by a locked internal passage. This allowed the residents to live independently, with a front door and garden path to the street, yet have full staff contact if they so wished.

Unusually, both the officer in charge and the cook were male which could well account for the fact that this was the only home in the survey where all the tools and woodworking equipment were in good repair and easily accessible to both staff and residents. Working together, residents and staff had edged and built walls round the gardens, made a bird bath and provided a shelter for the dogs who were regularly exercised by the residents.

Burn House was on the outskirts of a large city with a steep secluded grassy access on to a main road which held an excellent range of shops and services and a range of bus stops for the five minute journey to the city centre. It was a purpose-built two-storey building with separate male and female corridors for the 18 male and 2 female residents – eight of whom had been relocated from hospital. The building also contained two respite care beds which were used by 20 regular visitors. The integral design included a training flat for two people and a staff 'sleeping in' unit which doubled as a day training unit.

Interesting facets of the residents' social life included involvement with the local church which was within walking distance and attended by several of the residents. The minister visited Burn House every Sunday spending part of the evening with the residents and encouraged their participation in church coffee mornings and sales of work. Several of the residents also visited their friends with whom they attended the ATC in other group homes in the region. These visits, by public transport, took place both at weekends and on weekday evenings. As most of the region's homes appeared to follow a policy of sexual segregation, the visits tended to take place in the more public communal areas of the group homes.

Kirk House was a purpose-built poorly designed group home on the outskirts of a large city. Well situated in a poor area of the city surrounded by adequate shops, services and transport it housed 22 permanent residents of whom 11 were relocated from hospital. Two respite care beds accommodated 29 regular visitors. A separate day unit, the origins and purpose of which were unclear, catered for four day-care people. Kirk House seemed to have some community links in that three residents regularly attended church, the minister visited one Sunday in four and the Boys Brigade took residents out. Unusually, residents appeared able to choose their own doctor and dentist in the limited catchment area and were able to visit them on their own if they so wished. This was such a rare occurence in the ten group homes that it was probably dependent on the particular good will of a sympathetic medical practitioner.

Kirk House residents were not in segregated accommodation but eight of them lived in cramped conditions and some discomfort in an internal upstairs 'training unit'. The rationale for this would appear to be that real life was tough and they were in training for it. The author's personal response to this inadequate life provision was that in real life people had a reasonable expectation of personal living space, food was neither purchased nor prepared in multi-kilo amounts and that a microwave, far from being 'too dangerous' for the residents in training to handle, might well have ensured at least some effective domestic provision. The steep stairs up which these residents trudged daily, with their ready-prepared bulk-bought food from the central kitchen, afforded an entirely overlooked danger. The meagre supplies in the ill-equipped kitchen included salt in a container marked sugar and several other similar anomalies.

The Lomonds was a purpose-built group home sited in a large council housing estate on the outskirts of a prosperous town. The 23 residents were encouraged to visit the next-door pub and the small shopping centre across the road that had most of the facilities necessary for independent life. The permanent residents, four of whom had been relocated from hospital, comprising four males and 14 females, lived in various permutations in the building. One wing contained 16 residents of both sexes, another housed 4 female geriatric residents and a separate house in the grounds served as an independent training unit occupied by one male and two females. The two respite care beds coped with 26 regular visitors.

The overwhelming impression on visiting the Lomonds was of the care taken by staff and residents to provide a visually satisfying environment. The visitor is greeted by the totally unexpected sight of a dining room with small tables ablaze with vivid red table-cloths, each topped with a matching poinsettia, contrasting with the polished wood floor. Neutral walls, pine domestic furniture and well-designed print fabric, backed by net curtains, line the large windows. At meal times the table-cloth and real plant (as opposed to artificial) is replaced by a more serviceable check cloth matching the different coloured toning chair sets at each table. This visual impact is satisfying enough to camouflage the overlarge institutionally designed dining room with the ever present kitchen hatch. The interior decoration throughout the home is such that one becomes aware of contrasting colours and textures in very ordinary and utilitarian furnishings. This easy transformation of a standard purpose-built group home into such a welcoming environment raises many questions! Another unusual feature of this particular home is that once a year the entire home closes down and the staff and residents all go to a dinner dance in a 'posh' hotel in the town along with the general public.

The Ashes (for full description see Chapter 8) was a purpose-built two-storey group home situated at the edge of a small town within walking distance of the town centre. The town spread in a ribbon development up the main road to the group home which is close to the ATC. The 23 permanent residents, nine of whom have been relocated from hospital, lived in five separate internal flats. The two respite care beds had 15 regular visitors. There was a large and rather unwelcoming communal area containing an open-plan lounge and institutional-type dining room. However each flat had an individual lounge, dining area and kitchen. A small day training unit opened off the kitchen. Unlike the other group homes there seemed to be a floating population of live stock which at the time of the LOCO assessment consisted of a cat, six budgies, three canaries and a rabbit. Different animals and fish had been noted on other visits.

The Five 'Casual' Group Homes

Whereas the Scottish provision appeared to have a uniformity of both architecture and philosophy and catered for a well-defined population of people with either clinical syndromes or clearly defined severe learning difficulties, the English provision appeared more random. Training units were the norm in the Scottish homes yet only one British home made any attempt to provide one and this was mainly for people with moderate learning difficulties.

The Villa was part of a large mental subnormality hospital situated in a suburban area of a large industrial city close to shops, services and transport. One two-storey villa had been converted into four self-contained training flats for 16 hospital patients who shared the same staff. Each flat contained two male and two female residents who appeared to have little contact with the residents in the other three flats. Only one flat was assessed by LOCO but a brief look at the other flats indicated they were identical. The design of the flat assessed was hardly traditionally domestic, with four bedroom/cubicles along the outer wall opening on to a central lounge. The kitchen, bathroom and dining area more nearly represented domestic provision.

The four flats appeared to contain the sort of elderly resident who would not have been committed to a mental subnormality hospital in present-day society. The residents in the flat assessed consisted of a woman over 70 of normal intelligence who had been committed at 17 for having an illegitimate baby; a lady of 50+ who appeared to be mentally ill; a 27-year-old man who had been committed to Rampton on a murder charge and had eventually been relocated in the hospital; and a 65-year-old retired man with moderate learning disabilities who was on a regular state pension. All the residents were basically illiterate.

The disturbing feature of this training unit was the acute shortage of money, pinpointed by the LOCO assessment, which hindered staff in domestic training exercises. At the time of assessment each resident was allowed £11.00 a week for food, and received a personal allowance of £8.25 per week to cover all their needs such as holidays, clothes, toiletries etc. In addition each flat was allowed £5.00 a week for cleaning materials, replacements and additional purchases of household effects. The staff feeling was that the hospital had effectively cut off these flats, and the residents who arrived from the hospital villas had very little in the way of personal possessions and even less in the way of domestic necessities. This severance carried through to the hospital land on which the villa stood, in that the residents were not allowed to cultivate the surrounding lawns or annex a small area to allow them to make a garden. There appeared to be no effective community links to replace those of the hospital. There was also some suggestion that the people chosen for relocation did not include many of the younger, long-term 'easy patients' such as those with Down's syndrome who were well settled in their villas and of help to the nursing staff.

The Court group home was contained in a newly built, architect-designed complex off the main road on the outskirts of a large industrial conurbation within an easy bus ride of the city centre. Adjacent to a similar complex of sheltered housing for the elderly, both shared a local shopping parade that provided most necessities for independent living. The village, within walking distance, had been overtaken by urban ribbon development but retained a village centre, pubs, ethnic restaurant and take-away facilities plus many small shops offering specialist services. The Court was designed to house five internal independent units with a large central inhospitable dining and recreation area which featured the less happy aspects of institutional design. The local authority supplied contract provisions for all cleaning, cooking and gardening services for the entire unit adding to the institutional ethos.

Due to a complex rotation of respite care and training facilities it was difficult to estimate the number of permanent residents in the 24 bedded unit. Of the 15 more clearly defined permanent residents eight had been relocated from mental subnormality hospitals. The 12 respite care beds were evenly distributed between the units and used by 64 people on an irregular basis, all of whom appeared to be a part of the life of the home. Included in these respite care arrangements were 16 to 18-year-olds from the local special school because at the time of the LOCO assessment the hostels for children only accommodated children under 16. The management used fairly clear intellectual criteria when placing residents in the various units. The special care unit had four permanent residents and four respite care beds which housed 24 regular visitors for varying periods who were profoundly mentally and physically disabled. The intermediate unit had three permanent residents and four respite care beds used by 20 people. These residents tended to have fairly severe learning difficulties and were termed by the management as 'common or garden' learning disabilities and did not appear to get any training for independent living outside the group home. The training unit housed residents with mild learning difficulties for a two-year training course. Five of these are permanent residents and five beds are devoted to respite care training and used by 20 similar people who otherwise live with their families in the local community. The Court also contained two semi-independent flats for one and two residents which appeared to be stepping stones to community relocation with ongoing training programmes. a particular feature of the Court is the high staff turn over at all levels.

The Croft was a conventional purpose-built single-storey group home newly built in the centre of a rural council estate adjoining the local shopping parade to which it had pedestrian access. Near by were a seaside holiday town and a string of coastal holiday and caravan camps easily reached from bus stops outside the Croft. In an unusual development the nearby staff house had been taken over by the eight older residents who found life in the main house too fast and noisy for them. This would appear to be a thoughtful approach to the ever-increasing problems of the geriatric population by a new breed of manager who was a young male, highly qualified university graduate equipped with an effective computer programme for every aspect of group home life.

The Croft's 29 permanent residents, four of whom had been relocated from hospital, had profound, moderate and severe learning disabilities. Sixteen men and women with both mild and severe learning disabilities lived in the main unit while an additional self-contained unit led off the large institutionalised dining area and housed the special care unit. Both units had two respite care beds which catered in all for 59 regular visitors. The geriatric population of eight lived across the road in an ordinary house originally designed as a staff residence with regular domestic provisions.

There was no training unit although the Croft also had responsibility for a four-bedded group house in the community. The local authority provided contract cooking, cleaning and gardening services and also control a central purse that provided clothes for the residents. However the contract gardener was glad of the help of strong willing men to build a swimming pool and carry out many of his improvements to the buildings and grounds. The staff appeared to have some difficulty explaining the residents' frequent absences from the ATC which seemed to offer rather less stimulation than their current building programme! These residents were the rural population discussed in Chapter 1.

Beckside was a somewhat older purpose-built two-storey group home in a popular Spa town adjoining the ATC. There were 21 permanent residents, nine of whom had been relocated from a local mental subnormality hospital and three respite care beds. While still retaining the large kitchen and institutional central dining and communal areas, the progressive manager persuaded the local authority to allow her to redesign the rest of the building. Four small self-contained internal flats were provided for the permanent residents and one respite care unit. The flats all had basic kitchens and small lounges. Residents collected the ready-prepared food at meal times taking it back to eat in their flats. The central kitchen was open to residents with tea, coffee, fruit and cakes always left out so that they could help themselves. This was the only home in the survey where residents had easy access to the main kitchen at all times.

On Sundays all the residents came together for Sunday lunch in the main dining room, which was quite an occasion with tables nicely set with table-cloths and napkins and a particularly good traditional roast meal. Beckside served the community far more than the others in the survey by retaining close links with relocated residents and day-care people who were welcome to come along for Sunday lunch and were charged 73p. This hospitality was also extended during the week when former residents were often invited either for the evening meal in the flats by their friends or joined the respite care people in the main dining room before going to Gateway Club which was held in the ATC.

There appeared to be no recognisable training unit for community relocation but many of the residents had decorated their own rooms and with staff help had even built-in some simple furniture. All the residents chose their own furniture, curtains and bed linen. Many residents appeared to have either private incomes or access to family financial help for extras. The euphemistically termed training unit was occupied by residents who were marginally more self-sufficient and who made a reasonable job of keeping it tidy. At the time of the LOCO assessment the home was short staffed and the manager was about to leave to take up entirely different work having found the constant battles with the local authority over her dynamic and forward-looking management had made her working conditions intolerable.

Beckside had a particularly favourable location situated in a holiday Spa town with lovely gardens, shops, plenty of entertainment and a welcoming church all within walking distance. The ATC was on the campus, as was the special school many of the residents had attended as children, which added to the independence and mobility of the less able residents. All the residents seemed very happy, coming and going as they pleased and relating to the staff as one big happy family. They did not seem overkeen to leave Beckside to join some of their relocated friends in the wider community.

New House was a purpose-built group home situated in a specially designed neighbourhood complex two miles from the centre of a new town. It adjoined the community health centre, library, leisure centre and community worship hall all of which were off the main road and served by pedestrian walkways. However, apart from a small supermarket, other services were reached by a nightmare crossing over a main road and a three-quarter of a mile walk through confusingly identical roads and houses to another shopping parade. Any bus journey involved a similar expedition to the nearby main road. The local authority's decision to keep a central purse and control all the residents' pensions and savings books at headquarters may well be a reflection of the environmental difficulties the residents would encounter in any attempt to be responsible for their own finances. They were also provided with tokens for bus fares so had no immediate need for money. However, six of the more able residents handled some of their own money. There were 24 permanent residents, 18 male and six female, with two respite care beds which catered for 20 regular visitors. Two residents were in wheelchairs, although there was no special care unit, and the appalling poverty of their environmental experiences will be discussed separately.

New House seems to contain most of the worst features of institutional design, including a large dining room with long tables which are laid by the residents for every meal with a paucity of requisites. At mealtimes residents queue up with their trays at the kitchen hatch and receive a plated meal. Most of the staff appeared to eat separately and of the two on duty, one appeared to supervise the proceedings from an arm chair in the centre of the room and the other joined a table of more able residents. This regime was apparently dictated by the psychologist who had designed behaviour modification programmes for several residents to be implemented during mealtimes. At some stage somebody must have recognised the barrenness of this environment and a small room with a table for four off the dining room, which may well double as staff room, was an option for some residents. This area was also used by residents who have been preparing some part of a meal as social training.

At the time of the LOCO assessment there was no training unit or training programme. When New House first opened ten years ago there was plenty of housing available for community relocation and the more able residents were given intensive training and relocated in small unstaffed houses in the next street to New House. The author, having spent some time with these residents, was able to confirm that they were living successful and independent lives. Five years ago houses became in short supply and all training and movement into the community was halted as there was nowhere for the residents to go. One surprising aspect of local authority policy was their decision to employ two of these relocated residents as domestic staff in New House. They were paid in the same way as any other member of staff and their conditions of employment seemed similar.

The Assessment Procedure

The staff at all the group homes were unfamiliar with the LOCO assessment, as it was a relatively recent innovation, and consequently had no previous experience of it, nor did they keep similar records.

A standard procedure was adopted by the author who personally completed all the assessments to ensure uniformity of scoring. Staff and residents in all the homes were interested and cooperative.

It seemed important to view daily life from the perspective of both the staff and the residents, so where possible residents were asked many of the LOCO questions before staff were approached to validate their replies. The author accompanied residents on visits to the supermarket, the doctor's surgery, took bus rides in to shopping centres and walked with or without residents to local services. In many cases the residents had a clearer understanding of the local transport network than the car-driving staff who did not live locally. Every post office where pensions were drawn was visited on foot usually with a resident. It became apparent that what was considered reasonable walking distance to shops etc for one community was often regarded as an unreasonable distance by both the author and other communities who had better access to transport or more local amenities. The distances walked by the various residents to reach their essential amenities were mechanically measured. These measurements highlight the disparity referred to above.

The author shared at least one main meal with each group of residents, with the exception of the hospital unit, but observed both the initial preparation and subsequent clearing up in all the group homes. All the domestic rotas were checked. She visited, by invitation, male and female rooms in all the units, and where possible joined in free-time activities. All the group homes were surprisingly helpful and no restrictions were put on inquiries or information about any aspect of group home life. Most staff were relieved to find that their time could be saved by allowing residents to answer questions. The Scottish local authority were particularly helpful, with senior management taking the author by car to the more remote group homes.

Data were also collected on residents in all the group homes, including severity of disability, length of time in residential care, proportion of mental subnormality hospital release patients and how many residents had already been relocated in the community or were hoping to be so in the near future.

Analysis of LOCO Assessments
Differences Between the 'Unified' and 'Casual' Groups
(Readers should refer to Chapter 3 for a more detailed explanation of sub-scores and the full statistical treatment of the study can be found in Sinson (1990).)

The raw scores of the LOCO assessment total 100 enabling a general LOCO score to be estimated for each group home, consisting of the total marks gained out of the possible maximum of 100. This allowed analysis in terms of significant differences *between* the ten units in both the total general LOCO score and the totals of the four subsections. Because the group homes were also divided into two equal groups comprising the five units following a 'unified' assessment approach and the five units utilising a more 'casual' ad hoc approach' it was also possible to assess any differences between the two as well as differences between the individual group homes.

Table 1 Loco Score

	Casual					Unified				
	1	2	3	4	5	1	2	3	4	5
BTC	4	4	1	1	4	4	1	4	4	2
Essential	35	36.5	29.3	35	38.8	39.5	40.3	41	39.5	42.5
Additional	28	33	22.3	29.5	35.5	34.7	34	35.5	36	33
Total	67	74	53	66	78	78	75	77	80	78
	Median 67			*Range 25*		*Median 78*			*Range 5*	

As can be seen in Table 1 the five 'unified' group homes gained a median general LOCO score of 78 with a range of 5, whereas the five 'casual' group homes had lower score of 67 with the much wider range of 25. This indicated a higher general performance in the five 'unified' group homes. When the sub-scores were analysed the scores for essential CO (co-ordination) items were not significantly different in the two groups, indicating that all the ten group homes were comfortably equipped and had access to most of the facilities deemed necessary for twentieth-century comfort. The three remaining sub-scores showed significantly superior management practices leading to a far better lifestyle for residents living in the five 'unified' group homes.

Both the home and neighbourhood learning opportunity (LO) scores showed there was little environmental difference between the ten group homes. However, the neighbourhood CO scores showed that residents in the five 'casual' group homes were by and large not able to take advantage of these favourable locations as management practices restrained them from moving freely about their local neighbourhoods. CO scores also indicated that in four of the 'casual' group homes residents were not allowed to choose their own doctor or dentist, whereas the majority of residents in the 'unified' group appeared to be offered this facility.

An important comparative LO score difference between the two groups was in the provision of outside premises for storage and use of tools, paints, outdoor games etc all to be found very well equipped in the 'unified' group but non-existent in the five 'casual' group homes. In four out of the five 'casual' group homes management concurred with local authorities in time-saving/cost-cutting decisions to provide various contract cleaning, catering and gardening services thus, in one fell swoop, not only depriving the residents of many of the purposeful everyday experiences of their more able peers, but also denuding their domestic environment of any opportunity of learning life skills in a real life context.

Comparative General Trends Across the Ten Group Homes
There was little evidence of any major home or environmental inadequacies in the LO scores in the group homes. Negative points were scored in varying degrees by all ten in the organisation of meals. The visible absence of standard items to be expected on a domestic dining table represented a severe obstacle to informal learning, the general architectural design of the dining and communal areas reinforced the institutional ethos and contributed to an unnecessary environmental poverty. A similar problem in all ten group homes was found in management attitudes to the basic provisions for residents bedrooms and respite care rooms, which illustrated an initial environmental paucity which was sometimes overcome in time by the more able residents. CO scores across all ten group homes also showed that management did not allow residents to look after their own savings, thereby reinforcing former institutional practices.

Although the management of all but one group home had no overt restrictions on residents having visitors of either sex in their own rooms, the CO scores in the LOCO assessment demonstrated that only in this one home was this principle actually being put into practice. A further distressing fact to emerge from the analysis of CO scores was that although the management in all ten group homes encouraged residents to invite acquaintances and friends to their homes, in only one group home did residents actually have any visitors other than close relatives. In all but one group home residents also had to account for their movements when going out. A similar result showed that although management theoretically allowed residents to pursue their own hobbies and interests there was only evidence from three group homes that one or two residents in these homes were actually doing so.

The LOCO results emphasised the relative isolation, and absence of community contact, of all ten group homes although most were ideally placed within the centre of small neighbourhood communities. The inference drawn is that in the light of this community isolation, domestic life and individual leisure choices *within* the group home must become more meaningful to the resident.

Micro-Institutionalisation

The LOCO examination of the group homes identified management practices that limited the personal development and normalisation of the 212 permanent residents with learning disabilities living in these purpose-built group homes, facilitating a process that the author has termed *'micro-institutionalisation'*. The characteristics of which would appear to be the transference of those institutional practices found in large-scale institutions to their smaller community replacements, allowing management to assume total control over basic individual life and leisure experiences such as cooking, cleaning, gardening, decorating, financial experience and freedom of movement.

CHAPTER 5

Micro-Institutionalisation
Contributing Factors

In the light of the prevailing political policies for people with learning disabilities, and the resulting emphasis on the shift from large-scale institutional care to small-scale relocation within the community, current literature abounds with examples of normalisation techniques and projects (a comprehensive overview of this can be found in Chamberlain, (1988).) However, after a closer look at the results of this LOCO investigation, and also the more cautious research reports, the reader may well ask whether this so-called 'normalisation' within the community could become synonymous with community isolation and so give rise to its own form of *micro-institutionalisation.*

Felce and Toogood (1988; see also Felce 1989) in their well-documented Hampshire research project resettling people with learning disabilities in small houses within the community, stressed the need for:

> 'many more examples of high quality services and further work on what distinguishes a high quality service from a mediocre or a poor one before we can be satisfied that such services can be delivered routinely to those who need them'. (pp.9–10)

With this proviso in mind the LOCO assessment procedure proved to be an informative predictor of which environmental and managerial practices influenced the quality of services offered to residents in the ten group homes under discussion.

Group Home Training Units
In the 'unified' group homes, the use of a cohesive individual assessment procedure (P-A-C) in each group home and ATC may well explain the fact that, in line with their philosophy of community relocation, all five of the 'unified' group homes had training units where residents slept and spent a substantial part of their time. The efficacy of this training was proved by those residents who were then able to move on and live relatively independent lives in their local community. Four of these training units had staff available 24 hours a day and were assessed in a similar manner to the group home. The fifth (The Ashes, see Chapter 6)

was an unstaffed independent flat in the community and so not directly comparable to the other training units. This flat would have probably scored a near maximum LOCO score.

Only one of the 'casual' group homes made any attempt to provide a training unit although it is arguable that the hospital Villa could be regarded as such. In view of the financial restrictions and hospital services imposed on the already institutionalised residents, combined with their high staff dependency, it was decided to treat the Villa as a group home into which the residents had been relocated from the hospital.

An anomaly highlighted by the LOCO assessment was the performance of group home training units. As can be seen from the general LOCO score in Table 2, in the 'unified' group there was very little difference between the personal learning opportunities offered to residents in the training units and those offered to residents in the ordinary group homes. An enhanced score of +23. 4 in the only 'casual' training unit LOCO score indicated that the main group home was not living up to the better management practices applied in the training unit. Nevertheless, even this improved score failed to reach the general LOCO totals found for the five 'unified' group homes. This higher score was obtained by the residents being able to bypass some of the local authority contract cleaning and catering provisions imposed on the main group home by the local authority. This type of LOCO information highlights the overwhelming influence of managerial practices which often appear to go unrecognised both within group homes and by senior local authority management.

Table 2 Loco Score (Living Units versus Training Units)

	C1	U2	U3	U4	U5
Living Unit	52.9	78.25	76.5	79.5	77.5
Training Unit	76.3	78.50	81.5	79.5	85.5
Difference	+23.4	+0.25	+5	0	+8

Subjective reports and descriptions of training methods in the training units, both by staff and residents, bore little relation to the inadequacies revealed by careful LOCO assessment of day-to-day practices. As, in every case, both group home and training unit shared the same staff it followed that negative practices found in one environment were invariably transferred to the other. Many group home managers who wished to institute a more enlightened regime were in constant conflict with their local authorities over restrictive practices, and in these homes there appeared to be an unusually high staff turnover. Training units were virtually non-existent in the 'casual' group and only appeared to reflect the prevailing ethos of the main group home in the 'unified' group. Therefore it was decided it would be more profitable to limit the final LOCO analysis and look within the ten group homes for contributing factors to *micro-institutionalisation*.

Thirty years ago the plight of the mentally handicapped adult was described by Gunzburg (1968) in an innovative thesis introducing the concept of social education for mentally handicapped adults.

> A mentally handicapped person, whether child or adult, is in somewhat the same position as a tourist in a foreign country. He may not know the language or the customs of the foreign country and may have difficulties with the coinage and the decimal system. Being handicapped by his inadequate understanding of the language and perhaps slightly flustered by the demands made on his arithmetical prowess, many a holiday maker solves his shopping problem by dipping into his pocket and offering a handful of assorted coins to the shopkeeper, with the mute request to take his pick and be honest about it. However, no intelligent person will maintain this mode of life for any length of time...the mentally handicapped person is in a very similar situation...the difference between our handicapped adult and the tourist in a foreign country is, of course, the tourist's stay is temporary and many of the mishaps he encounters can be laughed off as being of no consequence...he has the intelligence necessary to adapt himself to novel, unaccustomed situations. The mentally handicapped lacks all these extra resources: *he is a stranger in his own country,* ignorant of its customs, imperfect in his command of its language and bewildered by the demands of changing situations. (pp.124–5)

Simplistic as this analysis may now seem in the light of the 1971 Education Act, our enthusiastic espousal of group homes with community relocation replacing institutional incarceration, some 30 years later adults with learning disabilities are still facing the same problems. The LOCO assessment indicated that there were several clearly defined managerial practices which deprived residents of any hope of developmental progress because they had little or no opportunity to learn or practice many of the basic principles of normal everyday living skills.

Negative Factors Contributing to Micro-Institutionalisation

Financial

Six items in the LOCO assessment probed the residents' familiarity with their own financial affairs (including the value and use of coinage) and group home managerial practices relating to these. In eight of the ten homes assessed, general managerial policy did not allow residents to keep their own savings books or to have any control over money due to them. In the majority of cases the local authority kept a central purse sending pocket money up to the group home on a weekly basis. This money was kept by the group home manager and handed out to residents either weekly or daily. Of the 212 permanent residents in the ten group homes, only 26 had control of their own savings books and some degree of autonomy in their financial affairs. Even more surprising was the fact that only three residents in the training units had a similar degree of control. Many of the staff would have liked to have given their more able residents rather more autonomy but were defeated by their local authority who were not prepared to take this particular financial risk.

Analysis of the 26 residents who were being helped to manage their own financial affairs indicated that some element of risk taking by local authorities could well be justified. The four residents at the hospital Villa, although previous hospital residents, who were of moderate learning disability and had had some experience of their own pension and savings books, constituted a minimal financial risk. However, the other 22 permanent residents managing their own money were part of the ongoing financial training programme at Braeside that appeared to be so successful that the staff did not even see the savings books of over 50 per cent of the residents. The Braeside population was neither more nor less intelligent than any other unit in the study. It should be said that in some cases residents did not have full control over their savings books until staff were convinced they were aware of the significance of their financial transactions.

Braeside demonstrated that residents who were given a careful teaching programme with easy access to post offices and banks were able, in time, to adjust to the complexities of their personal finances. Many residents were well able to budget their own money effectively. In Chapters 8 and 9, it will be shown that where residents are carefully trained to appreciate their financial status, and to handle their own pension books, given financial responsibility relative to their growing appreciation of the value of money, little difficulty is reported. These chapters will also demonstrate that in the private sector, when residents are freed from the negative financial practices imposed on them for administrative convenience, they achieve a favourable economic status and become valued customers in their small communities. It would appear that those residents trapped in their local authorities' cost-cutting exercises, where a central purse controlled the supplies of basic everyday needs such as clothes, food, cleaning materials and even bus-tokens in lieu of fares, were not only deprived of individual personal developmental opportunities but also of valuable opportunities for a visible and respected neighbourhood presence and consequent community integration. The purchasing power of the residents of Greystones was much appreciated by a number of local shopkeepers for whom they provided a small, but regular, source of income. This goodwill was probably effective in securing one or two jobs in the town for the residents.

Leisure

It was evident, from the results of the LOCO assessment, that all the group homes were comfortably equipped and ideally placed in the centre of small neighbourhood communities providing optimum leisure choices. However, only the 'unified' group (as identified by initial P-A-C assessment) recognised, and in any way attempted to provide for, the more subtle self-actualising leisure needs of their residents. Felce (1988) indicated that the major need of residents was to be meaningfully occupied for the bulk of their time, and provided with opportunity, choice and support to this end. The present author in an earlier study, reported cases of failed community placements and the subsequent return to institutions of developmentally disabled people in several geographically disparate parts of the country. Although initially domestically competent, they were quite unable to deal with their increased leisure time when faced with the isolation which has turned out to be inherent in community integration. As the visits from keyworkers and support services gradually tailed off, in the light of their evident competence, they also tended to lose many of the carefully taught domestic life skills that had led to their successful relocation (Sinson and Stainton 1990). In the course of this LOCO investigation the author noted some of the people already living in the community, gratefully returning to their group homes for Sunday lunch, transport to Gateway Clubs, weekday tea etc. Lonely and isolated, seemingly unable to make new friends, they returned to see those residents and staff they regarded as both family and friends. (The study of Mary in Chapters 6 and 7 can be seen repeated in many other parts of the country.)

Independent community living is not an option for the vast majority of older residents, and certainly most older people who have not benefited from the various legislatory measures over the years will end their lives in similar local authority provisions to those described. Many of them will have left the hospitals they regarded as home, and there is some evidence that in the light of their limited life experience, especially as far as social life was concerned – these were not such bad places after all. Residents from Greystones and The Ashes (Chapters 6, 7, and 8) provide an interesting picture of the full social life they enjoyed in hospital, while still being critical of punishment regimes, large multi-bedded wards and hospital food. As far as the subjective reports of residents can be evaluated, there were more opportunities for a gregarious and varied social life in the hospital than in their current community placements. They appeared to have enjoyed frequent and regular discos, bingo evenings, dances, in-house cinema, concerts, garden parties, swimming trips, night classes, directed hobby activities and in-house church services among other hospital provisions. In the ten group homes in the public sector there was no indication that any of the residents joined the general public in the usual community leisure facilities, with the exception of visits to the local pub. Visits to swimming baths, riding stables or leisure centres were invariably on days when special sessions were held for the ATC or Gateway Clubs. By contrast, residents in the independent sector made frequent visits to the theatre, cinema, swimming baths and leisure centres. They went individually or in twos and threes (not always accompanied by a member of staff) using the same sessions and facilities as the general public.

Two LOCO questions probed the friendships between the residents and people in the local community by asking whether 'residents may generally invite acquaintances (besides regular friends and members of the family) to their home'. Although the management of all ten homes were happy to encourage such a situation, not one resident in the ten homes actually did so, nor knew any acquaintances in the neighbourhood to ask. Burn House and Beckside were the only homes that encouraged residents to invite their friends from the ATC to visit and also to stay for meals. These were the only two homes where residents even invited their developmentally disabled friends for social visits. In contrast the homes in the independent sector fostered such links with the community by holding regular parties and social evenings to which they invited the local community and they also made a point of participating in neighbourhood events. Their strong social links with the church gave them an added entry into community life. In all ten homes the church was the main, somewhat tenuous link with an outside social life in their own community.

It would appear that meaningful leisure choices for residents can only be present if the environment (here in the form of the group home) provides the support which the majority of group homes in this study were clearly not facilitating. The LOCO results also emphasised the relative isolation in the form of community contact of all the group homes. The inference drawn is that in the light of this community isolation, individual leisure choices must become more meaningful to the individual. The independent sector appears to be providing a more flexible approach to leisure activities. Wentwood's somewhat fanatical training for leisure (Chapter 8) is counterbalanced by the realistic provision at Greystones (Chapter 9) of a member of staff whose sole afternoon or evening duty is to provide leisure opportunities for the residents. Both these group homes insist that realistic leisure choices can only be made when the residents have been taught how to participate in the various activities on offer. In both these homes leisure activities are timetabled, taught and documented as rigidly as any other educational programme, with staff keeping a written check on resident participation.

All five 'unified' group homes had well-supplied outdoor tool sheds containing hobby and games equipment, but there was little evidence of any spontaneous unsupervised use of these facilities by residents. Nevertheless, in the 'unified' homes there was clear evidence of garden and home improvement projects where residents worked alongside staff. The staff attributed this enthusiastic cooperation to the staff need to complete the annual P-A-C which required assessment of residents' hobbies and their manual dexterity with tools! Such facilities were non-existent in the five 'casual' group homes. All ten group homes encouraged residents to have hobbies and provided places where work could be left incomplete on large tables in small quiet rooms. In six homes there was no evidence of any resident actually involved in any ongoing unsupervised individual hobby. In the remaining four homes, one or two residents were completing easy painting by numbers, simple sewing pictures and some knitting. As far as unsupervised hobbies were concerned, passive television watching and constant taped music were the norm in all ten homes in the public sector.

By contrast, Wentwood's and Greystone's residents were too busy most of the time to watch television. The Wentwood students were not encouraged to watch any television. Staff at Greystones were interested to note how day-time viewing virtually ceased after the first year, when residents found other interests. However, for Greystones staff and residents, certain programmes such as sport and the various 'soaps' were regarded as sacrosanct!

In eight of the ten group homes residents were not allowed to leave the home without accounting for their movements. The reason for this was said to be related to local authority fire regulations. In the hospital Villa the residents had complete freedom of movement. In the other group home where this was allowed, very few people actually did go out on their own without telling anybody. Here, residents had a large name board in the entrance hall where they could slide a board against their names to indicate that they were out. Staff appeared to think the system worked well and that the residents probably reported their movements from habit. One explanation appeared to be that residents going out would often ask staff on duty if they wanted a newspaper or any personal shopping doing. The staff invariably availed themselves of these kind offers.

Contract Services

It seems almost unbelievable that in the 1990s this section still has to be included. In many group homes practices suitable for the large Victorian institution would appear to have been transferred en bloc to their supposedly 'normalising' community replacements. All the five 'casual' group homes were provided with various permutations of contract services by their local authorities. Such services effectively denuded their environment of any opportunity to experience and so learn these life skills in a real life situation. Contracting services included catering, cleaning, laundry, gardening, hairdressing, chiropody and a clothing account at a large old-fashioned department store that did not appear to stock the sort of 'gear' the younger residents preferred to wear.

It hardly seems necessary to point out the total stultifying effect this must have on any hoped-for 'normalisation' process when residents are unable to even comprehend the daily life experiences of their more fortunate 'normal' peers. Much of the residents aimless leisure time could be filled by merely being allowed to conform to the daily domestic duties of the average citizen. Even watching television failed to be a useful learning experience, as residents were unable to profit by the constant advertising and shop for the goods they were constantly being exhorted to buy. It is generally accepted that twentieth-century society has become a consumer-based society (blessed with built-in obsolescence of most material goods), but residents in group homes were still subject to the prevailing paternalistic Victorian values where most of their material needs were provided for them.

The 'unified' group homes fared rather better in that as they were committed to a regular developmental assessment for each resident (P-A-C), management felt impelled to provide the requisite developmental domestic experiences alongside contracting services. In the few cases where contract services were supplied, they were used flexibly and residents were not totally deprived of these particular learning experiences. In the private sector, the residents of Wentwood, CCC and Greystones shopped for food and cleaning materials and even appeared to develop 'brand loyalty' – to the surprise of the staff. Here residents and staff shopped, cooked and ate together with obvious enjoyment. They catered for similar numbers and appeared to have no problem with the domestic-sized kitchens equipped with ordinary domestic machinery, as shown in later chapters.

Special Care Residents in Group Homes

The 'unified' group homes had no particular provisions for residents with special physical needs and the manager of the Ashes had taken an early decision to relocate the four residents who had mobility problems and were dependent on wheelchairs. By contrast four of the five 'casual' units had a proportion of special care residents. A careful look at their daily regime raised the question of whether the specialised needs of such residents are best served by being included in this type of group home environment.

For example, New House had two young male cerebral palsied wheelchair cases at the time of the LOCO assessment. Neither of them had any effective speech or movement other than a little gross motor movement. They were both in standard single bedrooms with no special modifications. One was a local man and the other an immigrant teenager who knew no English. No member of staff at the home knew any Indian languages nor was anybody very sure of his name. The staff appeared to have given him an English name to which he made little response. His family spoke little English and no attempt had been made to find the services of an interpreter for either him or his family. His ethnic background was such that the food he was served was probably quite unpalatable to him.

These two men followed a similar weekday regime which involved getting them ready for transport to the ATC very early in the morning, after which they were then left sitting in their rooms for some time until transport arrived. The author watched their return home at the end of the day with some interest. Both men were wheeled straight from the bus to their own rooms where any physical needs were attended to. They were then left in their wheelchairs facing the window until the evening meal was ready. The ubiquitous tape recorder was then set in motion, but at the end of the tape nobody came to change it. Both rooms looked out on to an unstimulating view but given the angle of their wheelchairs and their lack of muscular control, it was doubtful whether either man could actually see out of the window. There was no attempt to provide any occupation or visual stimulation on the tray of the wheelchair. Walking past the rooms at regular intervals the author noted the total isolation of each man. Nobody visited, no member of staff called to see they were all right, no other resident looked in to see them. The walls were bare and there appeared to be no visual or kinaesthetic stimulation once the music stopped. An hour or so later a member of staff wheeled them into the dining room for the evening meal. The Indian was put at a table on his own, with his back to the majority of residents. Being a messy eater, due to his lack of fine motor skills, the psychologist had decided to isolate him from the other residents at a separate table. He received minimum help with his meal much of which went on the floor. A member of staff on duty idly watched the proceedings from a large armchair in the middle of the room while drinking coffee. The other member of staff joined a table of more able residents. The English man ate with a small group of residents and received some help from them but little verbal interaction. When the meal was finished the Indian was wheeled back to his room to sit yet again in solitude and the other man was moved to the lounge area of the room while the tables were cleared. Other residents rapidly left this lounge area and for the next 40 minutes the man sat on his own, facing a blank wall in an empty lounge. Nobody even turned the television on. In fairness, only two care staff and the cook on were duty and they were fully occupied clearing up the meal and helping the other residents. However, this appeared to be the normal staffing at this time of day both at this home and at all the other group homes visited in the course of the LOCO assessment.

Having noted similar situations involving residents from the special care units in the other group homes, the author decided to make some inquiries about policy relating to special care residents in this particular home. It transpired that both men were the recipients of individually designed behaviour modification programmes by the psychologist attached to the home. The author was amazed to find that the staff were well pleased with the way their special care residents were fitting into the daily regime. The plight of these two men locked into this inexorable daily routine, imprisoning them in such solitude, was the saddest sight imaginable in these days of 'normalisation'.

There would appear to be no excuse for this type of dehumanising treatment. These two particular young men would have already benefited from pre-school placements where a range of multi-disciplinary professionals would have started the type of stimulation programmes that would have been carried on in the special care units of their special schools. Almost certainly, at some time in their educational lives, they would have benefited from the advancing knowledge of cerebral palsy techniques. Physiotherapists, psychologists and trained teachers would have exposed them to intense stimulatory techniques enabling them to have some degree of autonomy in their own environment. This is no idle speculation. The author in her own pre-school nursery assessment unit (as far back as the 1970's) had subjected many cerebral palsied infants to specially designed toys, equipment and techniques. Various professionals instructed the post-graduate special education teachers training in the unit, who then took these techniques into schools and special care units all over the country. Such procedures have been the norm over the past 20 years in the English educational system but seem not to have bridged the great divide between childhood education and the more permanent adult special care provisions. It is fairly clear that both the pay structure and staffing levels in group homes, as they stand, are not adequate to support both special care and ambulant residents under the same roof.

Geriatric Residents

There is some indication that some group homes are starting to recognise the problems posed by an ageing population. Only three of the homes assessed in the LOCO survey had made separate living provisions for their older residents and these were forced on them by the awareness of staff of all levels of the increasing difficulties the older residents were encountering in daily life. In the 'unified' group both The Ashes and The Lomonds provided internal small easily accessible units for four residents and in the 'casual' group The Croft provided a totally separate house for eight residents. All three homes accepted that residents in these units may eventually develop a higher staff dependency. The Croft staff found that the older residents were upset by both the noise and fast pace of life in the main home but responded well to the small-scale quiet domestic provisions in their own house. Living with people of their own age, at their own pace, many residents were able to be more independent than before.

The lack of leisure provisions appeared to be an intensified problem for the older residents and only one home had made any provision for this. Most ATCs have long waiting lists for places and elderly residents already attending ATCs are encouraged to take 'early retirement'. Those residents who do not avail themselves of this opportunity have to retire from the ATC at whatever age the local authority decrees. They then lose their daily routine, their main source of social life, many of their friends and any opportunity for a daily change of environment. In most of the homes elderly residents were observed sitting around during the day doing not very much. Although there is an increasing awareness by local authorities of the need to provide unemployed, redundant and retired citizens with some way of filling their increasing leisure time, as yet this awareness has not filtered through in respect of the needs of the developmentally disabled pensioner. At the point where the average pensioner is provided with access and transport to social service day centres which provide good opportunities for hobbies and social contact, the developmentally disabled pensioner is excluded from exactly similar provisions at the ATC, and almost certainly has far less innate resources to cope with this isolation.

The Lomonds took in four older residents (one as young as mid 40s and all well below pensionable age) who for various geographic reasons had never attended the local ATC. On application, they were refused places on the grounds that they were too old. In a singularly forward thinking move the manager applied for help to the local basic education unit which ran adult literacy classes for illiterate members of the local community. An adult literacy teacher was supplied to the group home and provided a stimulating day-time educational programme for the four ladies. This was carefully designed for them and involved local and aural history, project work which included forays into the local community, basic health education and some basic literacy skills. This programme probably provided considerably more stimulation than the daily craft work at the local ATC. The author noted other residents (home for the day for various reasons) joining in with great interest.

It would appear that in respect of most negative practices discovered by the LOCO assessment, one group home in the private or public sector had found a perfectly good way to circumvent or overcome restrictive managerial policies that were unthinkingly being applied to whole populations!

Choice of Medical and Dental Practitioner

This LOCO area was far from clear cut and raises some questions regarding self-advocacy of developmentally disabled people. The British medical system is unique in that it still provides neighbourhood primary care facilities and patients are able to register with a general practitioner who serves their geographical catchment area. Medical practitioners are not obliged to accept patients on their lists, and theoretically patients also have a free choice of general practitioner. It has become customary for several medical practices to join forces and operate as individual practices from a central health centre. In the 'unified' group homes management agreed that all residents could theoretically choose their own doctor and dentist within the constraints of the medical system. In the 'casual' group homes only Beckside permitted this individual choice although New House was built virtually within the grounds of the health centre.

In the 'casual' group, management policy dictated that no resident was allowed to visit their general practitioner, for whatever reason, unaccompanied. The only exception to this rule were three residents with moderate learning disabilities in a training unit at the Court. The 'unified' management were infinitely more flexible and many residents were encouraged to visit the surgery on their own for repeat prescriptions or simple consultations that staff felt that residents could well cope with. Regardless of this flexibility on the part of management, only one sympathetic general practitioner in the entire survey was prepared to see patients with learning disabilities on their own. As he was only visited by the three residents of the Court, the remaining 209 permanent residents had no options other than compliance with either managerial or medical strategies.

Self-Advocacy, Normalisation and Micro-Institutionalisation

The common component of the negative factors cited above, which contributes to the ever increasing *micro-institutionalisation,* is the lack of personal choice afforded to most developmentally disabled people in most areas of their lives. However, the first requirement to enable a person to make a choice, is to be given the opportunity to do so. In each of the above negative factors one or other professional approach has imposed a professional-client relationship which takes no account of the individuality or uniqueness of the client. In every case it leaves the professional with the ability to explore and impose a variety of different approaches; the professional retains a flexibility of choice while the client's options diminish.

The contemporary concepts of normalisation and self-advocacy (in respect of people with learning disabilities) have emerged and developed in tandem. This rigidity would seem to have paved the way to many of the aspects of *micro-institutionalism* highlighted by the LOCO assessments. Brechin and Swain (1988) suggest that both concepts 'create a professional-client relationship which enshrines the professional in a world of exclusive and privileged knowledge, and consequently entombs the individual with learning difficulties in a fundamentally dependent role'. They propose a merging of the two concepts that would enable a working alliance with professionals to be seen to be satisfactory not only from the professional point of view but also *'from the perspective of people with learning difficulties'*.

CHAPTER 6

A Public Sector Venture

Because the author wishes in no way to misrepresent the nature and outcome of this project these two chapters are, as far as possible, related by the people involved, who prefer to remain anonymous. In this chapter Mrs F describes the background to the relocation process. The tape recordings were made during the years 1989–91. The local authority concerned were supportive of all Mrs F's decisions and gave her all possible help.

The Group Home

Mrs F, having had what she termed as her English adventure, decided to retire with her husband and come back to Scotland to live near her married family. They had both been involved in social work projects in London and the west of England where Mrs F held senior positions in assessment and family therapy units and had also been involved in setting up housing projects for mentally handicapped adults. Mrs F was also a trained councillor and had been trained in behaviour modification techniques. Seeing the post of 'group home manager to The Ashes' advertised, while in Scotland on holiday in 1987, she decided to visit the home with a view to taking up some less demanding work to compliment her husband's retirement and leading up to her own retirement.

> I came and saw an enormous sitting area with chairs round the edge and four coffee tables in the middle – that nobody could possibly reach from the side – and this dear old lady sitting there with nobody near her at all and getting absolutely no attention. The place was smothered in white net curtains and looked beautiful in many ways – it just didn't feel right. Males and females were living separately apparently because it 'causes problems'. I assumed at that time that they *wanted* an institution and that nobody who was managing something could possibly be letting that happen if that wasn't what they wanted. So I thought 'I'll go up there – and yes it'll all have to be changed but it will be nice and slow and gentle and be semi-retirement compared to my last job'. So I came up for the interview and found that what they were wanting was change.

> When I started work I discovered that things were a great deal worse than had appeared on the surface. The authority had presented the staff in a rather drastic light – but to be fair – I think they had started out with the best of intentions but things had not been easy. They had become disenchanted and now allowed things to happen that perhaps

they wouldn't have allowed when they first started. The staff and the residents had all been there for ten years since the home opened and the result was pretty disastrous.

I started the ball rolling by saying I hoped we could provide the kind of life for these people that they needed to live, because they had the resources they needed which were not here. That meant finding them somewhere else to live to allow them to be given the freedom and opportunities to develop as people. At least 50 per cent of the residents here when I arrived shouldn't have been here. That was a totally alien concept. Totally! For the first year, as long as the previous Depute was around, it was extremely difficult. If she had half a chance she would tuck them into bed at nine to half past. Finally she retired and I got a very good Depute.

Although Mrs F intended to make changes as slowly as possible the residents wouldn't let her. Once she opened the flood gates people moved into the community very quickly. The first to move were the people living in the lodge and bungalow in the grounds who had been on minimal care training for four and a half years. They had already completed their basic social skills training and it was doubtful how many of them were actually disabled.

They resented this length of time. The minute we offered them homes they couldn't wait. You get people to a certain crescendo point and up to a certain level of development and given these criteria you then have to move them on. At this stage the most important criterion is their ability to get on with their neighbours – it's nothing to do with whether they can scrub the floors. They have learned to recognise that they have to recognise the rights of other people and that is something that most people never teach.

If they've never had their own rights recognised you must teach them that as well, but you must teach them that other people possess the same rights.

After the residents moved out these two buildings were subsequently closed down as they were found to contravene the majority of fire and domestic safety regulations. When challenged about this the Authority said they had not upgraded the buildings as they wished to keep them homely! Several years passed before money was found to upgrade them to suitable living accommodation.

We were then left with 30 beds and residents with IQs under 50. I looked at each individual and set out with the original aim of finding the most appropriate setting for each client in order to enable them to live as normal a life as possible. They had all been here for ten years since they had been discharged from The Park (the local mental subnormality hospital) and those that hadn't came from the old Poor House. I spent a great deal of time wading through some absolutely appalling case notes, some of which were so bad that at the point at which we opted for open access – I removed the case notes up to that date and put them in a sealed envelope. They haven't been destroyed but they are not available because they are so bad. For example, some case notes, over a period of four years had not one positive statement. I don't think the staff even realised they were doing it.

I looked for diagnoses and mostly there were none. With the help of medical staff I attempted to ascertain a diagnosis for each resident and then attempted to ascertain whether there was anywhere else that would better meet the needs of this individual. We had one young lad who had been placed here for a fortnight when his mother died while they sorted out what to do with him and 13 years later was still here. He was not mentally handicapped and there was an entry in his case notes from the psychologist saying 'This man is not mentally handicapped and will not benefit from being so remanded'. He wanted to go out into the community and didn't know how to set about it.

We had three wheelchair cases and this building was not built or designed for wheelchairs. People were nobly struggling on coping but the staffing level was such that if two people were withdrawn to look after the physically disabled there was nobody to look after anybody else. We found nursing home placements at the rate of one a year and they were happy to go. Nobody was moved to anywhere they didn't like. In particular one lady with cerebral palsy should never have been placed here – she was so arrogant about the other residents 'I'm not like them' – nor was she.

I think there is a considerable dichotomy in the minds of most people who work in this field about whether it is necessarily always right to say people should live in the community. I think it's right for some and a question of looking at each individual. One of the major problems is that when you come to planning for this client group it's very difficult to plan on the basis of each individual. I use paediatric assessment methods to determine where the ups and downs are in each person's development. If you've got somebody who is presenting problems and is having difficulties adjusting, then the chances are you've got some very big down. For example we have a lady with a very big gap in her personal social development for perfectly understandable reasons, but the trouble is that she's now got to the age of 46 and nobody's done anything about it. It's a bit late. To make sense of that you also need to know the background from whence they came.

Left with her 30 beds Mrs F then proceeded to totally restructure The Ashes both socially and architecturally by creating five separate internal flats within the home with the individual names of Oak, Holly, Ivy, Beech and Thorn. She also sorted out the staff in the home who were interested in training and those who enjoyed being with the residents but wished to have no involvement with such schemes – and deployed them accordingly. She reduced the number of residents to 23 (although 30 beds were available) and provided two respite care beds. This enabled each flat to have a small lounge adapted from the five spare bedrooms. All these lounges had televisions, easy chairs and sofas and each flat had a kitchenette fitted into a convenient space provided with chairs and dining tables. Every flat had a front door with the glass windows obscured by transparent overlay. Fire regulations precluded locking the internal front doors but eventually bells were provided with staff and residents from other flats expected to ring to obtain entry. The residents had keys to their own bedrooms which they all appeared to use.

Oak was on the ground floor and contained three female and one male high-dependency residents. These people had a high staffing need but could still manage to provide for themselves in the same way as the other flats. Beech contained young males and Thorn female residents of mixed age groups. Holly and Ivy contained mixed male and female older residents which arrangements were arrived at after various permutations of residents were tried. People were initially put together and then had to be moved either because they complained or the staff became aware that they were not getting on with other residents in the flat. The main criteria for selection was whether people had the ability to get on with their neighbours as Mrs F believed that if she used this criteria there was a reasonable chance that people who then moved out into the community would succeed within that community.

Assessment at The Ashes

Mrs F effectively brought her extensive experience of paediatric assessment to her work with adults when restructuring The Ashes using similar developmental assessment techniques to those used in the author's pre-school assessment unit. Mrs F believes that developmental assessments are more effective than the conventional social skills inventories when considering both community relocation and interpersonal relationships within The Ashes.

> We use Gunzburg P-A-Cs. We sometimes ask the psychologist for IQs and I use a development quotient as well. The Deaf/Blind Association produced a developmental booklet which you fill in and I also use Mary Sheridan which works in a similar way. Basically what you get at each age are four different milestones and if you match up the four with the person you get a reasonably accurate estimate of where they are. It's extremely useful because you've got the very different strands in it you can actually match it much more closely to the person. For example, we had one Down's Syndrome lady who everybody was getting very confused about. Eventually I assessed her and she was functioning at five to seven years in the vast majority of areas, except for interpersonal relationship skills which were precisely at two years nine months.

I think people have great difficulty extrapolating developmental assessments for use with adults. Most of the developmental assessments are for small children and they have great difficulty recognising that these signs are still present in an adult. I say to my staff 'These are the signs present – what age do you think that applies to?' Then we discuss it. One lady of thirty functions very consistently at two and a half. As part of that she has tantrums and they are absolutely typical two-and-a-half-year-old tantrums. She kicks and she pulls hair, she lies down on the floor, drums her heels and bangs her head. All these things are things two-and-a-half-year-olds do. The staff can now cope with these things much more easily even though it's dangerous because they understand what's happening. They are not so frightened of her because there is a reason why she does that particular thing because its part of her developmental pattern. It's still got to be dealt with and it's still got to be diverted but we manage because we see the early signs and we divert her on to something else. But the staff need to know what they are diverting – what developmental stage – because there's no point in saying to her 'Look Joan, we know you're feeling off colour, but why don't you come and read a book or something?' She can't read a book, you've got to produce something to divert her and it's got to be at a level suitable for a two-and-a-half-year mentality in somebody of thirty. That's where the extrapolation is difficult.

Everybody gets confused with the business about the dignity of the adult. We get told 'You've got to take account of their disability but you've also got to treat them with the dignity of their chronological age'. To that we subscribe, but at the same time that doesn't mean that you give them activities which are appropriate to their chronological age because they can't handle them. What you have to do is work out how the activity that is appropriate to their developmental age can be extrapolated into something which is appropriate to their chronological age.

Daily Life at The Ashes

The large communal lounge and dining room were both retained to provide a focal point for social gatherings and a core to the home. Although the evening meal was centrally prepared the residents carried the food to their flats where they set the table and ate together. Each flat was responsible for preparing and cooking their own breakfast and ensuring that supplies of raw ingredients from the kitchen were always in the store cupboard.

Lunch was always served in the main dining room for those staff and residents who were in. This was a somewhat spartan self-service refectory meal, designed to familiarise the residents with the concepts of self-service canteens and cafeterias. The quality of the food was excellent with little convenience food in evidence. Although the author was surprised at this soulless deviation from the otherwise small-scale domestic provisions, there was no doubt that it was rather better than the college refectory or works canteen where their more favoured siblings would be lunching. A total contrast to this provision was the training flat off the kitchen and main dining room. Each night a resident prepared a meal from scratch, to which they invited a member of staff and two other residents. The table was set with a lace cloth, pretty china and glasses and whatever else the resident chose to add. This was supervised by the cook who having had no previous special training in mental handicap taught each resident the way she had similarly taught her own children and grandchildren. This one-to-one ratio was very effective and replicated any typical family session with a rather less harassed adult than is usually the case. Every resident made simple cakes or scones to compliment the menu he or she had chosen. Timing was important as the preparation only started when the resident returned from the ATC so there would be some realistic concept of the problems of getting a meal to the table on time.

> The Ashes is now a series of very small group homes and the communal area serves as a village hall – like a very small village with their own little houses and a central community centre. They have their own private lounges in the flats but they can also come into the semi-public areas where they can have a disco, play pool etc. The only meals they all have together are Saturday and Sunday lunch. We could move an Ashes flat into a house in the community provided we move with it the staff support it has already got. However you do have to create some sort of special social life for them.

An example of this special sort of social life within The Ashes is the attempt to start residents off on hobbies. The large table in the communal lounge supported plaster models in various stages of moulding and decoration. The shelf above the table held plastic bags of knitting, sewing and art work. The paucity of any opportunities for individual personal development in the group homes was noticeable in Chapters 4 and 5 where the LOCO assessments indicated an almost total lack of interest and opportunity within the homes for any type of individual hobbies.

> We're having a Christmas market and the staff are making things with the residents. It's so that they've got a reason to make things because they don't take up hobbies willingly. They're not self starting. We don't tell them to do things, we introduce them in a way that gets them interested. For instance I will sit and knit on an evening and watch television. I'm doing it so that they get interested in the knitting, so we have two of them at the moment who are actually knitting themselves a jersey – and that's quite a considerable achievement! I will sit with them in the group setting – I won't go into their flats because that's not my role – that's the flat helpers' role. I and all the other officers have to be very careful that they don't intervene in that relationship. The flat

helpers will sit with their groups in the evening – but sometimes they'll also sit with them in the main public area or anywhere they find their people.

Each flat has a flat helper. This member of staff acts in a similar way to a keyworker. There is also an attempt to give each flat a fair amount of autonomy, however Mrs F found real difficulties arose when trying to teach the remaining residents (who had IQs in the 30–40 range) to accept this level of responsibility;

> We've been working on self advocacy in The Ashes and getting absolutely nowhere. We have the flat system and were trying to get somebody to represent each flat but we could not get in any way the concept of one person speaking for the four of them. So then we rotated it and they came in turns but they still said only what they wanted. They could never say how anybody else wanted it. I'm trying to get over to them about speaking for oneself and also speaking for other people so that they have the same rights to have a voice as the staff. We have full meetings about once a fortnight usually just before Sunday lunch. What is interesting is that we've also been having little meetings on a rotational basis and we're actually getting far more from them in these little meetings of one representative from each flat.

Mrs F accepts that there is considerable resistance by society to the integration of people with learning difficulties into their local communities and acknowledges the key role played by public relations. If the residents are going to be accepted by the community it is important for the community to have contact with The Ashes so that they will have an understanding of the residents' capabilities and see that they can look after themselves. Fund raising ventures are open to the public and visits are welcomed from all sectors of society. There are also a number of regular volunteers working at The Ashes. These include prisoners on remand for armed robbery and other anti-social crimes, two of whom are always on regular placement at The Ashes and interact well with the residents.

The remaining residents living in The Ashes seemed well settled in their flats and talking to them revealed that they were content with their lives and had no wish to move into the community to live more independent lives. A surprising fact was the genuinely positive feelings the residents held for the Park, where the majority appeared to have what they considered was a pleasant life. Margaret's life perceptions may well be representative of many patients relocated from the Park which is due to close in two years time. The Park appears to be typical of most large Victorian institutions that changed only in name as the years progressed.

Margaret's Perceptions

Margaret was a large lady in her 40s with a diagnosis of epilepsy and severe behaviour problems. She had behaviour modification training in the Park in an attempt to curb her aggressive behaviour, which had generalised over into The Ashes setting enabling the staff to have some control over her behaviour. Margaret's IQ was below 50 but her verbal ability and communication skills masked many of her problems.

> My Mam and Dad took me to the Park because I wasn't behaving at home very well. I knew I was going there – I'd been there before. I got sent there because of my behaviour. I had attacks of shouting and bawling at Mum and Dad and I broke a window. I don't know why I did it. I did the same at the Park – and banging windows. Mum came up to visit me and they wouldn't let her because I was bad. They put me to sleep, gave me a lot of stuff and knocked me out. It was terrible. I went on to ward 23 first and after that I went to ward 6. Ten or eleven people slept there. It was all right. Sometimes the wee ones would make a noise. The small ones would shout and bawl. There were old people and young people all mixed up. The men were in different wards. It was quite nice. I wore my own clothes and I did my own washing. I like the Park – I'd have liked to have stayed there. I was there ten years. I got a lot of friends there. Some of them's here. I got come here because they said it was getting closed down. I went to the ATC in —— and stayed in the hostel there for a year. It was all right. It was a nice hostel and I went to the adult centre and back every day. I liked the centre – I got on fine.

> I came here and then I went back to the Park for a week and then I asked to come back here. I got a bed in a flat here and into the centre. I used to fight with some people. There were some I didn't get on very well with. They're in a house of their own now. I would have stayed there.

Which was best, the hospital, the hostel or here?

> The hospital. I liked the hospital. We had a lot. The nurses were good to you. I was crying, I didn't want to go away. We had a flat, there was me, another girl – there was four of us in the flat. There was plenty going on in the Park, plenty to do. We had a centre in the hospital but I always went to one outside in the town and came back in a bus every day. I enjoyed myself. At the hostel all you did was go to the centre and come back to the hostel. I did go out on my own – into town on the bus – I got on great. Here, after the hospital there's not so much to do. Here I go to the Centre three days a week and do cooking here other days.

Was there much more to do in the Park? Yes, you watched TV.

You watch TV here? Yes, you went out shopping.

You go out shopping here? Yes.

So what's the difference?

I don't know. I liked the nurses. I got on fine with the teachers as well. Maybe it's 'cause there were more people there.

What didn't you like about the hospital?

I liked it all. After a long, long time I could go out of the flat myself and buy my food and cook it all myself. The hospital food wasn't very good food – oh no! It was terrible food.

If they asked me to go back I'd go back, but I don't know. If they wanted me back I'd go back tomorrow. I like the staff in the Park – but I'll stay here because of Mum. Mum thinks there's much more training here and she couldna' manage herself on the bus to the Park. It's far away. When Dad was alive, Daddy drove you see, and he took me back and forth in the car on the weekends and that. Every weekend. I came back Sunday to the Park. Now I can go home the bus once a fortnight. I like going home. I wouldn't mind to live at home.

Who are your best friends, the staff or the residents?

The staff – I like the staff. The staff are very helpful. The staff are good to me here too. Mum feels I'm settling down well here. I don't want to get Mum upset, because if I upset Mum I wouldna' be back home again. Once I was home and I was upsetting her and Mum was crying and the wee cats were unhappy as well – and Mam says 'You're fighting again and I'm not having you back home for two weeks because you're fighting again.

Do you do any shouting and bawling now – here ?

Sometimes at the staff here and I start crying. I go to my room and I can't stop sobbing.

Why?

I don't know – it's just habit.

If you could live at home, the hospital, the hostel or here, where would you like to live?

I'd like to live at home. Mum misses me. I go home and I come back and Mum starts crying. Mum's 76 – Dad died at 71. I've got four brothers married. I'd like to go back to Mum at home. Mum loves me. I phoned Mum tonight. I go home for Christmas and Hogmanay.

Would you like to live on your own?

No, Mum wouldn't let me. I'd be frightened somebody would come in the house. I shared a flat at the hostel with my friend but I just couldn't get on her with her at all – it couldn't work. It was very hard for me to sleep with her and that – there were two bunk beds in the one room. It didn't work very well. I used to fight a lot. I wouldn't mind getting a wee house of my own beside Mum. Then my Mum could come and see me and get coffee and that.

But Mum won't always be here will she?

No, that's right. That's what Mum was saying to me before. When Mum dies – now Dad's away – where would I go?

The Flat

After resettling as many residents as were capable of independent living in the local community, Mrs F decided to apply for an independent 'training' flat from the local council. She wished it to be within sight of The Ashes and with easy access to both The Ashes and the ATC which was only a three minute walk up the road. Although the residents would lead independent lives the flat would be regarded as a stepping stone and realistic training for full community independence. A flat on the third floor of the local council estate became available at this time and the tenancy was taken in Mrs F's name. It was in both sight and easy reach of The Ashes and on the way to the ATC. She was then faced with the task of selecting residents from those remaining who would be compatible and capable to undertake such a move. After much assessment and deliberation she decided on Mary, Joan and Enid.

Mary, a lady with Down's Syndrome and scoliosis in her mid 40s with a working-class background had always attended the ATC in the town. After her parents died she came to live at The Ashes at the age of 30 because her grandmother and brother felt unable to cope with her. Until her grandmother developed senile dementia Mary had either visited or been visited by her family every weekend. A very small lady, she has a recorded IQ in the region of 35–40 and was subject to bouts of depression.

Joan is also a lady with Down's syndrome in her mid 40s from an upper-middle-class background and had been placed in a mental subnormality hospital from the age of nine. At a later stage she was moved to the Park and after her father died she came to The Ashes which had just opened in her home town. Joan had always returned home for weekends. Very small in stature she has a recorded IQ in the region of 35–40.

Enid is a lady in her late 40s from a middle-class background with a diagnosis of focal epilepsy and cerebral palsy. She had been placed in the Park at the age of 16 and had moved to The Ashes when it opened in her home town. She had always remained in close touch with her mother who lived in the town seeing her every weekend. She too is very small in stature with a recorded IQ in the region of 40–45.

We had been trying deferent groups together within the Gables and we identified this group by use of P-A-C assessments and by putting them together to see if they had the potential to get on in the training flat. We had to identify some people who were possible candidates and we wanted people who had families in the town if possible because that

argued the possibility of better community support mechanisms because all the families would have their own friends in the community
and there was a chance that they would be allowed to move into these
circles.

There were actually four beds in the training flat but we came to the
conclusion that these three were the best combination we could come
up with at that time. There was no point putting in a fourth who was
not going to be compatible. The flat was on the third floor but there was
a reason for that which has proved in some ways to be valid. One of
the reasons was that they wouldn't be so likely to be harassed by people
and that was the housing manager's decision. Unfortunately the
families didn't like it.

We asked them if they'd like to go and they said 'Yes'. I know that they
have a habit of saying yes to whatever you ask them but those three
seemed to have progressed to a point where they were capable of doing
more than just staying in The Ashes. In the long run – if they say 'yes'
to you, you have to accept it – estimating that they've got the ability to
say 'no'. By the time they were actually moving across to the training
flat they had developed the ability to say 'no'.

They didn't go until we felt they were ready. They were together in a
training flat within the building and they got exercises in shopping and
coping and so forth. They can't read and write so we made picture
charts and then they put little stickers on the things they needed to buy.
There are hundreds of people who are illiterate living in this area – it's
traditional. Mary had lived at home for a reasonable part of her life,
Enid and Joan had been in the Park most of their lives but had visited
home a lot, so they all had a fair amount of domestic skills – the one
that had least was probably Joan.

We asked them if they'd like to go. We took them and showed them the
flat and they were heavily involved in selecting things for the flat.
Picking curtains and carpets, pots and pans etc mainly by catalogue.
We said 'Wouldn't you like this nice wooden salad bowl and the little
bowls?' Not a bit of it! They said they wanted 'the cut crystal one with
the silver rim'. An outreach worker lived with them for about a fortnight and then just slept there for another fortnight. After that they were
visited every day, then every second day – and so it went on until they
decided that they could cope.

We respect them as people. Down's syndrome people on the whole
don't get respected as people. People think of them as cuddly little
beings. These three are not over bright but they're socially quite capable
and can conduct a conversation, which is something most of the others
can't. That was one of the factors about them. They each have good
reliable social graces and that is desperately important. It shouldn't be
but it is, because these are the things that the public appreciate. That's
much more important for coping in the community than how well you
scrub a floor. Being able to scrub a floor is useful but you can shut your

door and nobody can see what it looks like. They have to be *not as good as* but *better* than the average person. Most of the people left in The Ashes now have not got reliable social skills – they may have them part of the time but not consistently.

After they had been living successfully in the flat a few months Mrs F discussed their life.

> They go to the ATC. Enid and Joan visit their mother. Mary is visited or visits her brother and Grannie. There's family support. The outreach workers still go in though nothing like as much now. They visit them about once a week, apart from that if they've got any problems they're on the phone. The phone rings, a voice says – 'Er, um, well you see it's like this – '. We had a crisis early in the morning the other day. It was a very, very hot day and Mary woke up and went to the bathroom and somehow or other choked and that frightened her. Enid got all worried and phoned me – this was before breakfast and I was the officer sleeping in The Ashes so the assistant ran across. We have two members of staff each night, one waking and one sleeping in. Unfortunately their two keyworkers were both on holiday. We did actually have the outreach officer of the ATC looking on but it was a bit early at quarter to six in the morning! She found Mary in a state but not really ill, more in a panic. Enid had as result caught the panic. She calmed her down and then found her with the window tight shut, a duvet and a blanket and socks on, on this baking hot day. So she stripped her off, sponged her down and told her when she felt a bit better to come across and see us later. She appeared about ten o'clock and was fine. She does feel the cold but the outreach officers do keep removing bits and pieces of clothing!

Visiting the Flat

Shortly after Enid, Mary and Joan moved into the flat the author was invited to visit them for tea. The invitation was made the night before and as all three attended the ATC from nine o'clock the following morning there was no time for any undue preparation. Having no prior information about their lives she arrived about half an hour after they returned home and after climbing three very steep flights of stairs was overwhelmed by what she found. The first (and lasting impression) was of three very tiny, vulnerable ladies, who were barely able to reach the front door handle – two of whom had obvious minor physical defects of scoliosis and cerebral palsy – and whose combined intellects barely approximated that of a single individual.

The flat consisted of an entrance hall off which opened two bedrooms, an office with a telephone, a large living dining room, a bathroom and small very well-fitted kitchen containing the airing cupboard and immersion heater. The office was used by the outreach workers and as none of the three could read or write they put all their post on the desk. In due course the outreach workers explained the complexities of the various bills and letters that arrived. (A thank you card later sent by the author would receive similar treatment.) The author was perturbed to find that there was no chain on the front door, but subsequent inquiries revealed that none of the three ladies had managed to learn how to use the chain when taught at the ATC and it was decided the dangers of locking themselves in were too great to fit one on the door.

The whole flat was immaculate and the tea that was prepared by the three of them in many ways replicated their 'entertaining' exercise in The Ashes training flat. A lace cloth covered the table which they proceeded to set with a pretty china tea service. Home-made cakes appeared and the teapot was carried from the kitchen to the table and tea was then served in a manner that would not be out of place in any upper-middle-class home. The ease with which this was accomplished, plus the fact that the kitchen was too small to eat in, confirmed that this lifestyle was in no way contrived for the author's benefit and was their customary way of entertaining visitors. It transpired that both Joan and Enid enjoyed cooking.

Even more interesting was the level of excited conversation over tea. All three ladies vied with each other to explain about the flat and what each of their duties were, chipping in on each other's conversation to add and amplify various facts. On a more serious note, sitting round the table after tea, they told the author a little about their previous lives. As the conversation progressed it became quite clear that they had fused into some sort of complex family group. When Mary began to talk about the car crash in which her father died, in which she along with the rest of the family was injured, the story was taken up by the other two who added facts and details of Mary's life at this time. They now appeared to have a common, shared life history in which each shared a part of the others perceptions. The author remained silent, regretting her decision not to bring the tape recorder in case it could have been seen as an invasion of their privacy.

CHAPTER 7

'I'm In the Community Now – I'm Getting On With It Now'

The life perceptions, opinions and conflicting views presented in this chapter have not been subjected to any editorial influence, nor did the professional staff listen to the residents' stories (apart from one keyworker in one case) before making their comments. The protagonists, in this demonstration of community relocation, were part of a well-thought-out programme that had taken them from home, through 20 or so years of a large mental subnormality hospital; ten years in the group home described in the previous chapter; to an independent unstaffed training flat on a large council estate well supported by outreach keyworkers. After two years in the flat two of the ladies moved into their own homes in the community but the third was transferred to a private group home in the area after only six months in the flat. All three ladies still attend the local ATC together as they have for the past ten years. As in the previous chapter the transcriptions were recorded between 1989–91.

The author was expecting to pay a return visit to the council flat to see how they were all getting on. However, by 1991 the situation had changed considerably and by now appeared to beg the whole question of self advocacy for people with such limited communication skills. It is hoped that the views presented in this chapter will challenge the reader to reassess both current relocation policy and their own personal views on community relocation and self advocacy.

Six months after Enid, Mary and Joan moved into the flat Joan's mother decided to withdraw her daughter from the flat to live in a new group home run by her church that had just opened in the town. This was envisaged as providing her with a permanent and secure sheltered home for the rest of her life.

Mrs F

> It was solely because Mother wanted Joan to go. We said it was up to Joan because we couldn't say anything else. We didn't agree with it but at the same time Mother is a very influential person in Joan's life. Joan was seen by people at the ATC who were directly involved with her and they also talked to Mother. The keyworkers sat and talked with mother. Joan was the one for whom it opened the biggest door, and the tragedy was that she wasn't allowed to stay inside that door. She's regressed – her face has closed in again – she still smiles but it isn't the same. It's not acceptable for her to say if she didn't want to go.

The disaster was that not that they couldn't cope without Joan, the disaster was that emotionally they got rocked. When we lost Joan we then got some very considerable regression particularly from Mary. They took a long time to get over it. It took them a long time to adjust to the jobs she used to do – as to who did them. They had to reorientate their whole lives – although they had a rota system there were certain things that Joan did because Joan was best at them. Joan was best cook. They had a problem adjusting themselves to cover that. They did eventually but it took time. They didn't understand why she'd gone and it was very difficult trying to explain to them.

First we went through a period of trying to persuade them that they were still interested; then we went through a period of trying to find another third; but the interesting thing was the more we tried to find another third the stronger the relationship between the two of them became and the more rejecting they became of any third. We are now seeking a house for just the two of them. They are quite specific that they want a ground floor flat for just the two of them so an application has been made for that. Currently we do not have a group in The Ashes able to move into the flat independently.

Enid and Mary lived in the flat for 18 months remaining together for a further year before finally deciding to move on to separate accommodation.

They wanted to be on the ground floor and they wanted to be separate. At least Enid wanted to be separate and Mary was prepared to accept it. Enid is one of these people who does things in a house and then complains that she's having to do them. She's a 'put-upon'! She eventually decided that she was being so put upon that she couldn't tolerate living with Mary any longer. They moved Enid first because a house became available and because Enid was the one who more urgently wanted to move. Now if Enid has problems, Enid rings us up and tells us. She's got a phone and an alarm system. If her light bulb goes in her lamp or the toilet paper holder falls off the wall she rings us up and tells us and someone goes over and fixes it. Enid is coping a 100 per cent but nobody ever anticipated that Enid wouldn't.

Enid

The author had arranged to visit Enid at 8.45am and then give her a lift to the ATC. Enid's ground-floor council flat was entered through a lobby off the pavement and was close to the corner shop. The flat was in easy walking distance of The Ashes and the ATC. Enid met the author with obvious pleasure and showed her proudly round the flat, after first replacing the new door chain. There was a good size bed sitting room with her dolls neatly tucked up in the bed. The room was adequately heated by an electric fire with a couch, chair, low table, large TV and contained a homely clutter of ornaments and magazines etc. A small bathroom and well-equipped kitchen with a washing machine both opened off the hall which contained an airing cupboard and a large fitted cupboard that served as a wardrobe. One or two kitchen utensils were still in their original wrappings as Enid said she was so busy she'd not had time to use them in the eight months she had been living there. The store cupboard seemed to be mainly filled with cup-a-soup, biscuits and the odd tin of convenience food and fruit was ripening on the window sill of the living room. The flat was impressively well kept – but also showed signs of obvious use. When going into the back communal garden with seats and washing lines Enid was cheerily greeted by a neighbour hanging out washing and said she enjoyed sitting in the garden when the weather was good. There was an overwhelming impression that Enid was using every aspect of her environment – and well pleased with it all.

Enid's Perceptions

I lived with Mam before my brother died in a car crash, he was only 16. He was killed in a motorbike and a car crash. I was taking a lot of bad turns and things like that and Mam couldn't manage. I was 17 when I went to the Park, that's 35 years ago. Mam wasn't able with me, with Gran and things like that. After I was in the Park we had to go down on our knees – if we were bad and things. There was a big prison if we did something wrong. A room with just a bed if you were bad. You had your clothes.

When I first went I was on ward 11 with a lot of people. The thing is – the nurses was awful good to you. Then I got shifted from ward 11 to ward 12. Ward 12 was a locked ward and I went into the prison room. I couldn't even get out. You had to go out of it with the nurses and other girls. We'd just sit or watch TV. I was just there a few days I think and then they put me to ward 2. It was a good ward. After I went to ward 2 then I went down to ward 6 and that was a good ward. We went out. Ward 14 was the babies, ward 13 was the boys, ward 15 was they could hardly walk. We didn't see the men until we got out to the dance. Some of them had great boy friends – saw them at the dance or the pictures. We had pictures, dancing, bingo, concerts and things like that.

Then I went to ward 6 and worked and things like that. The things I did to the staff and things – they were all right with me. If you helped them and things like that, you could easy go on, but if you fight with anybody you're on punishment on all the wards. If you start with a boy or one or another patient you're on punishment for six weeks. Six weeks. You can't go to the dancing – you canna go to the concerts – you canna go anywhere. You had to get a pail and everything to scrub – for six weeks. For 25 years. I dinna have any fights but one of the male attendants told me to fight it out. There was another girl started on me at the dance and I just fighted back.

When I was on ward 6 we had a meeting with the staff and they told me 'There's a place Enid and you've been in here a long time luv and you no want to stay any more in here. Some day I'm going to see you get put out' – it was Dr M. There was a flat in ward 6 where we learned everything and staff said 'Enid, some day I'm going to see you put out'. My brother-in-law said to my mother 'You'd better take your daughter out – take Enid out'. We didn't ask to go out. That night Sister L said to me – I think it was the pictures or the concert or something like that – 'Go out with the rest of the girls' – so I went out with the rest of the girls but when I came back – I think it was the pictures that night – all my stuff was all packed up in sacks. It was on the Thursday night I went to the pictures, and came back with the girls and came up the stairs and all my things were all packed – everything was on my bed – packed up on the bed – the staff had to do it. I wondered where I was. I was shocked. I did get a shock, I was a bit upset. I asked Sister where I was going. She said 'Enid, come on and I'll tell you' and then the man came to see me – the social worker man and he said 'Enid, come on, you're coming down with me' and I said 'where am I going?'and he said 'I want you to go' so I went with him. Then he took me down to The Ashes. I left my bags behind. I saw all the rooms and things at The Ashes but I didn't know I was going. Then I came back and heard my social worker man say 'Please, that'll be your last chance Enid I think you'll be better in The Ashes'. I had to leave. My brother-in-law had said to Mam 'I think Enid will like The Ashes better' and I went to The Ashes.

I liked the Park, it was good. We did ever such a lot of things. The staff were awful good and things like that. I dinna want to go back because I have a step sister in the Park. Mum married again when I was in the Park. She was up at CCC for a while but she's been bad and struck people and they sent her back. She struck Mum and everything and I'm frightened of her. I've smacked her a few times and Mam's smacked her. When I had my last birthday at the flat she came to the party with my Mam and she just struck me but I struck her back. And then she struck Mam. Mam was upset and she was bothered by this.

When I got up to The Ashes I liked it so much. It was lovely. I was ten years at The Ashes and then I had to go to the flat and things like that. Pru *(keyworker)* and them had to put me out because it was too much and there were new people to come in. My room was number 8 and someone wanted it. I'd like to have stayed at The Ashes but Pru thinks it was too much for Mam and things like that.

The flat was too much for me and I had to do a lot. I think to myself that I did too much. I did like it in the beginning but I had to do everything. I had to do all the washing and making the beds. After Joan went away I did all the cooking. Mary did just sit – the both of them did just sit. I liked it at first but it was too much up the stairs. Mary has a home help now but I do all my work myself. She's lazy. I don't want a home help. So Pru went to my mother and said she'd seen another house and it was empty. Mam lives just up the road and I stay with Mam every Saturday and Sunday.

Here I do my own work and everything. I buyed my own furniture. I go to the bank – The Ashes taught me. I like to go to the centre every day, just walk back and forth. I go and see Mary on Monday and Wednesday night. We walk up to the club and get the bus back at night. I go to the leisure centre on a Tuesday morning by myself and go to the centre after I've come back from the leisure centre. We have games and things and the staff are there and I meet the Home Boys. They're the boys that have been bad and things like that and done something wrong and they're in trouble. They're awful nice. I was pally with a boy a long time ago but I'm not bothered.

I've got a phone here. See that down there – and that thingy up there. When I get any fits like that and I press that, it goes off at the Gables and they rush straight over. So I don't feel frightened. I've used it three times. They can talk to me through it. If I just want to talk to them I dial my own phone. My Mam lives just down the road. My Mam has been two or three times on a Sunday. I make dinner and tea and then I give Mam a cup of coffee. She's 81. Mam likes it here – she thinks it's marvellous.

What will you do when she's not here any more?

I'll just have to stay here.

When she's not here and you're on your own, would you rather be back in The Ashes?

No, I'll stay here. I'm quite happy.

Of all the places you've been, the hospital, The Ashes, the flat or here – which was the best?

I like here best.

Comments

Mrs F

I've been battling to go and see the client myself, often with the outreach officer for the contact, to talk to them and explain about The Ashes. Then to have them for a week or weekend at The Ashes to find out about it. Then to send them back to the Park or wherever it is, so that they actually have a cut off point to make a decision that is realistic. I am regarded as a maverick – a nuisance – and totally eccentric. A lot of people in the Park get moved out into the private sector on a sensible two-week trial but at the end of the two week trial they don't go back if everything's OK – they're just kept. This doesn't give them a realistic understanding of the fact that they don't have to stay there. Enid didn't say 'no' to going to the training flat. Enid has the ability to say 'no' but she never uttered a word. I think that what they do is that they rationalise from previous experience and produce an explanation.

Mary

Mary was interviewed at the ATC as she had recently had all her money stolen by a young local couple that she thought were neighbours and regarded as friends. She was very shaken by this and it was thought inadvisable to ask her to accept a stranger in her home at that time. She lived in a similar ground-floor council flat round the corner from Enid in the same development. Since leaving the flat her Gran had developed senile dementia and could no longer either visit Mary or cope with her at home where she was looked after by Mary's brother. In view of Mary's obvious distress about her money the author asked her keyworker (Sue) to be present during the interview. She sat, apparently working at her desk and out of Mary's direct view.

Mary's Perceptions

I went to The Ashes after my Dad died in a car crash. I was in the car as well. I was in the car crash too. Mum was at the back with Andrew and me and my Grannie. My Grannie had a broken knee cap and her forehead went through the windscreen. I got put in there after my Mum's death. She died later in hospital. I went to the Infirmary and my Auntie was hearing about us and I lived with her for a little. My Mother used to be a supervisor in Jones. She had two children, me and Andrew. We were both healthy. I was born in ——— Andrew was born in ———. I was born first, Andrew was born second. My school was at ——— and his school was at the Academy. Then I went to Ivy house when I was 16. When I was a wee girl I lived on the farm. I've finished with the farm now. My own home is 22 Carlton Ave and my Granny was not able for me. That's why I went to The Ashes.

I don't go home now, Andrew comes to see me on Saturday. On Sunday night Andrew and Gran used to come and see me or sometimes I go up for my tea and Andrew brings me back home. First I shared my own room at The Ashes. I cleaned my own room. My friends at The Ashes go to the centre. My first Christmas was at The Ashes and that was nice and Hogmanay I went to my Gran and Andrew. He's my brother – he no has a motor any more now.

I got put out of The Ashes and Joan and Enid and me went to the flat. My room was number 11 and they needed my room for somebody else. I've finished with The Ashes now and I finished with my trial in the flat. Now I'm with the town council. Me and Enid were happy in the flat, Enid did the cooking and I did the other ones. Enid did the washing, I dried them up and Joan put them away, I did my own washing and we used to have a keyworker who came over. There were 75 stairs and I got breathless. I was to go to the hospital for a couple of days, the stairs were too much for me.

Now I've got some visitors come up to see me. Sue comes up and Pru comes up *(keyworkers)*. On Monday night I go to Monday Club at the leisure centre. Me and Enid walks down. On Wednesday I go to social club at The Ashes. Tuesday night I watch the TV and make my tea. I had a cup of soup yesterday and I have an orange or apple for supper. I have my dinner here (the ATC) I just have to make my own tea and my supper when I go home. Some times I make burgers and stuff like that. Thursday I might go for a walk. Friday night I sometimes see Joan at CCC and have my coffee and that. I walk up there to visit them.

How do you get back? How do I get back?

How do you get back in the dark?...

Its a long way – how do you get back? I get back safe.

How? Do you walk? Uh

In the dark? Uh um. How do I get back Sue?

I do my shopping on Friday after I leave here. On Saturday Andrew comes to see me about ten. If he's working he comes in later. I make my own dinner on a Saturday, sometimes I have pasties or beans. Andrew rings my bell and I say 'Whose there?' I've got a chain now. When he's working he just comes between one and two. On Saturday I go for a walk again if it's a nice day – by myself. Sunday, sometimes I go to church or sometimes I go to the shop and get my milk and that.

Was there more to do at The Ashes on Saturday and Sunday? Oh at The Ashes I was with my friends.

But you don't do that now? No.

Don't you go to The Ashes on a Saturday and Sunday to see them ever? No. Sometimes I go to church with The Ashes lot if I want to. Where my cousins got married in.

This Monday and Tuesday it's a holiday at the Centre. What are you going to do? I'll do my housework and clean up my bathroom. I'll watch TV.

Would you go down to The Ashes?

No. I'm in the community now. On a Monday I go to Enid's house after we come home from the Monday club for a coffee. We go turn about, I go to Enid's house. We don't have our coffee there anymore as they have to get everybody home on the bus.

Who are your friends now you're in the community? Enid, and Pru and Sue (keyworkers).

What about the people who live next door?

I have my next door neighbour. Mr Young next door to me. Sometimes he speaks to me and I speak to him.

Have you ever been in his house No.

Has he been in your house? No. There's a couple upstairs above.

Have you been in their house? No.

Have they been in yours? No.

When the Centre's closed what do you do?

Do my kitchen work and clean my cupboards. I have my help on Monday and Thursdays early in the morning. Jennie goes out of the house with me – me and Jennie goes out together.

What will you do in the holidays – will you go to The Ashes?

Sometimes when I'm wearied I go down and visit them and speak to them. Sometimes I go on bus trips with my keyworker at the centre.

What are the good things about living on your own?

I'm getting on with it now. I'm in the community now. Enid's in it as well. Joan's in CCC housing.

Is that in the community?

No, CCC housing is not in the community they've got staff up there. Sometimes The Ashes' staff comes down to see me to see I'm all right. I went up to CCC housing for my holiday. They were just trying me out for a week – 'cause my keyworker was off with her husband – to see how I was getting on with it. I liked it. I got settled down fine with all my friends. Somebody else has got the room now.

Comments

Keyworker in ATC

Mary would just sit back in the flat and let Enid do everything. You'd ask her how she was getting on with her house work and she'd tell you all the things she was doing but she wasn't doing that – Enid would actually be doing it! She would just sit. Joan did a bit – Mary did nothing. She has a home help now two days a week – it's the only way Mary will cope on her own – that and back-up services. I visit, Sue visits. We're trying to get Mary to do as much as she can for herself but unless she has all this back-up help she can't cope. To go back in The Ashes would be a backward step for Mary. Mary doesn't want that at all. I think Mary is just existing in the community, she has got too much back-up. I think we might be looking at something like CCC for Mary in the future.

If you go to her house now she'll say 'This is my home' and she'll show you round the house and the garden. She's so proud of her home but I wonder if she's just existing there. When she comes home she does the same thing every time. She'll take her coat off and she'll switch on the television and that's time for tea. If you go in one day and then again the next day, you'll find her sitting in exactly the same place and everything in the same place – as if it hasn't been touched. In an ordinary house there's always something out of place. Like Enid's house – where she has to tidy up – that tells you an awful lot and that's normality. I wonder if Mary just spends her time just standing by the window – she misses company.

The bit I find is so difficult is that she's got plenty of lovely clothes and nice shoes but she doesn't want to wear them. She'd rather wear the same old thing day in and day out. Where do you draw the line here? You go up there and you find a nice skirt and put her on a nice tee shirt and she looks lovely and she does feel good. When she makes the effort she does feel good and it makes a difference. Then there are other times when she's a bit down in the mouth and a bit depressed and she's wearing the same things she's had on for a couple of weeks. I've left her – just to see how long she goes before she changes them herself but she never thinks of it. Then people come back at us – 'You're supposed to be caring people – you're supposed to be looking after her and you let them go about like that!' Then it's a personal thing against you. Then people talk about choice – but that's what happens. I find the job quite difficult sometimes. You just do what you would do yourself and how would you feel if somebody did this to you?

Mrs F

The staff are not friends, the role that staff play is much more subtle. They are much more substitute parents. I think a lot of them actually never reach the stage where they fully understand what friendship is. Friendship has the abstract bit to it that they don't have the ability to understand. I always use the quotation 'love comes from blindness, friendship from knowledge' and they don't have the knowledge of the way that people function to be able to develop a friendship in any useful way. They almost entirely remain in the stage of development where they extrapolate *from* – as in the child whose mother goes away to hospital who asks 'Why has Mum gone away and left me and what have I done?' The older child on the other hand says 'Poor Mum, what can I do to help?' They are all still egocentric and the whole concept of friendship is an abstract thought. At the flat she wanted to separate from Enid, but in fact the relationship with Enid served her better than it served Enid.

Mary has to be allowed to make decisions. The people outside don't understand. The community in which she believes herself to be still doesn't grasp that she has the right to do things that they find less than acceptable. It probably would have been better if her house had been nearer to that of her natural family but we couldn't get it at the time they had to leave the flat. They need a bridge to people. Not a professional bridge, that's impossible. It's usually a family bridge. We encourage the family and every Ashes resident has invitations to things for their family. We try to make it a family unit because if they are going to move outside The Ashes, they're going to need those families because it's the family links that make the bridge into the community. A good number of our families are siblings.

Mary is somewhat of a depressive, she swings a bit. When she's feeling off colour she is inclined not to do anything very much and forget to change her clothes and so forth. Then everybody descends on me saying she shouldn't be in the community because she can't look after herself. I point out that any depressive behaves like that and they will have periods when they are less able. People get confused between whether somebody has learned something and is able to do it but is choosing not to do it.

Should Mary have stayed at The Ashes?

I don't know. You have to give them the opportunity – and accept that it may go wrong. I'm not entirely sure that it's gone wrong completely.

What we need to do is look at it and see what can be done about it. Pru doesn't want to put her into CCC and Sue does, so you've got two keyworkers working from a different basis. Mary went to CCC because her two keyworkers were both on holiday from the training centre. There's no decision to even consider CCC for her.

Joan

Joan, the third of the original training flat residents, was interviewed at the ten-bedded group home where she had been living for the past 18 months since she left the flat. CCC was furnished to a high standard, with all the residents having their own bedrooms and much thought had obviously been given to the communal areas. The large domestic type kitchen was separated by a serving counter from the dining area – but access for carrying trays was possible at one end of the room. The design allowed the residents to cook with the staff in view of everyone and serve the meal at a long table screened from the cooking area. The lounge led off the dining area so that it was possible to walk through with tea or coffee from the kitchen when watching television. Staff and residents prepared and ate the food together in a pleasantly informal way. The table was well set and there was a fair amount of conversation over meals. The clearly visible daily menu was in large writing as was the domestic rota which was designed so that everybody changed tasks quite often. All the residents appeared to help prepare the evening meal at least once a week. The ratio of two well-trained staff to ten fairly independent residents over the evening period led to much staff and resident interaction.

It was particularly impressive that when the author (who no-one was expecting) was preparing to leave as the evening meal was almost ready, an invitation from the staff to join them produced an instant response from the residents who very quickly laid another place setting, found a chair, and slotted them into the existing settings. Tea was offered and poured at the table by the residents, condiments similarly proffered, and one of the staff volunteered to share his meal as everyone was ready to eat. The small-scale domestic preparation of the meal for 12 people (plus the unexpected guest) and the family atmosphere as everyone sat round the table asking the author where she came from was almost faultless.

It had proved very difficult to interview Joan due to her appalling communication skills. She was more than willing to talk but it was impossible to get any connected speech without resorting to direct questions. The little language she did produce was virtually indecipherable when replayed through the tape recorder. She had agreed to be interviewed and happily took the author to her comfortable well-furnished bedroom. Having first completed the initial interview, it was decided to ask a member of staff to repeat the interview using the questions Joan appeared to have already answered. This was mainly to confirm that the author's interpretations were correct. The information gleaned in the original interview came as a surprise to the staff at CCC who had worked with Joan for the past 18 months and thought she regarded the group home as her home. It was also surprising to the author that Joan remembered her coming for tea in the flat and spontaneously volunteered information about the visit that the author had forgotten.

Although hospitalised since the age of nine, Joan had always returned home every weekend from Saturday to Monday. This practice continued throughout her 20 years in hospital, 10 years in The Ashes, her brief 6 month stay in the training flat and the past 18 months at CCC. Her mother was a staunch church attender and as soon as the church opened its group home in the town she moved Joan there from the flat. It was felt that among other considerations she was also unhappy about her daughter living on the local council estate. It became quite clear as the interview progressed, as Joan answered each question with reference to what her mother thought, that she merely regarded her weekday placement as some sort of hotel accommodation which served rather like a boarding school. Her mother referred to the ATC as 'school' and Joan appeared to think that she had to stay in the hostel so she could go to school in the morning, which her mother had told her would not be possible if she lived at home. She enjoyed the ATC where most of the residents of her current hostel attended with her and she was also very clear in her own mind that she didn't need a home in the community like Enid and Mary. When asked if she too would like to live in her own home, on her own, replied very firmly that she already had a home with her own bedroom, all her clothes and a double bed at 7 Grange Street. On Sundays she went to church then her brother brought his children for tea and she looked after them. It was very difficult to establish what Joan really thought about anything as all her answers were reflections of her mother's feelings and prefaced by 'Mum says...': Mum didn't like the Park; Mum didn't really like The Ashes; Mum certainly didn't like the flat; Mum liked CCC.

Joan's life had a routine and purpose that had remained unchanged since childhood in that every weekend she was collected and driven to her own home by her devoted mother. Christmas had always been spent in whatever institution she was in while her mother visited family in Aberdeen and Joan then came home for the family Hogmanay celebrations. Joan's story raises too many problems for comfort. Each agency seems to have done their utmost to perpetuate a lifestyle that ultimately may well not have been in her best interests. The consensus of opinion is that Joan's life will collapse almost totally when her contact with her mother and her home is withdrawn.

The following questions, which replicated part of the original interview, were put to Joan by the CCC care assistant who had known her for the past 18 months.

She seemed to have as little success as the author and equal difficulty understanding the replies. Some questions were asked in two or three different ways to elicit an answer without unduly influencing the reply.

Joan's perceptions

Do you like staying here? Yes.

What do you think of this place? Fine.

What about Mum's house? Yes.

Do you like living there? Yes

Is that your home? Yes.

What makes them different? My sister comes. My sister's got three dogs and my brother has three children. I'm an Auntie. I go to church.

If anyone asks you where your home was what would you say? 7 Grange Street

Is that your home? Yes.

Is this your home? Yes. *Two homes?* Two homes.

How did you get on in your flat? Fine.

Is here better? Yes. Better here.

Did you like the flat? Sometimes. There were three girls.

Do you want to go back to the flat? No I like it better here. People better here. I do my housework.

Is it the company? Yes.

Did you not get company in the flat? No.

Would you like to go to the Centre and sleep at home every night? No I live here. I go home on Saturday.

Is that what Mum says? Yes. I go with Alec. Mum says to go every day.

If you got into trouble or if there was any bother at the Centre would you tell Mum or would you tell the staff? I'd tell the staff and I'd tell Mum at the weekend.

Would you phone Mum if there was bother? No, I'd just tell the staff.

Comments

Ashes care assistant

Joan is very mother dominated and it was mother's decision to remove her from the flat and go to CCC. Her mother didn't like her walking up the stairs. I thought that was a tragedy. My personal view is – although it's not really my job – I felt Joan took a step backward by going to CCC. However, when you get down to it, it was her choice. Maybe she would prefer to be where her friends are.

CCC care assistant

She very much gears herself to going home at the weekend. There's a work rota to keep the house tidy and right and she won't do her work on Saturday because she's going home.

I sent her to the chemist to get her prescription but when she got there and they didn't have it ready yet. And she stood and she bawled and she shouted and she refused to move from that chemist until they gave her what she wanted. Yet I've been hearing about her today at the ATC and she never speaks, and she's quiet and shy and she bounces about all cute and timid.

Where do you think she's happy?

I think she's only really happy at her own home.

Mrs F

The family aren't going to provide for Joan once Mum has gone. She will lose a large sense of her identity. Joan regards mother's home as her home not CCC. Mum likes CCC because she sees it as being a of a different social standing – that came over loud and clear. If Mum could find somewhere other than the training centre for Joan that was a bit more upper class that would be better too.

CCC was founded by the church and the one in the town was out of date when it was opened because it's a ten-bed 'place for life' unit. They also seem to have a policy of preferring certain types of resident – and they like Down's syndrome!

Joan's mother, being a church-going lady had been somewhat involved from the start. Even if Joan had still been in The Ashes when ARC opened it would have been quite possible that mother would have moved her. I still see Joan because the ARC people come to the social club we have on a Wednesday night. She's not the same – her face is shut down again. What I see is that when she went to the flat her face lit up and she opened out and behaved in a way she never had before. She's sort of shut down again.

People invariably move back towards their generic inheritance. They move back to the value systems of their home and family and cling on to those. Their social behaviour will be dictated by what happened to them as a child. We all of us carry in the back of our heads what mother said. Joan is clinging to that which has proved more powerful than anything else. You can't get away from people's inheritance and what this does prove is that it is vitally important for anybody working with people with learning difficulties to have some knowledge of their early life because you can't work effectively with them unless you've got some idea of what background they came from – and hopefully some knowledge of their family history. Otherwise you're fighting against something that you don't even know what it is. It's also about recording – getting trained social workers who realise it isn't just about filling in a form. There is a reason for providing this information. It isn't just that people are saying this client had a mother and a grannie and a brother etc and isn't that nice. It's that these things have significance in their life.

Overview

Mary's keyworker

> I'm sure we're getting some of these community placements wrong. No matter what's on paper. We've had so many people moving from residential care into their own homes and it looks very good on paper but if it doesn't work for that person – then it's a failure. If they're not happy – then it's not working really. We talk about trying to get groups of people with learning disabilities mixed up with ordinary people but they seem so much happier in their own groups. That's what they want. You say the community should get involve – but people don't want that. People with learning disabilities are not accepted by most people, they're treated differently.

Mrs F

> I don't think there is as anything as simple as the community. I don't think there is anything as simple as training people to live like every-body else because everybody else doesn't live the same way. I get very fed up for instance with all these statements about networking – i.e. they ought to be able to go to this club, or that club, or the other club. I don't belong to any club so why should they? Maybe Mary likes it like that. One would have to argue that given the opportunity if she's living like that – she may be choosing to. But I would agree with you – she may not! The problem is how you find out whether they like it or not – because they're not going to tell you. They will tell you things that are wrong – but they won't tell you they don't like the thing overall because they know that there's a drive towards it. I wanted them to stay together but they didn't want to. Mary made that choice as much

as Enid. They wanted to separate and they were very definite that they wanted to separate. They were quite keen at that point to get away from each other. They're both on the ground floor literally just round the corner from each other – not two minutes walk away from each other.

I think what we're into with this one is about the ability to live in friendship and that's actually why I had three of them originally and why the loss of Joan was such a tragedy even though Joan didn't see it as a tragedy. It's easier with three. It wasn't anything to do with the work it was to do with the relationship. If one wanted to be on their own the other ones still had someone to talk to. It's about how do you relate to other people. Two people on their own really have to have a very good relationship – living with one other person intrudes on you more. Whereas if there are three of you there is less pressure. You caught them in the flat in transition. They were bound to move over a period of time. They had to move on from there after two years and they would have moved on even faster had we not had the thing with Joan. We'd have got them a flat for three. We had an application in for Enid and Mary together, then Enid and Mary felt they wanted to separate. They were in fact the last of the residents that I thought were capable of moving on at that time.

The people in The Ashes now would only move if it were into a staffed house. We're still training, but you can train them till you're blue in the face but they don't remember anything. They don't have the capacity to organise their life sufficiently to be able to live without staff support. We could move an Ashes flat into a house in the community provided we move with it the staff support it has already got. We've got to the point where we've managed to move out all the people who have the capacity to live semi independently. The Ashes is now a series of very small group homes and the communal area serves as a village hall. What's gone wrong is Mary's perception of this. Anyone in the outreach can use it as semi-public lounge. Enid will come in if she feels like it.

There's a progression when you put somebody into a community situation. To start with they're very enchanted because they see it as social freedom compared to what they had. Then they realise that the freedom bears with it responsibilities and that's quite hard work because there isn't always somebody to pick up after you. They see that life is hard work. They go through that and then they come to terms with the fact that – yes it's hard work – but they do get something for the hard work. They begin to understand that rights bring responsibility. Now that is something that is never taught to people with learning difficulties. In their own homes, institutions or whatever, everybody excuses them on the basis that they've got learning difficulties and that they can't really understand that if they do so and so – that means they've also got to do so and so. Yet this is always taught to small children very early in the normal world. It isn't taught in the world of learning difficulties.

It's a dream thing. They talk, in the Park and places like that, about having somewhere of their own – and people talk to them about how wonderful it is. They don't understand because when they lived in the community before – as most of them have done at some time, whether it's only childhood memories – people did things for them. They didn't have to do things for themselves. Then they hit the reality of the fact that living in your own place means that you are responsible for locking the door at night, for putting out the rubbish, for cleaning every day – it's not just sometimes.

'The best laid schemes o' mice an' men gang aft a'gley' etc. You can plan as you wish but if you then say of somebody in the community – 'This person is a citizen' – they have the right to make decisions. They've got to make the wrong decisions if they want to.

Part Three

Patterns of Living
The Independent Sector

CHAPTER 8

Training for Leisure
Wentwood Education

The LOCO assessment of Wentwood Education, which has functioned as a private sixth-form college for adolescents with severe learning disabilities since 1980, also yielded a unique ten-year treasure trove of P-A-C assessment and training procedures. These not only related to the development of the student-centred curriculum but also recorded, in impeccable detail, the developmental progress of every student over the ten years. This impressive wealth of data highlighted the paucity of information from other group homes and hostels visited by the author. The effective curriculum resulted in students being realistically trained in life skills that enabled them to enjoy relatively independent lives within the college, and also to avail themselves of the local neighbourhood facilities. These leisure activities were incorporated into the curriculum in a way not found in any other group home or ATC.

Henrietta Reynolds (HR) established Wentwood Education in 1980 and subsequently worked there for the next decade. She set out to prove that an intensive residential pre-vocational course would give the young adult with special needs the ability and confidence to live an independent life within the community. It was also envisaged that this particular approach would extend the students' horizons beyond the somewhat restrictive world of the ATC. Wanting to control, and if possible eliminate, the overprotective background often experienced by students leaving special schools when they try to enter an adult world of growing independence, she decided that a residential setting was the most appropriate for her students. The intake was to be restricted to those students who were transferring from the then named ESN/S (educationally subnormal/severe) schools, or those within a similar IQ range from other sources. Thus the records analysed were from students with recorded IQ scores of below 55 or equivalent mental ages.

The material, which charts the development of young adults with severe learning disabilities through an intensive two-year residential social education course, was not originally collected for the purpose of research. However, it was possible to approach a subsequent research project with the confidence of reliability, as during the decade 1980–90 meticulous records and P-A-C assessments had been kept on all the students entering this private sixth-form college. The curriculum, teaching methods and assessments were based on P-A-C methodology. The students completed the two year course with regular six-monthly assessments, because of this it was also possible to use the records of the entire student intake over the ten years, without any strategic pruning of results. The only records not used were those for the handful of students who for various reasons did not complete the two year course and those students who had not completed the course by May 1990. Thus it was possible to establish a base line for every student graduating over the ten years, and so define progress from admission to departure.

The full research project which compares and contrasts the Wentwood way of life with that of the residents in the 'unified' group homes (see Chapters 4 and 5) is the subject of a further publication which covers a far wider range of data than is presented here (Sinson 1992). In that more detailed and wide ranging presentation it has been possible to present sound statistical evidence from both Wentwood and the five 'unified' group homes, of the efficacy of the entire Wentwood curriculum. However, as an antidote to the resulting *micro-institutionalism* of residents in all the group homes, who are subjected to the negative practices outlined in previous chapters, that part of the Wentwood curriculum relating to the teaching of leisure activities has been extracted from the wider research context to form the basis of this chapter.

As Wentwood is a private concern, combining residential training of life skills with a clear educational component, the cost of staffing such a college with a high staff/student ratio is unusually high. In the light of the current financial stringencies in the public sector, if the Wentwood method, and results can be seen to effectively equip the young adult with special needs to cope with policies of community integration, then it should be regarded to be ultimately cost effective. Almost certainly the controversy about the desirability and feasibility of such schemes will continue throughout the next decade. It may well be that a closer consideration of this particular forward-looking undertaking may add some positive elements to the debate. One indication of the success of Wentwood is suggested by the fact that the majority of students over the past three years have managed to achieve a measure of self-sufficiency. Most of them are living relatively independent lives in small community houses (with varying degrees of staff dependence) rather than in hospitals, larger group homes or with their families.

The Environment

The initial difficulties of finding suitable accommodation for Wentwood involved rejecting many different geographical locations. For the P-A-C training programme to be effective, students had to live both within a well-defined urban community and yet be sufficiently distanced from amenities. This would enable the training programme to be designed with realistic graduated progression and challenges. Effective transport links were essential to enable parents to visit easily and for students to be taught to travel home independently for holidays and short visits. A range of sporting facilities were required within the locality to enable students to experience the same choice of independent leisure activities as their more fortunate siblings. A large garden with outbuildings was necessary to develop those often tedious occupations of gardening and house maintenance which are usually substituted by contract provisions in local authority residential group homes.

The house had to be manageable and conform to concepts of ordinary domestic architecture in order to avoid the more usual local authority group home pitfall of instituting time-saving/cost-cutting contract cleaning, catering and services. Within the house there had to be accommodation for up to 12 residents as well as living-in accommodation for staff. The students' total environment had to provide every opportunity to learn life skills in a meaningful setting. To this end it was intended that the community would be relatively self-sufficient and employ no domestic or other maintenance staff.

Eventually such a location was found, comprising a large nineteenth-century rectory set in the original village square and adjoining the church and vicarage, around which a small market town had developed. There was extensive ribbon development leading to factories, housing estates, motorways, sports centre and all the impedimenta of twentieth-century urban life. Two years later the adjoining vicarage, the Grove, was acquired to enable seven students to spend the final part of their course living almost fully independent lives with a minimum of staff supervision.

The Students

Ninety students have attended Wentwood over the decade including those still completing their course. Their ages on departure ranged from 17 to 22 years. The majority of students have local authority backing with the main catchment area being adjoining authorities in the south of England. The social class distribution was broadly that found in the normal population with a slightly higher proportion of middle class students from the more geographically distant locations. This was not Wentwood policy, but was assumed to have arisen through the ability of articulate middle-class parents to persuade the funding authorities to co-operate in Further Education projects. Such parents also had a more ready acceptance of boarding school and college life. All the students were ambulant, although several had both sensory and minor physical disabilities, and were within the 40–55 IQ range.

Intending students had to spend a trial period of assessment at the college. The students who were not accepted at the end of this two-week trial were those students who appeared over sophisticated and already competent in some of the personal and social skills needed for both leisure and work. It was felt that, although currently attending special schools, they would feel understretched by the Wentwood curriculum which was designed for the more severely disabled adolescent. Students were never rejected because they had too few skills, but some students were turned down due to their physical disabilities requiring more space than was available in the domestic setting of the college.

The Staff

Fourteen members of staff were employed which gave a staff/student ratio of one member of staff to four students during the day. This ratio decreased during evenings and weekends, to two staff in the main house for twelve students and one in the annexe for the seven more independent students. This decrease during the students' leisure time resulted in students in both houses having to cope with areas of their daily life with very little supervision. This was a deliberate and planned policy. Because there were no domestic or maintenance staff, this so-called leisure time was filled with the sort of domestic and personal tasks that would have normally required staff supervision or have been performed by domestic staff in local authority group homes.

Staff were employed both to teach a special subject and to be a general member of staff. The policy was for each member of staff to wear a different 'hat', with their special subject title drawn from the P-A-C section headings. For example, an individual member of staff was responsible for each of the main P-A-C areas of Self-help, Communication, Socialisation and Occupation. Within these confines, different staff members had a responsibility for the more specialised subsections. For example, 'travel' taught by HR was a subsection termed Mobility within in the P-A-C Self-help sector. This led to a novel approach to the curriculum, in that when staff were on duty, the lessons the students had during that period reflected the 'hat' of the teacher. As all teachers did equal time on the rota and students worked in small groups of four, this became a very effective way of teaching. The staff rota dominated the curriculum and as their duty time included a selection of day, overnight and weekend periods, this ensured that effective teaching went on throughout almost every minute of the students' waking day. Each teacher also had an equal amount of day rota time for formal academic-type group teaching. Not only did each member of staff have to teach a special subject in the P-A-C area but they were also responsible for making small-step teaching breakdowns for each skill in their P-A-C area. They were expected to record and inform every other member of staff, on a daily basis, of each student's progress and level of achievement in their own area. This enabled staff on duty at other times to decide which students they could send shopping with £10.00 in their purse and which students they had to stretch to count the pennies – and similar decisions. As they all needed money every day for bus fares, shopping, sports centre and the like, the result of such an integrated curriculum was that not only financial dealings, but all other areas of the curriculum, were applied both in the classroom and wherever they were a part of everyday life. An important result of this type of staff unity was that no time was wasted by a teacher sending a student off to do a task below their ability. Consequently, students' abilities were permanently stretched.

Weekly staff meetings were held. Alternative staff were employed to work with the students during this time to enable all staff to both attend the meetings and to have a break from teaching. Two students were discussed each week in the staff meeting. The discussion focused on an assessment form which had been left out all the previous week, for each student. Every member of staff had to complete their own subject listing current progress, achievements and immediate goals. HR insisted that there was no room in a well-run curriculum for woolly thinking or the concept of staff all 'mucking in together'. She felt that her approach to staff accountability, with its meticulous recording and assessment procedures, although generating a large amount of paperwork, was in the best interests of her students.

The effect of such careful attention to detail was to ensure that every member of staff had access to all relevant information about each student. This was often pinned behind doors or otherwise strategically concealed in kitchens, bedrooms, bathrooms etc and reflected the current ability and immediate goals of each student in that particular social skill area. One of the main objectives of this type of procedure, in relation to the staff, was to ensure that every member of staff was involved in realistic follow up teaching in every P-A-C area. A typical example is students who were unable (or unwilling) to wipe their own bottom. This information was up on the wall in the toilets and all staff were requested to go to the toilet with certain students whatever they were teaching. Many teachers find the concept of being employed to teach a special subject, such as gardening or communication skills, and also to be responsible for the toileting of an adult student, an appalling concept. This type of procedure required both the most intense communication between all members of staff and also relied on the absolute necessity of all staff carrying out this procedure. If a student went to the toilet five times a day his own way, but was only supervised at bedtimes, he was not going to learn. If however, every time he went to the toilet every member of staff, both male and female, applied the same rules, then the student would eventually learn.

No student was ever allowed by any member of staff to do any task incorrectly. Contrary to much of today's educational practice, Wentwood staff did not believe in students learning from their own mistakes, but that the correct habits must be instilled and constantly repeated from the very beginning of the learning process.

Evolving a Curriculum

The curriculum was designed to incorporate basic scientific learning principles into every-day living so that social skills would be meaningfully acquired. It was also realised that one of the salient features of such a programme was the assessment of each student at regular intervals, so that both progress and regression could be carefully monitored from a previously obtained base line. This information was then fed back into the teaching programme. This base line would enable Wentwood to recognise any basic social skills that were either missing or very weak, in each individual student, at the start of the course. Also to establish whether these were due to lack of previous opportunity or genuine inability. It was hoped the final assessment would measure both the student's progress and the effectiveness of the two-year teaching programme. Because life at Wentwood was based on the P-A-C recording system for social and personal development, it was possible to design an entire curriculum on this diagnostic tool. This initiated standard assessment procedure from which the curriculum would be evolved. To this end, it was particularly important to site the students in an environment which would enable them to experience all the relevant independent life skills as a regular part of their day. This would facilitate a continuity of approach for both teaching and assessment methodology.

As Wentwood was a pre-vocational course, emphasis was only placed on those academic skills that were directly relevant to social and independent living. By using the P-A-C developmental approach, based on standardised well-documented levels of attainment, six-monthly regular assessments enabled each student to be taught to maximise key developmental skills at the appropriate time in conjunction with other relevant social skills. A unique feature of the unified curriculum which finally evolved was this use of *assessment as the starting point of the curriculum* rather than the more usual random fragmented procedure found in most training schemes involving young adults with learning difficulties.

Parents were asked to continue certain learning programmes in the holidays, usually concentrating on leisure activities from the P-A-C areas. This not only gave parents positive objectives to aim for, but also introduced them to the concept of assessment. Many letters from parents, to be found in the students' records, outlined holiday successes could almost have been direct quotations from the P-A-C manual.

The P-A-C method was not designed to provide a comprehensive curriculum in a strict academic sense but to provide the individual with at least the minimum amount of social knowledge necessary to live a reasonably independent life in the immediate environment. However the Wentwood approach extended the method into an effective curriculum. Recognising that the P-A-C analysis of skills was to be the starting point HR realised that the scoring criteria and breakdown of skills was not detailed enough to serve as a teaching method. Over time, she and other Wentwood staff examined each skill and produced detailed breakdowns to enable teaching to proceed in logical graduated steps. These were incorporated into the curriculum to be used by all staff with each student. On the simplest level, there were 28 steps identified when students learn to clean their teeth including the use of excluding tablets so that students can see what they were cleaning. A far more complex road safety and travel programme was used by more advanced students. All kitchen skills were illustrated with simple stage by stage pictorial diagrams displayed on the wall alongside cookers and kettles etc often illustrating negative procedure with a cross through the incorrect picture. This ensures that students always have a quick reference point when working on their own.

A singular feature of the Wentwood way of life is the incorporation of these carefully designed procedural programmes into every aspect of the students' daily life, with relevant programmes displayed on walls and checkcards in every room in the house. Students always followed each step of every teaching programme in the correct context. In the early stages of training no attempt was made to either generalise or transfer aspects of training to any other skill. The author had personal experience as to the efficacy of one of the domestic training programmes and consistency of staff approach. On her first visit to Wentwood the staff on breakfast duty were called away to an urgent problem. The group of students who were detailed to clear and clean the dining room seemed unsure what to do. It transpired that one had only arrived the previous night and the others were relatively new to the rota. Picking up one of the many checkcards in the room, she found it possible for a complete stranger to implement the procedure and enable the students to work through the rota and finish in time to attend their morning meeting as usual.

Since 1950 philosophy and research in the field of mental retardation has concentrated on the rights and the abilities of people with learning disabilities to make individual and meaningful choices in their daily life. This ethos is particularly prevalent in the current swing away from institutional life and the concept of community integration. The Wentwood philosophy, by initially placing the student in a rigidly controlled environment, with little or no choice allowed in any aspect of daily life, would seem to be a negation of these principles. Yet the ultimate aim of the Wentwood two-year course is to enable each person to realise their full potential for independent living.

Implementing the Curriculum for Leisure

The curriculum provides an intensely active day which challenges a students' physical and mental resources. The hope is that this will also break the more usual lethargic dependent lifestyle of the adult with developmental disabilities and encourage the use of leisure time in a more personally beneficial way.

Surprisingly, for such a innovative college, the Wentwood day would be easily recognisable by anyone who had spent their formative years as a boarder in a British public school. The student's day starts very early at seven o'clock and finishes equally early. All students attend the nine o'clock morning meeting where the day's activities are discussed and any student problems are sorted out by the member of staff detailed for that day. Students also give brief reports on varying activities and are encouraged to communicate with both staff and each other during this time. In the main house the mornings are devoted to educational and social skills and the afternoons, from two until six o'clock, mainly to sport and some group activities. All the students attend the local sports centre and also practise other forms of sport such as riding, swimming or cycling.

After the evening meal the students have appropriate domestic tasks and hobbies to do under the sort of general staff supervision that their public school peers would recognise as supervised 'prep'. The evening drop in staff/student ratio to one to seven ensures that students work independently and have a fair amount of friendly contact with the other students in their shared bedrooms. Most students appear to be in bed by nine o'clock and there is little communal evening social activity during the week. The exception being birthday parties which are always held in the evening when there is a special meal of the student's choice, birthday cake, dancing and games. The student concerned plans the party, shops for the extra foods such as crisps etc, bakes the cake and organises the games. This gives every student the experience of throwing a party on their own birthday. Television, regarded as a 'time waster',

is not watched during the week and only a very few selected programmes are allowed at the weekend. The majority of students have
their own personal radio/stereo systems and no restriction is put on the
use of these, so long as they are used with discretion and not played at
full blast to disturb other students and staff.

The Wentwood Week
The weekly and daily timetable remained much the same over the ten
years and ensured that the expectation of every student would be to
participate in working day that lasted from 9am-6pm, with one hour for
lunch. They worked in 'groups' from 9am to 1pm, consisting of four
students who would work with a member of staff in the relevant
teaching subject. Lunch would be from 1pm-2pm and would have been
prepared and cleared away by whichever group were working on that
social skill. From 2pm to 6pm students also worked in groups with the
four members of staff on duty.

On Monday two members of staff would take ordinary group work
while the other two would take half the students riding for the first part
of the afternoon and then bring them back and take the other half riding.
The groups left behind would probably be involved in gardening,
woodwork or house maintenance depending on the special skills of the
staff on duty. On Monday afternoons groups usually worked on money,
language and literacy sessions. All areas of the timetable were accorded
the same weight and were regarded as work by the students whether
they were taught in the building or (more usually) participating in
shopping and travel lessons in the town.

Group sessions were held on Tuesday mornings and everybody
walked or cycled to the sports centre in the afternoon. They returned for
group sessions from 5pm to 6pm during which one group would be
preparing the evening meal. Wednesday followed a similar pattern with
all the students going swimming from 5pm to 7pm at the local baths.
Thursday afternoon included a special session of group movement for
all the students which involved five participating members of staff. Sport
was regarded not as a playtime but as a deliberate structured educational activity, with five staff involved every afternoon.

Friday's particular activity was a session of language and literacy in
which every student wrote a letter home, regardless of their level of
proficiency. Students who had achieved reasonable typing skills used
the typewriters with help; those that could write a little, wrote by hand
with help; and those who as yet could do neither, dictated their letters
home. The words were often drawn out of them with great difficulty.
Typing was a special subject on the curriculum and regarded as most
important in that it provided every student with a standardised form of

communication that could equal those of their more intelligent peers. Every student sent at least one piece of typing home a term, whatever their standard. The letters were supervised by HR, who was in charge of this particular activity and knew whether students had said similar things the week before. She insisted that they used a fair amount of communication skills to remember and relate the week's activities in a way that would be interesting to their families. The students' main topic when left to themselves was food, but if they really insisted on this area they would be encouraged to describe the fact that their home-grown cabbage came from their own garden or that they had actually been shopping themselves for it. By the end of the two years many students were capable of writing long and interesting letters home.

Life in the Grove, where students spent the final part of their two-year course, was less rigid and in the ten years covered by this study only three students failed to proceed to this final area of the course. Part of the day was often spent participating in a work experience scheme and rather more time was given to the running of the house. These students were encouraged to be virtually self-sufficient and make the majority of their own decisions as to food, shopping and financial budgeting. They also had a greater say in the use of their leisure time and where possible attended local community clubs in the evenings or weekends alongside the general public. They still attended the morning meeting and some academic-type lessons with students in the main house and always participated in the afternoon sports group sessions. Taking their turn in the rota they had to shop for, prepare and cook the ingredients for all their meals and also wash up afterwards – which made for a hectic schedule if they were to be ready for the statutory two o'clock return to work. The early bedtime still applied to the Grove but there were signs in 1990 of a more relaxed approach to watching the occasional early evening television programme. Many of the students came from homes where the television was on for most of the day with meals merely punctuating the transmission rather than halting it.

Training for Leisure

Probably the most effective way to illustrate the teaching of such an integrated curriculum is to take the particular example of training for leisure activities. Before students were able to benefit from neighbourhood leisure facilities, they had to learn how to travel by foot, bicycle or public transport to the required destination. Travel, which obviously also comprised road safety, was a particular interest of HR, who always taught this subject herself. The aim was to ensure that all students would have travel as part of their life repertoire. This would have both social advantages and lessen the burden of the carers usually responsible for this problem in the life of adults with learning disabilities. The ultimate aim in the Wentwood context was that all students should travel independently to and from Wentwood each term. In the ten years in question no student had ever travelled independently before they arrived at Wentwood, most had never even walked up the street without their mother. In the light of their previous experience parents took some persuasion to agree that such independence could be possible. The result of this teaching was that some terms every student left Wentwood and travelled, at least part of way, on their own. The more advanced students completed the entire journey home while the beginners, as a preliminary exercise, would travel the six miles to Devizes to be met by their parents.

Just one of many case histories serves to illustrate the efficacy of the teaching and the eventual generalisation of these learned skills. The parents of one very overprotected Down's syndrome student finally reluctantly accepted that she was competent to travel to London by coach quite independently. Accepting HR's advice, they met her at Park Lane for the first few journeys and showed her how to catch a connecting bus to Golders Green, gradually standing back and observing her from a distance to be certain she could cope with the transfer. Finally she was allowed to travel the entire complicated journey home from Melksham quite unsupervised. On one particular journey she arrived at the correct bus stop without realising there was a bus strike. She waited – and waited – and after about three-quarters of an hour asked somebody why there were no buses. On being told of the strike she telephoned her father (a learned Wentwood response to an emergency) and said she would get a taxi home. This she did. The principal's delighted response when informed of this incident at the start of the next term was not directed towards the student, who was already deemed competent in travel skills by the college, but towards the parents who confidently allowed their daughter to make her own decisions.

When referring to this type of incident HR termed it 'the outside of the book' – i.e. the edited version. The inside of the book was her meticulous teaching approach which involved parents from the very beginning. The first exercise in the curriculum was to teach the students to travel to the nearest pleasant place where they could take their parents out for a pub lunch. When parents came to visit the college to discuss various aspects of a student's development and future plans, it was automatically assumed that at the end of the session the student would then take them out to lunch using a bus to get to their destination. They were told to allow time for this extended visit. Parents would leave the premises having no idea of where they were going, with only the student knowing the final destination. Staff said they could see the worry and unease in the parent's walk as they left the college. Unknown to the parent and in case of emergencies, the student always had the plans for the day in a pocket. Parents would be taken by bus to a nearby National Trust village to sightsee and then go for a pub lunch, eventually returning to Wentwood by bus. On the next visit they would go further afield and eventually the student would phone the parents and make quite independent arrangements to take them out. They would meet in Bath which was a yet more complex expedition. Over ten years every student (bar two) eventually managed this progression.

Teaching Leisure Skills

As ever, the teaching consisted of doing and then talking about it afterwards. Four students would first go on a bus ride round the town while the principal observed their behaviour. The next phase was to board the bus together but allow one of the group to complete the journey alone while being followed by car or on foot. An expensive and time-consuming part of these travel exercises was the need for member of staff, with a watchful eye, to follow by car. Members of staff often preceded the student to a destination such as a bus station, to observe more complex travel behaviour. Students also had to master the speech requirements of unaccompanied travel which was no mean achievement for people with so little linguistic competence.

The students would then return to the classroom where they used a toy bus to practise the relevant behaviours. If their speech was not adequate for role play then a tape recorder was used to help them practise, with the HR taking the roles of bus driver/conductor. The lesson started with the students being made aware of the self-help skills necessary before going out, such as going to the toilet; doing up their flies; looking in the mirror; finding money; taking medication and checking that they had the list of things needed to go on a journey. Earlier road safety lessons were recapped and students learned the Wentwood way of asking for a ticket; asking for directions; whom to ask and where to go in an emergency to telephone Wentwood. Train journeys were also included in the syllabus and the more advanced students studied the local bus system, using timetables and transport-service maps to appreciate the relative distances of familiar places.

The ultimate test in the travel course came after students had fully mastered the intricacies of travel to and from the nearby city of Bath. When they were able to find a particular shop or cafe, where HR would meet them, they were each invited to find their way from Wentwood to her own home in Bath to join her for lunch. This journey was deliberately not included in the training programme and involved changing buses in the bus station, having first asked which bus to take to get to the destination. The address was only written down in cases of severe speech impediment. Having travelled from Wentwood to the bus station in Bath, the student then had to catch a small city minibus and ask where to get off. Having got off at the correct stop, it was necessary to ask for directions to the house. (The author can validate the difficulty of this particular journey having got lost in a similar attempt by car.) All the students over the ten years managed to complete this journey (dressed in their best clothes as befitted such a special occasion) where they were rewarded by a favourite lunch of their own choice. They were also warned that if they didn't manage the journey and the principal had to turn out to find them, they would not get their lunch. In ten years no student missed their lunch even though some were a little late!

In her travel lessons with the students part of the curriculum included learning to ask for directions from strangers. To demonstrate this aspect she used videoed scenes of friends of her own children (who the current students didn't know) asking for directions to the sports centre and other venues in the correct manner. The video was shown to the students who then had to go out and repeat the exercise in the same location using the same words. Students were informed that they wouldn't be videoed until they carried out the complete behavioral sequence in the correct manner. Videoing the students making fools of themselves seemed in this situation a singularly inappropriate way of teaching and merely reinforced the students' mistakes; whereas to use it as a reward for correct learning seemed a more positive approach.

A factor to be considered in video teaching was that the students often didn't relate to strangers in the more complex behavioral situations. The video, of necessity, used crowd observation techniques which students found confusing with no familiar cues to which they could relate. For example, when trying to teach students the correct way to join a queue in the post office or similar situation, if they were asked to analyse the behaviour of a woman in a red coat to see if she was standing well or badly etc, they failed to relate to or define the situation. If someone they knew by name and were familiar with was filmed standing in the same queue, preferably someone the same age from the local school, then the students identified the salient aspects of the behaviour being taught, quickly and with interest. In this context the widely used MENCAP 'Let's Go' films meant little to the students, proving useless until the students had experienced the activity in question. Wentwood reversed the usual procedure with this series by going out and experiencing the activity and then using the film as a basis for discussion.

Students were also taught not to approach strangers for information but always to approach either someone in uniform, or in an obvious position of authority such as behind a counter. If this was not possible they were taught to ask women with either children or shopping bags.

Physical Exercise

The effect of physical exercise on students' general development was of particular interest to HR who considered the effect of walking to be far the most beneficial. As such she gave it a special place in Wentwood life. Without the necessary physical abilities most students would be unable to participate in the leisure opportunities on offer. Many regular and routine practices at Wentwood evolved from the needs of particular students. Early in the development of the curriculum, Wentwood acquired a couple of 'lumpy' students that were unable to keep up with the others on the regular outdoor travel, shopping, post office and library trips. Teaching staff found this a problem and the other students in the group suffered as a consequence. In trying to solve this problem she started to take the two slow students out on regular shopping trips and walks and soon found by making up a game of brisk walking round the town they could improve their stamina. These trips took place on a daily basis first thing in the morning and proceeded at what she considered was 'a decent social pace'. The spin off appeared to be (as she had long suspected) that this exercise was successful in improving both their bodies and their minds. This then became a regular part of the curriculum and she always took new students walking first thing every morning, with entirely beneficial effects. The rationale for placing Wentwood in the centre of a small market town was the ease with which students could walk to every place they needed to visit. Shops, doctors, dentists, clubs, sports centre, church and village hall were all within walking distance.

Cycling was another important feature of Wentwood life. Students were trained initially in the local school playground at the weekends, until they actually learned to ride. They then progressed to the small lanes in the square outside the college. Eventually students cycled to work experience and often cycled behind the minibus if it was too full on an outing.

The afternoons at the sports centre gave students the choice of a wide range of leisure activities. Having previously assembled any special clothes or equipment, they walked the one and three-quarter mile each way to and from the sports centre, accompanied by a member of staff. The walk went through the main street of the busy market town and involved negotiating a large dual-carriage trunk road carrying traffic heading for a nearby motorway. The centre offered a choice of activities and students were encouraged to sample all of them. They attended the public sessions and were responsible for changing their own clothes, showering and using the lockers and keys correctly alongside the general public.

Weekend Leisure Activities, Evening Classes and Clubs

It was hoped that the concept of leisure would become part of the weekend and holiday lifestyle in the students' adult life. Cycling and horse riding were encouraged as weekend activities. With the help of a teacher with a particular interest in cycling, students joined in events with local cycling groups. The weekend activities were planned in some detail. Wentwood staff were aware that, left to themselves, students would fall into the usual inactivity which was a particular feature of their home lives. An added reason for HR seeing every student in the Friday letter writing session was part of a deliberate policy to keep both staff and students 'on their toes'. She expected every student to be able to tell her during the afternoon what they were planning to do at the weekend. This should have already been discussed and planned with the members of staff on weekend rota. Students were not allowed to be told by staff what to do during the weekend but were expected to plan these activities during the previous week. This anticipatory work towards weekend leisure was designed to overcome the inevitable weekend inactivity usually experienced by residents in group homes.

The local village hall/community centre displayed a list of all clubs, concerts and other activities on an outside notice board. Students were encouraged to find out about suitable weekend and evening activities listed on the board and attend with the general public. Several of the students attended the camera club and by using the local notice boards they also found out about the bazaars, jumble sales, films, exhibitions, coffee mornings and discos which are a feature of life in any neighbour-hood community. In the summer, many picnics and walking trips were planned with great care. The students began to realise that the planned use of local transport could take them away from their current environment to somewhere more pleasant on a warm sunny day. An added incentive was the visit to a local pub and finishing the day with a meal in a cafe or restaurant.

All weekend activities were structured to take due regard of financial restraints, so that students would realise that the relative cost of some activities make them unsuitable on a regular basis for people living on the type of income they will eventually have to budget for themselves. It was hoped to provide an extended repertoire of outdoor and indoor activities. To aid this type of thinking the MENCAP 'Lets Go' series of slides produced by Brian Rix were frequently shown as a starting point for discussion. This type of weekend activity was a considerable challenge to students who have spent their formative years watching sport and films on the television at weekends.

At various times over the years Wentwood has introduced students to evening classes in an attempt to involve them in leisure activities after the working day. Typing was initially started as an evening class where students would go to a neighbour who taught typing in her own home. Two students went in rotation after supper from 7pm to 9pm with an able student taking a more dependent student. Before attending classes all the students had to wash themselves and change their clothes and ensure that they were clean and tidy after the day's work. Gateway Clubs were also visited in the evenings but the staff had reservations about the students using a facility solely for people with learning disabilities, rather than the excellent local facilities. Several students attended St John's Ambulance Brigade evening classes which entailed wearing a complex uniform which they had to cope with by themselves. One student joined a local swimming club which involved a member of staff having to collect him at 11pm. The Girls Brigade, Venture Scouts and the local youth club were also local evening activities that students attended as regular members. Initially students were accompanied by a member of Wentwood staff who in exchange would offer some input into the organisation. As students became involved and integrated into the activities in their own right, this staff input was withdrawn. In all extra curricular activity the policy was for staff to teach students the correct behaviour and then withdraw. The policy continued as each new group of students joined an activity.

If students were unable to attend the various clubs independently after the requisite time then they were withdrawn. Community integration rather than community tolerance was the Wentwood aim. An example of this was the local keep-fit club where students were withdrawn after a term because they were unable to follow the verbal instructions quickly enough. Therefore they would never be able to cope successfully on their own. One or two students always attended local adult literacy classes. This was thought to be important as a social activity and would also make them aware of something else they could do on their own in any community. Although the students didn't need the service from a literacy point of view, their own classes being superior, it was used as an entry into the system. Wherever they then saw the book logo they would know they would be welcome to join in, thus extending their repertoire of things to do in their free time.

Community Life

During their leisure time at weekends and in the evenings, there were several other extensions of college life into the wider community. Students participated in the 'clean up Melksham scheme' regularly instituted by the Rotary club. This was merely an extension of their outside maintenance and gardening group work and gave the students a practical generalisation of their often tedious and repetitive college experience. Wentwood regularly assumed responsibility for two streets in the annual Red Cross flag day and staff were insistent that this task was carried out in exactly the same way by the students as by the general public in the other streets. For many years the college was also involved in the Kennett and Avon canal scheme and from the early days of the college, students regularly attended with a member of staff who was involved in the reclamation work. All these community activities were carried out by very small numbers of students at any one time. Wentwood had no wish to overwhelm the local community with an obvious presence.

Holidays

Wentwood particularly stressed Bank Holiday outings and hoped to train the students to use their leisure time effectively so that at Bank Holidays, and other times when their ATC or college of further education are closed, they will be aware of the opportunities for recreation in their own environment.

An extension of the integrated P-A-C approach was the annual term-time holiday which all the students took in small groups. The planning started well ahead with maps, pictures and lists of things to take with them appearing on the dining room notice board some weeks in advance of the holiday. Students were involved in all the usual travel and accommodation bookings and routes were planned in detail. They travelled to their holiday destination unaccompanied using the public coach service. When they finally arrived at their destination they had an excellent opportunity to generalise all their previous leisure learning skills to a totally new environment.

The final-year independent Grove students were expected to take rather more responsibility on their holiday and each student assumed responsibility for one day's catering. They were expected to arrive with a whole day's menus prepared, so that they could shop locally for the ingredients. They were expected to prepare the food, unaided, in a strange kitchen. Last year everybody coped well with this exercise, except the least efficient student who opted for a pub meal which was enthusiastically supported by the other students – and endorsed as a realistic choice by the staff!

Parents were kept fully informed about the student's progress on the holiday and invited to visit the students for a day, joining in with the activities. It was hoped that this experience would encourage both parents and students to implement a more independent life style at home during the Wentwood holidays.

Utilising Leisure Training in Work Experience

Although Wentwood stress that the college is running a pre-vocational course, it is nevertheless thought appropriate to give students some experience of a working day. This becomes another opportunity to generalise domestic and leisure skills learned in the Wentwood context, to a wider setting. Work experience also allows the students to realise that the unremitting toil involved in real work can be boring and requires great attention.

All students, regardless of sex, are taught simple gardening, horticulture, woodwork, house maintenance, domestic cleaning, cooking, laundry and all the various additional skills needed to run two large houses and gardens with no outside paid staff. This makes for a considerably more realistic life style than is provided in most local authority group homes. Wentwood students can see an added point of the rigid programmed teaching of these areas when they are able to use them in a genuine work experience project in the wider community. However, there was another aspect of work experience Wentwood felt they had to build into some part of the course, enabling the students to have an extended experience of sheer solid directed group labour every day for two weeks. It was felt that students must learn that work was not just a treat that took them out of Wentwood a day a week, but that it went on and on and on.

Once a year the college found a genuine project work experience within the grounds. One year it was taking down and building a new greenhouse; another year the redecoration of two rooms; the next year building a patio etc. For this exercise, two groups of four students and two members of staff were taken out of the Wentwood timetable completely and worked on the job from 9am to 5pm every day. They became quite separate from the Wentwood routine, missing lessons, sports and both the fun and the tedium of their everyday lives. The students made their own sandwiches the night before. Dressed in overalls with the statutory thermos flask, they were ready to start work at 9am each morning. After finishing at 5pm, they showered and were able to rest, until the others finished group activities before joining them for the evening meal.

Two or three days into this novel experience the students invariably decided they had had enough! They would get tired, cold, or wet and decide they would prefer to go riding or visit the sports centre. Grumbling would be endemic and the staff concerned took a very tough approach, insisting the work continued. Other staff would visit the project, taking photographs of progress and heaping praise on the students. This would help them to get through this stage and begin to experience the pleasure of completing a task which left a tangible record for everyone to see. At the end of the two weeks they knocked off at mid-day on the final Friday and had a celebratory lunch with the principal at the local pub. a photograph album was compiled of the various stages of the completed work and the trustees of Wentwood would personally visit the project and thank the students. By the end of this time not only had the students learned about work, but the staff had also learned just which student was capable of sustained work. They were often surprised which students could and could not cope.

The Church

The church was also an important part of Wentwood life and several studies now show that one of the few agencies to facilitate community integration of the developmentally disabled is the church. As with all other practices, Wentwood tried to instil habits at first, until students were aware enough of the concept to be able to make informed choices. They were only allowed to choose when their behavioral skills were adequate for them to carry out such a choice successfully. All students were expected to attend the church of their own denomination on Sundays. The organisation of this was considerable, as students often went to as many as five different churches in the town, one of which adjoined the Grove. They would go with whichever staff was on duty and whose church it was. If this was not possible, Wentwood would appeal to a church to find someone to initially be responsible for the student and then gradually reduce the dependence. As the church habit became instilled, inquiries would be made of Wentwood parents as to why particular students had not for example, made their first communion, been confirmed, had their barmitzvah etc. Eventually there were groups of students attending local confirmation groups, first communion Catholic groups, Baptist and Congregational teachings as part of the local church congregations. A social spin off was that as students went round the town on their daily lessons and social activities, total strangers to the staff would know the student from church. This enabled the student to have their own tiny part of community individuality, quite separate from the Wentwood world. Staff would go to great lengths to ensure that students attended church social functions even if this meant missing part of a day's group lesson or activity. The church was seen as a very suitable area where students could develop their own individuality, personal relationships and self-importance.

This emphasis on church attendance had a particularly beneficial effect on parents, many of whom revealed their own religious 'hang ups'. Although not themselves ostensibly practising any religious beliefs, they had felt that their child could never be a Christian (or whatever faith they subscribed to) because he was mentally handicapped. The fact that as an independent student their child was having a similar religious upbringing to that given to his siblings, appeared to be a tremendous relief to many parents. This often brought out religious practices in the parents that they had put aside because they had felt they couldn't share the experience as a family any more. Many families reverted back to regular church attendance in the holiday times with their student off-spring. Difficulties arose with various non-believing staff who could only see it as a religious exercise but they were finally convinced of the benefit to the student in the areas of social and personal development. Churchgoing could be seen as a valid weekend activity.

Overview

Sinson (1990) found many cases of severe depression and isolation occurring in people with learning disabilities (who were relatively well settled in the community) over Christmas, Easter and August Bank Holidays when their ATCs were on holiday for an extended period. In all cases they were totally unaware of how to avail themselves of any alternative leisure occupation in their own neighbourhood during this time.

One of the more disturbing findings to appear in recent studies of community integration is the increasing number of failed community placements and subsequent return to institutions of people with learn-ing disabilities who were totally unable to deal effectively with their increased leisure time. The long lonely weekends experienced by many people led to increasing feelings of isolation and alienation from the community, rather than increasing community contact. The inference drawn has to be that in the light of this community isolation, individual leisure choices must become more meaningful to the individual – how-ever abstract this concept may appear to be. In the light of these findings the Wentwood concept of leisure seems justified, but must have come as somewhat of a shock to the system for many students. It is particularly interesting that HR appreciated and implemented this concept of leisure in 1980, some considerable time before any literature was available on the results of community integration. Leisure is an integral part of the curriculum and also provides a cohesive way of generalising skills learned in other areas. The P-A-C method, from which the curriculum was evolved, has a considerable emphasis on the assessment of leisure activities.

More remarkable is the pitifully low academic and communication ability of these students as shown on the P-A-C assessments and student records at the end of two-year course. This aspect is considered in more detail in the research report (Sinson 1992). All the Wentwood students came from special schools and had IQ measures below 55 with a very

few exceptions. These seven exceptions had behavioral problems that belied their IQ assessments in the mid 60s and were not capable of living independent lives. The appearance of all the students was similar to those young adults with varying mental and physical disabilities found in the various centres for people with developmental disabilities. By and large they had very poor verbal communication skills which did not show a significant improvement over the two year course. What they did seem to have acquired was an immense amount of social competence and the personal confidence to implement their carefully learned life skills.

CHAPTER 9

A Home for Life

Introduction

In 1987 Sister X took 12 long-term institutionalised patients from the wards in a large mental subnormality hospital and in a private venture relocated them in a remote north of England country residence adjoining a farm and over a mile from the nearest houses. Sister X had trained at the local mental subnormality hospital and had worked there with these patients for 17 years. They had been in the hospital considerably longer. She particularly chose older institutionalised patients, who had been in the hospital most of their lives and who would not otherwise have been considered for relocation into the community. She intended to provide a secure environment for them that they could regard as their own home for the rest of their lives. As the main aim of the venture was deinstitutionalisation, the isolated position of the house was not seen as a drawback as it was not intended to further relocate the residents into either the surrounding hamlets or nearest towns.

For the first two years Sister X lived there with her small daughter and husband, who continued his full-time job as a charge nurse at the hospital where they had both trained as student nurses. The house was staffed with her own father, brother-in-law and another Sister from the hospital. The birth of a second child made a move from their very small private living quarters within the house to a nearby house imperative. By this time the residents were all securely entrenched into their environment and the staff and residents were able to put the extra space to good use.

These 12 institutionalised adults would appear to have been dumped in the middle of nowhere and were now in a segregated society and to an outside observer might well appear more alienated than they were in their original institution. There at least they had been part of an overlarge community. Despite these initial impressions they appeared to be living the happiest and most fulfilled lives of any of the people covered by this book. They were also living more satisfying and independent lives within the limits of their potential than any developmentally disabled adults relocated in the various large or small community living units visited by the author.

The reasons for this unlikely success seem to depend on a complex interaction of environmental factors and the decision of Sister X to disregard most of the accepted mores of current relocation theories, about which she appears to be singularly disinterested. The author visited Greystones over three years from 1989, when the initial LOCO assessment was carried out, and followed the progress of the residents through 1990 and 1991. Of necessity the location of the venture and its protagonists remain anonymous.

When Sister X was asked why she had undertaken such a daunting prospect with so little financial capital, professional help or backup, she gave a forthright and honest reply.

> Well obviously, the crux of it is business isn't it? You want your own business. This is what we know and this is what we enjoy. You felt that you could do better yourself…outside the confines of the hospital and could provide a better life for the patients. You were just frustrated with the system…knowing you could do better yourself and obviously reap the benefits at the same time. We couldn't do it if we didn't enjoy it. We've sunk every single cent we had in it. We've been very lucky…we've had no trouble because we're aware of the type of residents we have and we're aware of their feelings. You've got to gear it to the needs of the residents. If we had the money we'd have more staff…to do more things with the residents.

Although the home was set up under the auspices of social services as a registered residential care home for the mentally handicapped (with a social services certificate), the relationship with any professional body was nonexistent. The residents were on the list of the local GP and social services did a routine inspection once a year and a supposedly 'surprise inspection' at any other time. However Sister X was on good terms with the local social services officer and would occasionally phone him if she had a problem. He would invariable respond with 'OK I'll pop up and do your surprise inspection and we'll discuss it then'. If too much time went by without the surprise inspection she would remind him that Greystones had not had their annual surprise inspection.

Both Greystones and Wentwood were originally intended to be included in the study described in Chapter 4 where the Greystones' LOCO score was higher than the other contributing group homes. However, the idiosyncratic managerial strategies of both these private sector ventures was such that there was little point subsuming them into the pervading apathy of local authority provisions. Depending on the reader's perceptions Greystones, as described, could represent an act of faith, a commune, an idiosyncratic extended family, or yet another institution. Sadly, neither the author nor Sister X have the necessary skills to subdue such abstract complexities into the current form of conventional relocation literature.

The House

Greystones was a well-established country residence by 1510 when local history books indicate that the owner's initials and date of the building were inscribed on the lintel of the principal door of the house. It was still a family home with well-developed gardens, substantial outbuildings and stables, standing in three acres of land when Sister X acquired it in 1987. A narrow house, the architectural construction allowed every room to have panoramic views of the beautiful gardens and unspoiled surrounding countryside.

Sister X was quite determined that the external features would be matched by similar internal decor and furnished the entire residence in typical country house style. Regardless of the expectations of her previously institutionalised residents the living rooms with their parquet floors were furnished in pale blue chintz and pale pink velvet with swagged curtains and china lamps with delicate shades. Each bedroom was decorated and furnished in a different style with individually patterned bedding. Before the patients moved in they visited the house, saw their rooms and were able to chose their own furnishings in an attempt to start the gradual deinstitutionalisation process. The house was filled with flowers, ornaments and delicate china. Bowls of fruit were always out in the living rooms and table-cloths always on the dining room tables. When the author queried the sameness of the two pale blue three-piece suites and the two sets of matching occasional tables, feeling that a contrast in size or texture might have been more exciting (as specified in LOCO) she was firmly told that the house had been furnished to conform with people's expectations of country house living – where it appeared that three-piece suites of furniture with matching occasional tables were mandatory! The bathrooms were carpeted and one bathroom was pine clad throughout. The kitchen was fitted with high-quality wooden fittings with both a solid fuel and electric cooker with laundry facilities in a separate room. The domestic scale of the provision was impressive and there was no attempt to make the facilities anything other than would be found in an average home. Even the food appeared to be purchased by the residents in usual amounts and there was little evidence of bulk buying except for larger than usual tins of baked beans and soup.

Over the three years that the author visited there was no sign of deterioration. Residents and staff were involved in constant decoration and took a pride in keeping their home in good repair. Even the pale suites, which took a daily hammering as the residents sat there to watch television, showed no signs of damage.

One outbuilding had been originally converted into a cottage for three of the male residents and comprised two large bedrooms upstairs (one shared by two people) a bathroom, lounge with a television, kitchen and games room with pool table downstairs. The aim of this separate building was to give the residents some idea of social living so that they could invite each other over to play pool etc. These three residents ate their meals in the main house. One other bedroom in the main house was also shared but both these shared rooms would revert to single rooms with the new building programme which was due to be completed in 1991.

Every resident had their own belongings in their bedroom and over the four years since Greystones had opened all of them had acquired radios, clocks, hi-fi, personal televisions, musical instruments etc. Many residents had also replaced their bedding and furniture with items which they had personally chosen and purchased. Photographs of holidays and friends were in every room and each room gave an indication of an individual lifestyle which must have been a difficult achievement for these previously institutionalised people. When they had first arrived at Greystones the only luggage they brought was a plastic bag containing a few clothes.

Initially Sister X had banned posters on the walls as it spoilt the decorations but by 1991 when her own daughter had started school and arrived home with pictures, and Wendy (a new resident) was about to move in, she despairingly changed this policy:

> I'm even coming to terms with posters on the bedroom walls. Wendy's moving in soon and she said 'my bedroom's going to look nice with the all the posters up'. So I said 'well I suppose so but I'll just have decorated your room', but she said 'I know and they'll make the bedroom look nice' and I'm thinking Oh God give me strength!

It appeared that Sister X had to come to terms with deinstitutionalisation in her own time. The other members of staff did not have this problem as being unaware of the residents previous life styles, they merely applied their own norms to the Greystones regime.

A new building programme was under way in 1991 which would allow two of the younger residents who wished to live together to move into their own flat in the converted stables. They had been 'going out' with each other during the four years they had been at Greystones and had had previous heterosexual friendships when in the hospital. These two people had chosen all their own furniture and decorations, even including the bathroom suite (mainly from catalogues) and watched them all being delivered and fitted. This flat would have one bedroom upstairs and a downstairs bathroom and kitchen/dining room which would enable them to live as independent a life as they chose. This flat would free a single room for one of the residents who currently shared a room. A further two self-contained flats were being built leading directly off the main house. It was envisaged that these would enable four residents to move to more independent lives from the main house and also free the other shared room.

The Staff

In 1989 there were five full-time and two part-time members of staff. Sister X was the Officer in Charge with a Sister who had worked with her at the hospital acting as her deputy. One care assistant and Sister X's brother-in-law (Leslie) and father (George), who had both previously worked in the car trade, made up the full-time complement. A local lady from 'the church' was employed part time as a non-trained care assistant and Sister X's husband did part-time weekend duty. As most of the staff were untrained Sister X trained them as and when it appeared to be necessary.

By 1990 the nursing sister had been replaced with a non-trained care assistant (Lynne) and the part-time local lady had left the area and had been replaced by another similar unqualified local lady. No domestic staff were employed as the residents were trained to be responsible for looking after both themselves and their own home.

In 1991 the position was slightly different with regard to qualified staff. Sister X was now part time and her husband still held his job at the hospital. Her father, brother-in-law and the non-trained care assistant were still employed full time and they had been joined by a full-time Youth Opportunity trainee who had worked for the previous year in the local ATC where she had known four of the residents. Sister X's husband's brother (Keith) now also worked full-time while waiting to start his nursing training at the hospital. There was a new part-time care assistant to replace the local lady who had done the cooking. The three part timers appeared to make up one full-time position. A brother-in-law of the full-time care assistant worked on Sundays so that someone was always available to take the residents out. Unlike the constant staff turnover in the ten local authority group homes described in Chapters 4 and 5, there was a reassuring stability in the continuing familiar staff over the three years, and their interrelated backgrounds made an effective extended family for the residents. By 1991 the two children aged one and five years were an integral part of this extended family as they joined the residents in shopping trips and afternoon outings whenever Sister X was on duty. When she was busy Sister X invariably asked a resident to see to their not infrequent demands and they were accepted as younger siblings in a family group.

By 1991 Sister X who only worked part-time was the only qualified member of staff and with her husband tended to work the weekend shifts moving their two children back with them at the weekends. Greystones were able to pay good care worker rates but for the ratio of staff to residents they required they were unable to afford more qualified staff although they would have welcomed them. Each member of staff served as a keyworker for two residents and was responsible for helping them develop a more independent personal life.

As far as job satisfaction was concerned the staff were unanimous in enjoying the personal rewards of their working lives but rather less satisfied with the financial remuneration. When asked whether he regretted leaving his former long-held job with its attendant social life and responsibilities, George summed up the attitude of all the staff:

> I didn't think twice about it. A body shop manager is one of the worst jobs in the garage. Here you can work the 15-hour shifts you want and have the time off you want. It's harder work because you're stretching them all the time... If this place belonged to the council I would treat it as a job – nine to five or whatever. There wouldn't be the same commitment. Yes I want it to go well for my daughter, but really it's these lot, the home itself that matters. I tuck them all up at night, see they're all right. You don't treat them like patients, you try to give them their independence and only give them help when they ask for it.

The Residents

Jill, Down's syndrome aged 31, had been in the hospital from birth. When she first arrived at Greystones in 1989 she found work in a café one day a week. She lost this job when the café changed hands, the new owners wanted someone who they could leave on their own and who could cope with the money. It was also rumoured that they were frightened of her. By 1990 she had found work as a home help two days a week and in the local hairdressing establishment. In 1991 she was still holding down these jobs four days a week.

Peter, Down's syndrome aged 33, had been in the hospital since a small child. He too still held his 1989 four-day-a-week job in the local haulage firm in 1991.

Jill and Peter completed a two-year special education course during 1989–90 at a college of further education. At first they were taken in by car but after a short time they were trained by the staff to use public transport catching the 7am bus and didn't arrive back until 6pm.

Norman, aged 48, had been in the hospital 23 years but had come on from a previous subnormality hospital where he had spent his early life. In 1989 he found daily work at the local chicken farm until it closed in 1990 when he was employed at the market garden on a similar basis. This was less successful and he gradually built up daily gardening jobs (by personal recommendations from satisfied clients) which he had also done at the previous hospital where he had been the only one of the residents to have outside work.

Barry, Down's syndrome aged 31, had been in the hospital for ten years. In 1989 he found a job in the pub which he still held, with increased hours to five days a week in 1991.

Ian, deaf/mute aged 65, had been in the hospital for 42 years. In 1989 he was employed in both inside and outside work for the church. By 1990 he was also doing two days in a small holding and by 1991 he was working in the market garden five days a week.

Colin, Down's syndrome aged 41, had been in the hospital since a child. He worked in the church and the house in 1989 but by 1990 he had found work in a café three days a week. By 1991 he appeared to be fully employed still working at the café two days a week and now also working in a social club three days a week.

Brian and Joseph in their late 50s had been in the hospital since childhood and over the years Joseph had 'talked' for Gerry. Since arriving at Greystones they had both worked at the church and Joseph also attends the ATC two days a week. By 1991 they were continuing the church work and David now attended the ATC three days a week.

Jack and Jo, both aged 51, had been in the hospital since children. On arrival at Greystones they initially just helped in the house and gardens but both now attend the ATC three days a week.

Gerry, aged 53, has a withered arm and minor physical disabilities. He originally helped in the house and now attends the ATC three days a week.

Sister X had never intended to send residents to the ATC but found that they needed the experience of some outside occupation if only to equate their life style with those residents who went out to work. However for this group of less able residents the ATC was a last resort and being increasingly dissatisfied with the stimulation it provided, by 1991 Sister X was actively engaged in finding other provisions.

Rose, aged 44, was another less able resident who had also been at the hospital since childhood who arrived at Greystones in 1989 and died of heart failure on the way to hospital in May 1990. Sister X had been surprised how little her death had affected the other residents. Interest was shown in who would have her room and her weekly wage. Jill shed a token tear, most probably influenced by similar behaviour she had seen on the television. 'Because she felt she had to'. None of the residents attended her funeral or inquired after her in any way. This general behaviour bore out Sister X's long-held belief in the emotional flatness of institutionalised mentally handicapped adults.

Louise, a tiny lady aged 51, who had been in the hospital for 38 years, replaced Rose in 1990. She had known all the other residents in hospital and although a recent less able arrival appeared to have settled in well by 1991 and was currently helping in the house.

Arrival at Greystones

George, who arrived at Greystones after 12 years in the car trade and with no previous experience of adults with severe learning disabilities, described the moving in process:

> They didn't all arrive together – they came in threes. When they first came, they came here and they had all their clothes just in a sack. They went upstairs to their room and all the clothes they took out were rolled up and put underneath their pillow, and they slept like that for a long time. They made their 'bundles like they did in hospital so no-one would steal them. They just couldn't trust anybody. Basically it was the same with the lot of them. Everything they had they carried around with them. They wouldn't have keys and they wouldn't have locks. They felt safe in their rooms. Even now if they want to get away they go up into their rooms.

> When they first came they just sat and watched television regardless of what was on. They wouldn't move around freely. Now they don't watch during the day at all – there's too much going on. They'd been in V for such a long time that they would accept everything that was put down in front of them. There was only one nurse in charge of two houses at the hospital. Now if they don't like something they'll tell you they don't like it. When they first came you didn't know what they liked. It's just this last year and a half we've started to find out. It's harder work now as they move around and you're never sure where they are. When they first started we knew exactly where they were – they sat down and they stayed there.

Sisters X's description of Louise's arrival at Greystones was occasioned by Louise's sheer delight in showing the author the new shoes, cardigan and beads she had just brought for her impending holiday.

> When she first came she looked like a woman of 80 year old. I couldn't wait to get my hands on her! She looked like an old lady and she's only in her 50s. You can jazz Louise up a bit. She had shapeless old frocks and things.

By 1991 Jill, the other female resident, had blossomed into a trendy young lady in the statutory smart jeans.

> Jill is adamant what she wants. She looks her age now and she takes care when she's getting herself ready to look trendy. Although we give them guidance when shopping she usually says 'No. This is nicer!'

And George's description of the men:

When you saw them at V their trousers were halfmast every one of them. When they first came and you saw them on the street that's the first thing you'd notice about them.

By 1991, hairdressers, barbers and trendy clothes had totally transformed all the residents into very acceptable, casually dressed adults. Several of the men had beards or mustaches and the women had well-groomed hair. Particularly noticeable was the fact that they all looked equally presentable in the house even when they were not going out.

Communication

In view of the currently available facilities all the residents would appear to have been rightly placed in a mental subnormality hospital at the time of their original psychometric assessment and certification. They all appeared to be well below IQ 50 and had virtually no communication skills. The author believes that the residents would still be assessed as mentally disabled by contemporary standards. Even with modern educational facilities it is doubtful whether any resident would have been able to achieve an independent life. As can be seen, the majority of residents shared a common history and had spent most of their lives as well as their formative years together in the hospital. Several remembered going to school in a blue uniform with short pants and sleeping in large 12 bedded wards. Most of them had lived together at some time in their lives during their progression through the villas to the smaller rehabilitation units in the grounds. Only Norman, who had transferred from another hospital, had worked outside the hospital and most of the residents attended the adult workshop on the premises doing fairly low-level undemanding tasks. The hospital from which this group of residents originated appeared to be no better or worse than any other large mental subnormality hospital of its type.

Conventional communication skills were virtually nonexistent in the majority of the residents and the author (who has reasonable experience of similar restricted communication skills and signing) had to resort to a translation situation. A resident would translate for a less able communicator, and would be questioned carefully by staff to ascertain that they had arrived at a correct interpretation. The residents had known each other for many years in the hospital, often living together in the same villas for some years. They had attended the hospital school as children together and they had common recollections, the veracity of which could be checked with Sister X who had shared the last 17 years of their lives. The four Down's syndrome residents had limited but more conventional communication skills and seemed able to understand the others. Over the years in hospital Peter used to talk for Gerry. It did not seem appropriate to use the various types of photographs of sad and happy faces adopted by other researchers when trying to establish relocation measures (Booth *et al.* 1990; Conroy and Bradley 1985). The residents came to know the author and were happy to try to communi-cate. They would probably not have understood the picture cards, mistaking them for some sort of game, and chosen cards at random in a desire to either please or win. Real life seemed to be something they knew about and their achievements would have been diminished by converting them into an imperfectly understood game.

Before visiting employers the author attempted to get a clear picture from each resident as to how his or her working day progressed. As each resident's job was not shared by the resident or member of staff attempt-ing the translation, there was no other source of information about the daily routine. In every case the employer verified the routine the resident had outlined. There was clear evidence of some type of non-verbal communication existing between the group which was not dependent on either conventional language or the conventional and personal sig-ning they also used when communicating with the staff and other adults.

Employment

Sister X decided that part of normal life for the residents would include work outside the house as far as each resident was capable of working and happy to do so. It was agreed from the outset that if they were not happy in any job then they would be taken away from it. She approached potential employers asking if they had work they could offer each resident with the proviso that:

> 'If you could take him on trial – we'll see how it goes'. I never push any pay at the beginning. Then I say, 'well this is what they're capable of and it's up to you what you give them'. Usually they come round and take them. You're not getting a full job out of them. But if it's useful to the resident and useful to the person concerned – money's not the be all and end all. If you were employing and paying a proper domestic or home help...you would want perfection...but you don't get perfec-tion.

> People are wonderful with them...really good with them...and they wouldn't be anywhere where they didn't want to be or where the people weren't keen on them. There's no way they're being exploited. They get a reasonable wage for what they're going to spend each week. If they were doing anybody out of a job – then they don't need to be where they are – They're not giving perfection and they're being paid for the type of work they're doing. They go to work when we feel they should go to work – not when the employer wants them. It fits in with their lives and not the employers' lives. If they were going to be working nine to five every day – they couldn't do it. I'd be pushing for

full wages probably then. They do a useful good job for a reasonable amount of time…and not to great perfection.

Financial arrangements

When Greystones was first opened Sister X received no financial help from any health, social services or local authority agencies. The residents had few clothes and very little money in their personal savings accounts when they arrived, so had to save quite hard in the first year to buy all the things they needed now that they were no longer provided by the hospital. They also needed enough money for holidays. By 1991 Sister X had heard of the Community Care Act but was unsure whether it applied to any new hospital residents she was hoping to get to replace those moving to the flats and had no idea how to find out.

The complexity of the financial arrangements are such that it took some time to work out how the books balanced. When the author finally realised how the system worked it became clear that it illustrated many of the difficulties of a financial system in which developmentally disabled people currently find themselves trapped. The majority of residents were in receipt of wages working in the community in part-time jobs. People with severe learning disabilities on a disability pension are only entitled to earn £6.00 a week otherwise they forfeit their pension. Without such a pension they are unable to provide for their daily living expenses or pay their board and lodgings.

When the author first visited in 1989 all the residents received the current pension rate and merited no 'top ups' in the form of mobility allowances etc. (Sister X pointed out rather bitterly that the whole scheme was 'done on the cheap' as far as the authorities were concerned.) In 1989 this amounted to £190.55 each week. Those residents who were capable went personally to the town post office every Monday morning and collected the entire amount. They then paid this into the bank in the town where the residents have their own personal accounts. Their board and lodgings money are deducted on a standing order and paid direct to Sister X. Each resident deducts £10.00 which they also pay into their personal bank account as pocket money. This £10.00 is used to save up for the two holidays a year they all go on, their clothes and any other necessities. Residents who can handle their own accounts sign out their own money and cheques and keep their cheque books and bank statements. Those who are genuinely not capable of handling these complexities have their accounts in Sister X's name. She pays the money drawn from the National Giro Bank (post office) into the bank and signs the cheque for them. This part of the proceedings is relatively straightforward and the need to bank the personal money was explained by Sister X because – 'savings and cheques are something far beyond, it's not real money if you're writing a cheque. If they need anything back that week like for horse riding or something they keep it back themselves'. All the residents are responsible for their wages and their own personal money which Sister X insists they keep themselves. If residents want any special furniture for their own rooms they are expected to save up to buy it.

The subsection of the financial arrangements is rather more complex and neither staff nor employers were at all keen to talk about it. When wages were mentioned several employers attempted to terminate the interview! Because the residents are employed in various jobs in the nearby villages and town many of them work several days a week. However, as they are only allowed to earn so little Sister X finds some employers feel guilty about paying them such a small wage for their work. Both employers and Sister X wish the residents to retain their dignity and not suffer any exploitation while still enjoying the satisfaction of working. They also wish them to get 'a fair reward for a fair job done'. In the light of their limited communication skills it is unlikely that any of them would be able to complain for themselves if they were underpaid, nor have they any idea of the correct hourly working wage. Some of the residents who work are paid directly by their employers on a daily basis but nobody seems sure how much they get as all residents keep their own wages! Some are given a weekly wage, amounting to the pension earning requirements, by their employer regardless of how many hours they work. Some employers send a cheque (based on the pension earnings allowance) on a weekly or monthly basis to Greystones. In other cases, such as the church cleaning and gardening, Sister X submits a record to the church of the hours worked by the three men but still only asks for an amount within the statutory allowance. By 1991 she was no longer charging the church for work done there and had stopped sending statements as these men were also paid for gardening and other jobs in the villages. A certain amount of produce would appear to find its way to Greystones, which is gratefully received.

The less able residents who are not able to work attend the ATC two days a week where they receive 50p a day. Sister X also makes their wages up to a fixed amount on a Thursday so that they too have a wage for the week which they can live on. Because they do not pay transport or have other work expenses their needs are less than those residents who are in outside employment. Theoretically this enables all the residents to have enough money each week for out-of-pocket expenses.

The Greystones Regime
House Meetings and Residents' Reviews
House meetings for the residents are held about every two months as neither residents nor staff are particularly interested in them and they

are held 'when we remember to have them'. The main domestic rota jobs are usually decided at the residents' meeting. The residents refused to have keys to their rooms or cupboards even when pressed to do so at early meetings. Marty was the only resident to have a lock on his cupboard but after he lost the key and the staff had to break it open for him he refused another key.

One problem addressed at a house meeting was that of evening entertainment. Being previously institutionalised the residents were neither used nor able to make individual leisure choices and waited to be told what to do.

> ...this was a problem. So we held a meeting and said why should we be saying 'Why not go to such and such tonight. Why don't you come to us with some ideas?' Because we were racking our brains trying to think of where to go. We've found now, in the last year or so – some of them like Marty will say 'I'll go to the pub tonight'. Now Peter and Jill will say 'We'll be away to the pub' – so we say 'Get away then'. With the likes of Gerry and John, the less able ones, you still have to structure something for them.

Reviews are held once a month so that there is an annual review for each resident. No formal or standardised records are kept as Sister X believed that social training should be directly relevant to each resident's life style. Progress is briefly noted on individual forms relating to domestic tasks but there are no measures of progress over time. Sister X is averse to this type of paper work and totally resistant to any form of assessment. Invitations are sent to the few surviving relatives but none have ever attended. Social service representatives are not invited as Sister X feels 'they are not particularly interested'.

Social Training

Having had some years of experience in the rehabilitation unit of the hospital preparing more able patients to take up life within the community, Sister X was unconvinced by such training and conventional forms of assessment. She designed her own social training programmes to take a realistic account of the residents' individual abilities. She required them to be a reflection of normal day-to-day living as experienced by each resident and is happy to let each individual programme grow informally out of individual needs. By mid 1990 she felt that some progress was being made.

> The beauty is moving out and looking back seeing what it was... and comparing it to what it is – and trying not to fall into the trap again. What annoyed me about the hospital was that if they were on a programme for boiling an egg...they had to boil that egg through Hell and high water, rather than doing anything different. They had to do that damn programme for boiling an egg over and over again and have

it recorded...that's not normal. Its a farce. You can get bogged down by all the paper work. We have to cram so much into every day here anyway. You know yourself what they can do – and you put into their files what they can do.

The untrained care staff appeared to have some literacy problems and confined their comments to the minimum, even in the day book.

All the residents clean their own rooms, do their own washing (using the washing machine) and ironing. Even the less able are expected to complete their own personal laundry although the staff have to help them complete it step by step every time. After four years of such daily supervision one of the less able residents, with a withered hand, can now iron his own shirt – except the collar. 'The times you've had your hand ironed' was a complaint echoed by most staff!

Cleaning

There was a rota for cleaning and each resident's social training tended to be designed around their own particular domestic job. These jobs changed little as the residents enjoyed their particular responsibilities and tended to be given ones that they were capable of doing. One resident who worked five days a week with only Thursdays and Sundays off; when asked what he did with his spare time said (in a happy mime) that he ironed all the sheets on his Thursday off. He clearly enjoyed this, was proud of his skill and considered it unthinkable that sheets need not be ironed! All the residents seemed to take a pride in keeping their home spick and span. a constantly changing rota, other than for washing up and clearing the tables, would have detracted from the residents' pleasure in the effective contributions they made to their home.

Cooking

Mealtimes are flexible with no set times, and tend to be served when everyone is finally in and ready, often depending on what is cooking. The weekly menu is displayed on the kitchen notice board. Staff and residents eat together in the dining room. Breakfast is usually cooked solely by the staff who also make up the lunch boxes for the workers and ATC people. The residents prefer to take a packed lunch to work and eat together at night. Although all the residents have alarm clocks it takes them all their time, with staff help, to get up and be ready to go to work or the ATC. Two residents have their social training day each week where they do domestic training, washing, ironing, shopping, baking, cooking, prepare the lunch for those that are in and all the normal domestic duties of the house. They also shop for the ingredients and cook their own evening meal on this day, having budgeted for the food out of the daily housekeeping money. They eat their evening meal when it is ready and don't necessarily wait for the other residents. Every resident has a social training day each week and their progress is recorded in an informal way in their file. Gastronomic tastes are respected and Jill who does not like chili con carne will usually make herself an omelette instead as do others who are capable. The less capable residents have a substitute meal of their choice prepared for them. There are no embargoes on residents helping themselves to food from the fridge and bowls of fruit are out in all the living rooms and the hall. Initially they needed a lot of encouragement from staff to help themselves to food that wasn't actually on the table. In the early days they also tended to follow hospital routine and put all the food on their plates at once, piling bread, sandwiches and cakes on to their plates before starting to eat. 'They were selfish, they just looked after themselves. Now they wait'. It took two years to break all the residents of this habit and to substitute a more relaxed regime where they would offer food to others before taking it themselves. It was impressive by 1991 to see the obvious pleasure with which they poured the author's tea from the individual pots on each table, before serving themselves – having first inquired if she would like some.

Social Rota

A prominent feature of the kitchen notice board displayed alongside the menus and domestic rotas for washing up, cleaning, social training etc is a social rota with a large daily square for each resident. It is mandatory to go on some social outing at least every three days and the days when each resident has been out are coloured yellow so that it is possible to easily ascertain if a resident has been staying in the house for too long. In the early days the institutionalised adults were unable to ask to go anywhere because, having had no experience of making individual choices, they had also no idea what the social options were – as Sister X explained,

> What was happening in the early days was that you'd suddenly say – 'When was Ian last out? When was he last at the pub?' Sometimes you'd find you'd missed somebody out because they're the type that can't come and say, or one of those that can't go out on the bus themselves. We found that if we made it conspicuous on the wall we weren't missing anybody out.

For the same reason baths also appear on this chart. Not because there are regular bath nights, residents are able to choose when they bathe or shower, but if a note is made it is possible to ensure people don't miss out baths altogether. Sister X is ambivalent about this fact. 'You want to get away from the institution – but you've still got to check'. Most of the residents need some supervision in washing and dressing especially those who have epileptic fits.

Gerry has a bit of a withered hand and he gets a bit dirty down below as he can't wash himself properly – and you've got to help him wash himself. Usually you just pop in and out and ask if they want a hand or anything.

Weekday Routine

Staff usually come on duty at 8am although two staff always sleep in at night. The staff usually work 15 hour shifts and sleep in on their duty day which adds further continuity for the residents. The four residents who go to the ATC are picked up by local authority transport by 8.30am. As these are the older, less able and still somewhat institutionalised residents who are unable to go out on their own, the staff usually have to make sure they are awake and getting ready for breakfast. However, within a year of coming to Greystones one of this group who had never been out of the hospital on his own or been on a bus in his life, was able to accompany the more able residents on the bus when they went on their Saturday afternoon outing. It was hoped, given time and training, that the other three would achieve a similar measure of independence.

The other residents are then dropped off to work by car. Although they are capable of going by public transport, the infrequency of such transport and the relative cost means they are unable to use it as the cost would exceed their wages. The three-mile return journey to P costs £1.60 and one car trip to take everybody to work is found to be economically advantageous. On pension day they will call in at the post office on the way to work to deal with their finances. Due to the differing days and times of employment, different numbers of residents are home each day and the rotas are carefully arranged to allow two residents to remain at home for their weekly social training day. Lunch for those at home is a light sandwich type lunch often made as part of social training day and eaten sitting at the dining room table.

Weekends

Although the week is fairly structured due to the demands of work the weekend is fairly free. The routine differs at the weekends, except for those who are working. People got up as they please and eat whatever breakfast they want – or not. Everybody has 'little jobs' on Saturday such as tidying the fireplace etc. Lunch is usually made by the staff at the weekends as there are no residents on social training duties and is served when both it and the residents are ready. The residents appear to sit in the same places at meals by their own choice except for those who are attempting to cut down their food intake with a view to losing some weight. They usually sit together at the same table 'as they were looking at the chips the others were eating'. Nobody is put on a diet but if overweight they are encouraged to substitute salad for chips and are usually agreeable to this.

On a Saturday afternoon those that are capable walk up to the main road and go into the local market town on the bus that stops at the top of the road. This bus runs from the east coast to the west coast (linking the villages to the shopping centres) is the only public transport in the area. The author accompanied some residents on one such snowy Saturday and stood hopefully at a place in the road that was apparently an unmarked bus stop. The driver appeared to know them and took their fares without comment and also the author's who was quite unable to find out the fare from either the resident or the driver. When she asked the residents no-one had enough language to explain so one of the residents selected a 50p piece from the author's purse and indicated she should use this.

The residents do their shopping in the town, buying cigarettes, sweets, toiletries etc and then go to the café (where one of the residents worked) for their tea where they are expected to pay and order like the other customers. The proprietor seemed to know them well enough and they were treated like other customers, causing no comment. When finished they walked up the road and caught the bus back to Greystones some three miles away. There were no timetables displayed but both residents and locals appeared to know the times of the infrequent buses.

Those residents not capable of going out on their own are taken out by car by the member of staff on duty each day whose main job is to take out those residents who wish to go. Others stay at home to watch sport on the television. At night those residents capable of taking themselves to the pub go either with a member of staff or by themselves. Sometimes there are outings to the pictures or theatre in the town.

Sundays are equally free, with residents getting up when they wish. If they want to stay in bed they can – but no breakfast is saved. All residents can make tea and coffee whenever they want in the kitchen as long as they clear up afterwards. Sunday lunch is usually cooked by the staff with help from those residents who have been out at work during the week. The afternoon is quite free and some residents go to church at night.

Holidays

The residents usually have two holidays a year and all the staff go with them. In 1990 they went to Spain at Christmas and Blackpool in the summer. In Blackpool they stayed in two separate hotels as Sister X didn't want them grouped together on holiday. In Spain, as this wasn't possible they split up into small groups and went out separately.

Shopping

Residents all choose their own clothes and their keyworkers took them all shopping individually in 1989 and 1990. By 1991 those who were capable had graduated to doing some shopping for clothes on their own. They would go to P (where they were now known through work and their Saturday trips) each taking their cheque book and a note from Sister X indicating that the resident was coming to buy slippers (or whatever was required) and how much they could afford to spend. The shop-keepers were asked by the residents to write the cheques as none of them could write, but they were able to sign their own names. Before setting out on such a trip Sister X would go through the residents' bank book with them and try to explain how much money was available making sure that they realised that money would also be needed for future shopping and holiday spending.

Occasionally this system fails due to still imperfect understanding of the abstractions of 'savings' as opposed to wages paid directly to the resident in real money. A kind shopkeeper recently phoned Sister X to tell her that Jill had purchased a hairdryer and other unaccustomed luxuries, for which she had paid by a cheque in excess of the amount usually spent locally by the residents. After a serious discussion with Sister X Jill was made to realise that if she kept these purchases she would be unable to go on holiday as she would have no money. The purchases were eventually returned to an understanding shopkeeper!

Sister X is also concerned that when handling money the residents should not be flustered or made to look foolish. After four years teaching at Greystones and a life time of social training in hospital, it became clear that for the less able residents handling money was an intractable problem. After some difficulties with a new bus driver, who was una-ware of the residents' problems, she decided that for their own peace of mind they should be taught to offer a pound coin for bus fares and any small purchases that they were unsure about. This would save exposing them either to personal uncertainty or public ridicule. The pervading Greystone philosophy is to ensure that the residents fit comfortably into their external environment.

Life Stories

Peter's Life

Peter, aged 30, agreed to tell the author about his life. He had control of the tape recorder having been shown how it worked and listened to himself talk. He agreed to the author's suggestion that Lynne, the care assistant, was present to help translate. His communication skills were slow, limited and indistinct. Although the result has been pulled into connected prose Peter thought long and hard over each sentence and the entire recording took over an hour to complete. Being a Down's syndrome baby he was placed in the hospital at birth by his parents. At the time of the recording neither the author nor the care assistant knew anything about his life in the hospital. Sister X eventually confirmed the basic facts were correct – although she was surprised to hear how much he understood about his own background. The only inaccuracy was to call Nessie his sister. She was in fact his mentally handicapped aunt who was on Sister X's ward for many years. Peter's family visited her although they never came to see him – merely sent him a Christmas card each year. Peter visited her in her ward every week – on the correct visiting day. After finishing the hospital school Peter passed through various wards and finally reached one of the rehabilitation villas where he was trained in independent living skills.

> The hospital – it was a good place – yes. I liked it there – yes. I was in Bawn House a long time ago. Yes…remember the school – wore uniforms. I had a cap and a blue colour short trousers… Slept on Rose villa at school – a lot slept there in big rooms. Put my clothes on the hanger in my wardrobe. Slept in the corner bed. I used to cry when I was a baby. Sometimes the others cried. Here there's two in my room – just two is better. It's better here at Greystones.

> Came here four years ago – like here the best. Barry, me and Norman came first. A long time ago I was at school with Andrew. It was noisy – more people there. I was working on the transport – I took the dinners round. Aye – the food was good at V. I worked on the dinner van. The food was in boxes and I put it on plates – all the potatoes and carrots. I served the tea out. Here I do the cooking. It's better here. Curry and chile con carne. We didn't get that there – they're too soft at V. Curry nice. Had it here first. We made cakes at V but we make proper cakes here. Went out myself at V to do shopping just like we do here.

> Went to college here – staff helped at night with my homework when I came home. I liked that.

Would you like to go back and live at V?

No. No chance. *Why?* I live here. This is my home.

Was V your home?

Yes V was my home. I've finished with there now. This is my home now. Finished with here in the summer. End of August I'm moving into the flat – finished on Friday – with my girlfriend Jill.

When you were in V did you have a girlfriend?

Yes Lea Walker. She's finished at V. She went back to her mum and dad.

Have you got a mum and dad? Yes, at home.

Do you ever see them? No I haven't.

Does Carol look after you like your mum would? Yes.

Who looks after you here?

Could be George, could be Carol, could be Lynne, could be Keith.

If you got into trouble at work who would you tell? I'd go and tell the staff here. I love Elizabeth.

Did you love the staff at V?

Yes. Elizabeth was on Bawn house with me. Elizabeth was on Ceders with me. She was there when I was at school. I said yes to come to Greystones.

Would you like to live in L by yourself? NO.

Who are your friends?

I've got friends, Jock, Alf at work – just see them at work – not at weekends. See people here at weekends. Go out to L at the weekends.

Do you remember when I went with you two years ago?

Aye – I remember – we went for coffee on the bus. Miss my friends at V – got friends at L.

Have you been back to see them?

No. We have social night here every other Wednesday – we have bingo, dancing, skittles. Sometimes Elizabeth comes.

Did anybody hit you at V?

No. Sometime ago I bashed them back when anybody hit me.

Did the staff hit you?

No, the staff were OK. I broke window. I lost my temper.

Why – who with?

Myself. I lost my memories. Of Jessie Rogers. My sister.

Did you lose a picture of her? NO. Jessie died.

Is that why you broke the window? YES.

Did you tell anybody why? NO.

Did you get into trouble?

No. They sent me to get a cup of tea from the canteen. She died on the ward. I was at school.

How old was she? A big girl.

Did you ever break any more windows? No.

Have you lost your temper here? No.

What will you do in the flat? I'll take all my own things to the flat.

Why will it be different?

There'll be different type of food, curry and chili con carne every day and salad. Jill'll cook the tea because I go to work.

But Jill goes to work.

Aye she does. We'll come from work and get washed and get changed and make our suppers. We'll watch the telly, we watch *Neighbours*, *Home and Away* and *Coronation Street*. Then we'll do resting – in that big bed.

How will you get up in the morning? I'll kick her out of bed in the morning to make my breakfast.

I can see you going without breakfast.

Aye!(laughter) she'll say – get on – you make it? There'll be just two of us me and Jill in a big bed.

Have you ever slept in a bed with somebody else? Yes, I've done it before.

Won't you get cross if she wakes you up? No, I didn't get cross with Lea.

But you didn't have two of you in bed there in V did you?

Aye. I just snuck into Lea's bed when the staff were at tea. Just me got in. When staff weren't looking – I'd just snuck in, lift the covers and snuggle in. She liked it. At tea time every day – aye. It'll be nice and cosy in the big bed with Jill.

Norman's Life

Norman, aged 45, was happy to talk about his life – it was however very difficult to understand him, and not having the powers of concentration exhibited by Peter, it was a tedious task to piece together all the disjointed information he delivered at great speed. His early life had been in another hospital before transferring to V 23 years ago.

A long time ago I had short pants and went to school before I came to V – at J. Used to take the coal to people's houses at J. Put all the coal on the lorry – for the next morning. Filled a big sack – put sack on back and carried it. Lived on a big villa.

Me, Peter and Barry came here first three years ago. V was a bloomin' dump, a nut house. Not a lot liked it. There's not a lot there. There's a lot going on here. We go all over and that here – V we just went to the pub. Here I do gardening work and worked egg farm here. At V got a job doing the grounds, did weeds and bricks and that. Do the big garden here too, turn the soil, dig. Grow cabbage and potatoes here. There's nowt to do at V. Not much there .

But there are a lot of people there.

Some of them there been there when the war started. They are all bored. Peter and Ian and me were in a house where we did our own cooking.

Did people's gardens in V. Had an interview, a woman came round and said no more gardening jobs – had a list of jobs – one was K *(a nature reserve)* – went on Training course there. Didn't go to the Adult training Centre at V.

Did you like J? You can't complain.

Did you like P? I don't care about V. No.

What do you call your keyworker here?

Sexy. When she came for interview I called her hotlips. It's better here there are more people to do things with. You're not tied in. When you're going anywhere you ask the staff. Not like V. If you want to do something you tell someone – then when you come back you tell them what you did. Its nice to live with staff. Dad comes and puts my telly off at night. I like it – not like V.

Rather more informal conversations with Norman, Peter and the other residents about life at Greystones revealed that they were trying to express a concept that was totally beyond their comprehension. It became clear that one of the greatest pleasures common to all the residents was coming home and sharing the independent part of their lives with staff and other residents. Fumblingly expressed pleasures included shared holidays where staff came with them, living on a daily basis with the staff who shared both the fun and the trials and tribulations of their everyday lives. Having their own keyworker who cared about their individual lives. The fact that someone came into their rooms each night to tuck them up or turn off their television and say goodnight was mentioned by several residents.

When asked about the 'staff', they called everyone by individual names but still subsumed them all under the generic term because, in their limited experience of life, adults of normal intelligence had always been hospital staff. Unwittingly they had created a family but had no way of recognising this unfamiliar entity and no words to express it.

A Home for Life

Asked about realistic plans to eventually move the six more capable residents into the community after further years of training Sister X expressed severe doubts about such a policy.

Would you feel easy in your mind to see any of them living in the community without maximum support?

I'm not totally against it – but they're not the *crème de la crème* from the hospital. We've been terribly lucky to have gone so far with what we have – who we've worked hard with. NO. To be honest I can't even see Jill and Peter coping with being totally independent at the present, however much they would like it and however much I would support it if they wanted it. They couldn't cope if they were on their own and there's no way they could handle their own money and plan. They'd live on tins of beans every day or spend a fortune and have a lobster.

Here they've all got their friends around them and they're totally relaxed as to what they're doing. They communicate with each other, do things together and they plan going out at the weekends together. In the cottage and the new flats I think it's nice for them to have more privacy, more time to themselves. They've got a place to go to rather than the main sitting rooms or their bedrooms. But we still find they come over here to do their socialising – this is the core place really. They choose to come over here – they do what they want really. I think they've got a firm commitment. This is their home and they're secure.

Sister X envisages that when the 1991–2 building programme is complete she will be able to contemplate a further expansion of the Greystones' provisions. She originally envisaged that Greystones would provide a self-sufficient environment for the residents. However, due to the incapacity of some of the residents she was unable to find outside employment for them. Although the domestic setting provided a far more stimulating environment than the hospital she reluctantly fell back on the local ATC but was disappointed with the level of stimulation provided there. The YTS care assistant who had worked with the residents at the ATC in 1990–1 confirmed Sister X's initial impression and was surprised to see the difference in the residents when she came to Greystones. The ATC days are spent in aimless, wandering inactivity, from which no-one dissuades them.

CHAPTER 10

The Village

To the informed reader this chapter may appear as tale of simple countryfolk and surprising in the naivety and passivity shown by both villagers and professionals. The author is committed, as in Chapter 1, to presenting the unvarnished views of the participants with no editorial connivance. Rarely do ordinary people have a chance to say, quite simply, how the relocation of what they still call 'village idiots' affects them. Even more unusual is the presentation of such positive acceptance in a community. Current relocation literature pays little attention to this aspect while often giving detailed plans of how to hold public meetings etc to influence and reassure the general public. It is interesting that Sister X has distanced herself from all professional theories of rehabilitation and relocation (having had experience of them and the professionals implementing them) and merely approached the villagers as if it were the most natural thing in the world that, non-communicating institutionalised adults with severe learning difficulties (whom they had never seen before) should work alongside them. Many questions remained unasked and some which were asked unanswered as the author had no wish to disturb the even tenor of village life.

The Neighbours

Greystones' only neighbours were the White family with whom they shared a common unmade cart track from the main road to their adjacent farm. Greystones was set inside and completely surrounded on all sides by two farms owned by the Whites. These farmers, being the only neighbours for at least a mile and a half, were the only people to raise any objections to the initial plans to site the relocated hospital patients in the area. They wrote to the parish council but were overruled at the informal hearing. Not wishing to make any local trouble the White family didn't pursue their objections. They felt the legal fees would be prohibitive and they would almost certainly yet again be overruled. Their original concern, which was not unreasonable given the location of the farm, had been the danger from heavy farm machinery which would be freely accessible to the 12 institutionalised adults if they wandered off their own land.

Mrs White had been born on the farm and all her family were local farming people as was her husband who moved on to the farm when they married. She had never left the area and had worked on the farm and lived in the same house all her life. The eldest son worked the farm with them and when he married he too would continue to live there. By the time the author spoke to them they had been living in close proximity to the Greystones population for four years and their objections were if anything far stronger – but for entirely different reasons. They had no complaints about the residents whose behaviour was impeccable and had caused them no problems at any time. However their stated objections seemed quite valid and highlighted the sort of problems that can arise when 'town people' try to relocate a residential venture in a well-established rural community.

Before Greystones had been sold to the present owners the water pipes from the main supply were in poor repair and constantly springing leaks. The Whites had asked the previous owners to contribute to shared new piping but as they were about to sell they refused. The Whites stood the cost of a new system themselves but made a single supply line bypassing their neighbours who were left with the old leaky pipes. The recent expansion of Greystones twinned with on-going land problems had caused the Whites much anguish and they were concerned about the future of such a community now sited in the centre of their land. Coming from generations of local farming families Mrs White was loquacious on the subject.

> There's no problem with them at the moment – but our biggest problem is what's going to happen to them in ten years' time, when Sister X gets tired of doing that sort of work. Eventually they'll not be as many handicapped people about – what with scanning and that. They've just put up another flat to take another six people…two of them are getting married to go into what was the garage…that means there's going to be another eight to go across there… They were meant to be coming out into the community to live in a family home…but that's in the middle of our farm…it's our land right round it. Fair enough they're no bother and they haven't been any bother…none at all. Seemingly they've been told…and they don't come across the road. But when they (the X's) decide to call it a day – that's going to be a little village in the middle of a farm…I think that when this job over there folds up there's not going to be the number of mentally handicapped people about and it might not go for handicapped people when they all die off. Somebody else might buy it up for something else.

> They haven't co-operated. When they came here four years ago they were supposed to put up a proper fence right round the garden. It's crumbling down and the bull could walk in there any time it wanted…into their back yard. Plus the fact that for the last 18 months they've had a burst water pipe and it comes out through our road side

so we can't bring a tractor through or even bring stock through. The water's too deep. Their water is a private supply. We've told them 40 times and they're supposed to be putting a new pipe down...but we don't want to cause any unpleasantness. The parish council didn't do anything for us in the first place so it's no good going to them...they're hopeless. In the Spring their drains overflowed and all the spaghetti hoops came out in the middle of our yard. It wasn't ours as we don't eat spaghetti hoops. We asked them to repair it but they said they couldn't do anything for three months...and they just left it. So we had to put it right...it was disgusting all the water was going right down to our back door and coming in. We couldn't tell anyone as it would be waste of time...they are all for them. If it had been the farm they'd have come and turned our water off, the amount of water that was wasted.

Farmer White took up the story

I don't like to cause any unpleasantness and what's the use of fighting – I've been and told them twice and all he said was...'What the hell are you bellyaching about – look at the roofs on those buildings of yours, they're making my outhouses damp'...So the next day I employed a tractor to come and take the roofs off completely so as he couldn't complain about them. His roof is so dilapidated the chimney stacks will roll down anyway in the not-too-distant day! He's the sort of chap that thinks he knows it all anyway. We've tried to be friendly with them...asked them to come over...asked them to our daughter's 21st... She would come but he wouldn't – so she couldn't.

What we don't like is the way they expanded... We don't hit it off with them – it's their lifestyle. They're not country bred you see.

This system here is where they were keen on getting the mentally handicapped out into the local environment into families...but they (the X's) bought and they came and they lived there for six months. Then they bought a house and moved out...I don't call that living with the family...it's not a home now, not a family home...it's a mental home now, nothing else...with staff. They're making that much money they've bought a house and moved out. Some day they're going to get tired of that place. They're getting them out of an institution but they're still taking them out to the ATC every day by health authority transport. It's really a money-making racket for the people who're creating these sort of homes.

They both then continued:

You should see the fence in the back yard...they're just packing all their stones and rubbish against the fence...it's ground level on their side so all the stuff's going into our field. Our field's full of their builder's rubble. We don't want to cause any unpleasantness...perhaps they're going to put in a new water supply soon.

The patients are no problem...what we're frightened of is if they keep expanding...they've built that into a mental home...they are the only mentally handicapped that are out here. If they'd done what they were supposed to – to have a well-fenced enclosure...it would have been better. One day when I've a bit of time I'm going to take the tractor, take their broken fence down and push all the rubbish back and build the fence up from our side. The bull and the cows could easily walk in. But what happens if he walks in at night and walks straight up on to the main road and causes a massive traffic accident which could easily happen...if the cows went we'll lose our stock.

They've employed very few local people...no-one from the community...they import all their staff from round the hospital or their own family. Only one girl from the village. They've made no attempt. They asked us if we would take on one of the lads but it's no good with livestock...no good at all. The trouble is here there is only the three of us...we're that busy that by the time you explain and tell somebody, you could have had the job done. One of the lads works in their kitchen garden...goes down there and scratches on...but he even took the gate off and chopped it up...and now our stock just walks in. They don't want to know if you tell them those sort of things...They don't understand because they're not country people and you've got to be born and bred in the country to understand the countryside,...honest...I'm not joking. They have a different outlook really. We try to slow the pace down. It's just these little bits of things. The patients are no bother whatsoever.

The Villager

I was born here, down the road at my parents – they still live there. My Dad was a miner and these houses were built by our colliery as miners' houses. The majority of the village were employed at the pit until it closed down in 1973. I went to the old school here – a church school – it's now a house. The vicar baptised and married me and baptised my two children and confirmed one and will do the other in the church where we were married. I go to church about three times a year. Three-quarters of the people have lived here all the time that I've lived here – some of them are elderly – but the village still remains the same people. A lot of them still use my maiden name. We were all at school together.

Living locally here, everybody passes the time with everybody else. We're just ordinary people – if I pass somebody on the road I say good morning or good afternoon – 'cause I've done this all my life...even if they're complete strangers.

I lived in the town six months after we were married with my husband's folk. I found it very unfriendly. Here there's usually someone popping in – or you can pop in at a friend's. They just didn't do that in the town. I felt like a fish out of water...everybody was rushing here, there and everywhere in the town. Rushing down to the shops, rushing back home, where here everything goes at a slower place. Newcomers move into the village and they move out – they don't seem to stop.

One of my neighbours up the road was getting Norman down to do her garden – she said the more he has to do…he's happier when he's busy. So I said if it'll help he can do my garden so she said she'd have a word with Elizabeth or Leslie and see if he could come. With me being caretaker of the school I need to know when to be around to supervise Norman. He doesn't always get to the right house. They drop him off and he used to come here at 1pm and I'd go back to work at 3pm and then he used go up to Pauline's. He knew his way to Pauline's – it's only two houses up.

Elizabeth or Leslie used to come around to see me and check he was all right. You have to be careful because they told me he's not allowed to use any electrical tools so he can't cut the lawns because I've got an electric lawn mower. Pauline has got a pushy lawn mower so he cuts her lawns. He's a lovely fellow. I can talk to him and he answers. When he first came up I used to struggle a little bit – certain words I couldn't pick up, but I can talk quite well to him now – we have quite a good conversation. He was telling me that they were converting two new flats and that he was hoping to be one of the ones to go into it – that he'd make his own breakfast and his own dinner. There's one that's deaf and dumb – I couldn't have coped with him. I'd have hated to have had somebody here that I couldn't have communicated with at all. My son – he's 14 – used to get on like a house on fire with Norman if he saw him outside – even at Pauline's he used to go and have a chat with him.

I don't borrow the pushy mower as I feel I'd be putting on him. The thing is, when he started to come I asked how much I was allowed to give him and they would never ever state a figure which I found a little bit awkward really. If you asked them at first they said either a little or nothing at all. He comes for two hours on Mondays and Tuesdays and then goes on to Pauline's. You can't let anybody do it for nothing, so the way we got around it was to give him a couple of pounds each day for the two hours and then he loves sweets so I'd buy him a family pack of Mars bars – I think he'd take it back down there. By the time he'd been here half an hour I used to ask him in for tea or coffee and he'd have one then instead of a biscuit. He brings his dinner with him and has it in the house with me. I don't know how much Pauline gives him – she's never ever said. I know they are only allowed to make a certain amount or it affects their benefit. I'd have rather they'd said what he was allowed to make and I'd have had a bit more idea of what to give him. I'd have said he was worth at least two pounds an hour. He was doing as much as my son would have done – except the lawns. My land was just rough out at the back. He did an excellent job, he dug all the garden and nothing was turned in, every weed came out. I said 'just turn it over Norman'. I didn't tell him to take the weeds out – he used to put them in a pile and I'd go and help him put them all into sacks.

He's as strong as an ox – where he gets his strength from I don't know. He cut all the branches off a tree and he literally dug the roots out. From what I gather that was part of his training but I never quite got to the bottom it. He even dug the garden sideways so that he wasn't walking over the piece that he'd dug. I used to find it quite fascinating the way he did everything. He said he liked coming here as my garden's not as bad as Pauline's. He used to go on to Pauline's and if he wanted anything – or if he was stuck with anything, like the roller or the saw, I'd leave the shed open and he'd just come and get in from the shed and put it back when he'd finished.

I don't ever see any of the others except Barry – who works at the pub – on the bus sometimes. I was in the pub one day for a coffee and I found Barry harder to talk to – whether it was cause I was used to Norman I don't know. The woman who lives opposite me works at the pub and he just came into the conversation.

There was a little bit of objection when it was first going to open. People were worried how it would affect them having the mentally handi-capped about here as there isn't a lot of people around here that are handicapped or anything. It's not like a town where you see them every day. I think parents were frightened of the effect on the children around. They're used to just going where they pleased – everybody knows them – you look after everybody's children here. Its very much a community – a lot of these people have been here all their lives – like me. They didn't do anything official about it though.

The first I realised they were here…I was on the bus and there was three of them got on – and struggled a little bit to make the bus driver understand they were going to the next town (about ten miles away). Now it's a case of the bus driver knowing them. It was then that I realised who they were. These three had nobody with them – they seemed to manage that as well. Everybody on the bus just seemed to accept them. Nobody here has really objected to them because they haven't caused any problems. The bus drivers know them now. Kids stop and pass the time of day with them – everybody knows Norman now with him coming here and to Pauline's. They all know when he goes to the wrong house and they send him to the right one.

When you first read about it in the paper that it was going to happen – I'd have said no – they wouldn't have accepted them in the way they've done. They've been quite useful to the community. They do quite a lot and they don't seem to bother anybody. They go down to have a drink at the pub – somebody usually takes them.

The Church

Greystones was part of a sparsely populated rural parish set within mainly open land and one of five Anglican church parishes with only two churches and one small combined post office and shop between them. The Anglican parish runs from east to west about three miles and from north to south (going by car) about eight miles. The five villages have a total population of 1200 people who split between small hamlets and the outlying farming land. The vicar lives in the vicarage of one of the churches in a hamlet of less than a dozen people which is not served by public transport.

The Anglican Vicar

The Anglican vicar had been there for 32 years and had baptised, married and buried most of the inhabitants during that time. Roughly 20 per cent of the parish occasionally attended the two churches set at each end of the parish but the congregation was often in single numbers due to the majority of the villagers being what the vicar termed 'non-playing Anglicans'. However the majority of these non-playing Anglicans were baptised, confirmed, married and would probably be buried by the vicar, who celebrated seven or eight weddings a year. There was a regular confirmation class of 18 people of various ages comprised of people he had baptised and whose parents he had married. The divorce rate appeared to be low. Very few of the village people who employed the residents were regular churchgoers.

> With it being in the parish you see, we heard about it coming and I know the neighbouring farmer, he came to church for his wedding. I married the farmer and his wife and baptised their children now in their 20s. Some people were a bit uptight about it coming here. I went and saw the farmer just before they moved in. They thought some of the residents might get mixed up with the machinery and the animals. One or two people round about didn't know what was in store for them. I had a word with them to reassure them and that sort of thing.

> I've been going regularly to visit Greystones all the time they've been here. I take the church magazine there and go in twice a month and talk to the residents or staff or whoever's there. I was there yesterday talking to Jill, Peter and the one that works at the pub while they were all in the kitchen. They make a sign when they see me – like cutting their throat. If Ian has seen a grave being dug he makes that sign and wants to be out of the way – so perhaps it means death, or perhaps just my collar. I was asked to take the cremation service of the girl that died and the obituary was in the parish magazine. They go to the Methodist chapel. There was someone working at Greystones who was keen Methodist and she took them off there. I married some of her family and baptised some of them. Her husband's probably a non-playing Anglican.

> When they first arrived Sister X came and asked if there was anything they could do. So the completely deaf man works out in the church yard and as he's stone deaf you can't give him machinery to use or he'd chop his fingers off–not being able to hear the machinery. The other two work

inside the church dusting and polishing. They do a good job. They've come in two or three times a week for the last three years. I didn't have any worries about them...I don't think they would have been at Greystones if they'd been dangerous. I didn't know any of them before, staff or residents but I don't think they'd have been brought out here if they'd been dangerous. They would have been kept in the hospital. I know the chaplain there very well, we sometimes have a study group meeting in the hospital and have lunch in the canteen. Having known the hospital for the past 32 years I knew that everything would be OK. Perhaps if I hadn't taken them to work in the church at the beginning...I don't think they would have integrated so much. Obviously they may not be doing a terrific amount in the community...but Rome wasn't built in a day.

Someone brings them in the morning and they're left to work. The staff at Greystones took them at first and trained them in the work. They decided what was needed we didn't give them any instructions. These days the church is kept locked but a key is at the farm just near by, They help themselves, it's in an outhouse hanging on a hook. I often see them walking back along the road to Greystones from the church by themselves. We used to do all the cleaning on a voluntary basis. The people who did the flowers helped with the cleaning.

The treasurer pays them...they don't want much because of their pension. I don't know what the payment is – you'll have to see the treasurer...he sees to it – I don't quite know...the money comes from church funds generally. There are no local authority things out here. It's just up to local people to organise things for the children in the holidays. For the adults the pub plays the social role with the sports teams and leek growing. There's the Young Farmers...they are very active.

They seem to be integrating extremely well so I think the Anglican and Methodist influence has a lot to do with it. There's an official linking of Sunday schools taught by some of both. There are very few United Reform people here and very few Catholic people here. Even though we may not do a lot, what we do helps them integrate and be welcomed in the community. People here have not had contact with people with learning disabilities until Greystones came here.

The Methodist Minister

The boundaries of the Methodist ministry were geographically different to the Anglican parish system and founded on a circuit whose centre was originally some 30 miles distant and derived from a split between Primitive and Wesleyan Methodism in 1870. The minister covers four churches sited in the small market town and three villages with 140 communicant members between them. He also has a community visiting role and contact with a further thousand people who he visits at some time. One of the churches was near Greystones. The Methodist minister had been in the post for six years but had not been aware of the arrangements to relocate the hospital patients in his particular parish.

One Sunday I went to the church, and then in trooped in about six Down's syndrome young adults with their helper. At that time she was one of my church folks – an Evangelical Christian, full of enthusiasm. I gathered that she worked down there when they just appeared in church. I smiled at them and of course I got smiles back. So I said 'hello' and carried on with what we call the normal hymn sandwich. I gathered that they'd been going to the Anglican church which was the full order of liturgy which didn't seem to click. They came along because we were a little bit freer. I was interested because the church they came into was a congregation of only about seven or eight elderly people. The membership is only twelve in that church. These youngsters came along and you could immediately see these people didn't know how to react to them,...because elderly people don't know how to react to them. The fear is there. Of course Jill is so extrovert...she walks into the vestry generally when she arrives now and flings her arms round me and gives me a big kiss and I give her a kiss. Peter who's there asks me about Michael the Anglican chaplain at the hospital. The others don't communicate. If you give Gerry a big smile he'll smile back. So they came to church.

I had wanted to organise joint ecumenical services with the Anglican vicar for some time. In my mind I call these family services. Now we have joint services once or twice a quarter in an afternoon for the family – with children. In my mind I call these family circuses and it worries me at times as I'm as much a liturgy man as I am free and easy. But how do you communicate to little ones and to the Greystones gang? The vicar comes and shares a service with me. He uses the book and gives the prayer and the lesson and I generally give the address. In one family service I took my putter and ball and talked about aiming for things – the right things – and said to the Greystones gang 'come and have a go'. We've now started an ecumenical Sunday school and we had one service on a Sunday morning which filled our chapel.

So now we have the Greystones gang coming. After the initial shyness from our group they've brought a new spirit to that church. As a Christian and spiritualist, theologically I believe that God is working through these young people because of the very nature of who they are and the very fact that they exude love. We've not lost any congregants and one or two more have joined us as well. They make the most horrible noise in the world when they sing – and it's hilarious. They bawl out but why should I worry about it. It doesn't worry anybody and I've never raised the issue. My attitude is – I might think I can sing but to some people it might be a cacophony of sound so why should I take exception. The other interesting thing is that they have been schooled in a simple liturgy when they were in hospital and I think they've been brought up to make certain responses. When we use the liturgy for communion it's not all that much different to the Anglican. The hospital chaplain is most ecumenical.

One of the things that always confronts us with the Greystones people is how much are they taking in? I just don't know. In our church council once or twice I've said to my members 'What do you think about the way I'm coping with this as minister. Do you think I'm being patronising?' One of the ladies said she thought I was. So I thought I'll have to watch that then, I won't have to patronise. I try to communicate. So what I do is talk. In my sermons – talking to about a dozen congregants – I tend to come out from behind my little lectern and converse. We also have the bidding prayer 'Lord in Your mercy' and the Greystones people know this from the hospital.

They all come to communion and they all receive communion. We have it generally once a month. We have no rubric which sets down whether people have to be confirmed. Last Sunday we had communion and I don't use a full liturgy, I vary it and at the moment I'm doing a theme on reflections in all four churches. I only go to their church once a month, the lay preachers do the other three.

The Greystones people are members of a Sunday congregation. If there's anything going on at the church they come. We don't have a lot going on at the church but they love to come to bun fights. In our church life we don't pick them out. If I address some of them it's just as if I'm talking to my other folks. Fifty per cent of that congregation are now mentally handicapped and the major way one communicates is by sheer friendship. Intellectually I don't know what I'm really on with. My style has developed more – I've never had to preach to so few people. We have quiet worship and they don't make any noise that is different to people who are not mentally handicapped. The only thing you notice is at times the raucust singing. The 'la la la-ing' and really that's no problem. We've got a pianist who cannot read music and plays by ear. We had a pianist who was 90 who could transpose the music in the middle of a service if it was too high. Poor soul she's in the old folks home now. I ring this new pianist up with the hymns and she sorts out her own tunes if she knows them. If she doesn't know them she doesn't play, so I sing it and get everyone to sing it after me. Flexibility and adaptability is the name of the game. The other week there was a song that some of them knew but not others. They all had their papers but the Greystones can't read – but they still have to have their papers – even if they're upside down...it's all part of belonging. So we started to sing and we had great fun. If God doesn't accept this as our prayers and worship what are we on about? God isn't schooled in the Anglican, Methodist, Jewish or Christian tradition. This is our offering and it's a wonder. There are times when I'm so moved by it all. There's a mystic nature about it that we can transcend. A lot of religion is cerebral religion and one of the interesting things is that to do a good thing – to do something which is an enjoyable experience – has a spirituality.

Folks better than me ought to write some theology about this. The acceptance that goes almost beyond the reason.

The worship we do, there is some hint they know. At the outset it concerned me, so I had a word with the hospital chaplain and he came up and talked to my lay preachers about some of the simple things we can do. That we accept them as adults and try to talk to them because there are things they will understand. But before even you come to mental disability there is the receptivity of a congregation mixture of so many age groups. You have different mental abilities anyway.

I never go into Greystones because with four churches I've too much to do and I know the vicar goes – but if any of them went into hospital we'd be first there. The fact that they are about – the fear factor has been diminished. People living in the area see them arriving at church every Sunday. When the Methodists get together and have joint services with the other Methodist chapels in the circuit, Greystones are always in the congregation. We had a great national jamboree and we had a bus and we went round to Greystones with the bus and picked them up. There were 2000 people there and we were singing 'Shine Jesus shine' – it was a bit charismatic – some had their hands up – and I looked over and there they were, making the sounds and the noises. I'd go so far as to say that our people in the Methodist circuit will fiercely accept them. Our Methodist people will tell you that they have changed the atmosphere of their church. In a sense they've given some hope to this little church that was just plodding along. We now have this joint Sunday school of 18 children. It's all bound up.

The minister concluded the interview in a rhetorical vein that inadvertently echoed the authors own concern.

It seems to me that this so-called deinstitutionalisation has been done without any real understanding of what we are doing with people's lives. How do they cope in these ones and twos in the little flats? The trouble with professionals is that we're separated from the non-professionals and we assume that everybody's come along the same road as us – with enlightened attitudes. What is normal?

The Parish Councillor

The apolitical elected parish council which meets three or four times a year is the lowest level of a three-tier system being 1 of 51 parishes under the local district council. A purely rural parish it is said to be one of the biggest in the country although sparsely populated. This is in turn administered by the county council and the parish council receives a precept of three per head for the 445 adults amounting to 1335. The 1991 census is expected to record over 600 people in the parish. Neither the Anglican vicar or the Methodist minister are on the council. This parish councillor who has lived in the area all his life and been on the council for 20 years was the key figure in squashing any local opposition to the proposed planning application for Greystones. He lived in the centre of the village, opposite the pub which was the focus of the village social life with several teams playing competitive sports. There were also social events like Country and Western nights. His view would appear to accord with those of other people in the parish. An interesting point common to all the villagers was the way they identified the residents not by name but by where they worked.

> Born and bred just five miles up the road…but we emigrated here when I got married…when we moved here we moved into strangers even though it was just five mile up the road…our daughter got married here.

Asked about Greystones:

> The first thing we knew about it was we had a planning applica-tion…most of which have to come through the parish council…the district council send the application in, where it's viewed and con-sidered by the parish councillors. Then you have recommendations or objections or whatever needs to be said. Then we send these back to the district council where they look at our comments but very rarely act upon them. Often we make recommendations about planning applica-tions when they come in…like we'd like it be connected to the main sewerage rather than a septic tank…but we've very little power…they don't take any notice. We maintain the footpaths and certain lights the county council won't put up for us. We lost the bottom of the playing field and we had to be compensated but there was no problem there.

The Greystones scheme may have been mentioned in the local paper along with the proposals to shut down the hospital…or to phase it out…and among one or two other applications the clerk brought it up. It's normal procedure for outline planning applications to be sent to the parish clerk and it's read out at the parish meeting. We got notice of the application to turn the house into 12 planning units for mentally handicapped people. Along with their application there was a letter of objection from Farmer White. The letter stated one or two points, one, that there would be a possible fire hazard from people smoking near his hay ricks and that they may leave gates to the fields open and let the stock out – and that having tractors and machinery there they would be a hazard to that. There were one or two nods of agreement when that was read out…there were three or four farmers on the parish council and they would tend to agree from the farmer's point of view. But I didn't quite agree with that. I said that as regards the inmates being a danger to the machinery you just had to walk or drive around the country lanes an hour in the summer when the slow moving farm machinery was on the road at two miles an hour and that was more of a hazard than ever they would be to the machinery. And I said that these people coming here would be by no means dangerous. They'd just be like little children that hadn't grown up…and that if you scraped a mark on the road and told them not to go over it they'd go up to it probably and stand at the toe of it but they wouldn't go over it. They just need to be told once and have it in their mind.

In fact, something quite funny happened a couple of years ago, when Norman, who does the churchyard and a few of the gardens must have been working hard in the garden on this hot sunny day and his reward was to go down to the pub for a pint...but don't be too long they must have said...and he must have jogged down the road, came up to the bar, got his pint of beer and downed it in one go and said 'I've got to go' and ran back up the road. It did him more harm than good I think! But because he'd been told not to be too long...he'd rushed away back. That was the only occasion I've seen any of them there without somebody with them. They usually sit in the lounge, chat among each other...we usually have a chat with them. If I see them there I go and have a word with them. They're usually there in the evenings, not often on the weekend. They all have their purses and look after themselves.

I haven't heard or been aware of any objection to them. We even have a couple of our own local village idiots that are much worse and there's no bother at all between them. They mix with them. We'd never be aware of them if they didn't work around. One works in the pub. Norman does a bit of gardening. One at the nursery...we never hear any complaints. It hasn't made any difference at all. I think it's made a big difference to them. They can nicely be out because anyone who does see them knows who they are and where they're from.

In the early days, before we knew who they were...you know Norman, he's a bit of a wild look about him and he was working in the churchyard and my wife had gone in there and got a bit of a shock when she saw him...a complete stranger in the churchyard...but it was all right. The first time I ever saw them was in the bar and I was walking along with two drinks and the young girl that works up at the nursery turned round and bumped into me. Maybe half an inch of beer spilt out of the top of one of the glasses and she was very sorry and most apologetic. 'Don't worry pet' I said and went to put them down...and she came over and said would I have another drink and she was most insistent. I let her buy me one...I said it wasn't necessary and 'a half would do' but it had to be a pint. I had more than I wanted that night! She was most insistent putting right what she'd done wrong and it wasn't her fault – just an accident – just a simple bump.

The Market Gardeners

The market garden was set into isolated country some two miles from Greystones and the owners had moved into the area some 14 years ago. Mrs Green had kept on her job as a teacher in the town travelling 30 miles each way to work until she took early retirement. She was a highly qualified and experienced teacher and had also worked in the remedial section of the large comprehensive. Over the years the Greens had employed several residents in the market garden and Jill had been cleaning in the house for two years. Their own family had grown up and left the area.

I think it was Leslie that came in first with Norman. Now we did employ Norman for a while but he was so limited that it was impossible to let him work on his own without supervision. He was doing damage and it was impossible for him to follow instructions. He doesn't understand the simplest concepts like large, small, up, down. You don't get that impression at all when you're talking to him and he was causing us more work than he was worth. We had him for about a year. We liked him, he was very very nice. Sister X was collecting him one day and said did we know anybody who would like someone to do housework. Jill had had a job along in a café and Jill had lost this job because the café had changed hands. I said well I don't really need anybody but she can come along here a couple of days a week until you find her something else.

Actually she's taken the place over, as if it belongs to her. She comes about ten o'clock in the morning and sometimes they collect her at two in the afternoon, sometimes we take her home. She brings her lunch with her. She's like a little clock, she always knows when it's time for food – she's very fond of food! We put a little diagram up on the clock as I was out one day and my husband was working outside. So he made a little diagram on the clock to show her when it was time for lunch and we've left that. She's very very good, her speech is poor, very indistinct. I can't understand her but my husband can. I showed her what to do and now that she's into a routine she tells me when she wants things. She likes certain brands of polishes etc.

Mr G reluctantly took over as his wife was called to the phone to explain about Ian the deaf mute who was working there.

Ian works here five days a week. He's very good. We've established a good sign language between us. Certain signs I understood that he would use – like for the toilet and that sort of thing. Being deaf and dumb all his life he probably hasn't been taught the official language. We pay him on a daily basis carrying it over to the end of the week depending on how often he's been here. We give it directly to him.

(At this stage – as with most of the employers – the conversation ceased and Mr G asked for the tape recorder to be turned off. It seemed that any discussion about money would lead to the end of the interview so yet again the author abandoned that particular line of inquiry.)

He works with the motor mower and I insist that he wears protective shoes. You have to take some sort of precautions. He got a very bad cut working at the church with the hand scythe. He's perfectly capable of working with machinery but they won't give him any...I know he's not supposed to have supervision there but I've always said he should have supervision. I'm sure it would be against the law in a factory to have somebody like that working unsupervised. Without at least somebody there to hear a scream if something does happen.

Mrs G continued but again the interview was nearly terminated when Jill's wages were discussed.

I just give the money to Jill, it's hers – it's their pocket money. We give them whatever we can afford at the time. Certain times of the year we have more than others. They always get something for Christmas and I bake for them.

It's difficult to ascertain Ian's level of intelligence. It must be quite high. He makes desperate sorts of noises, awful sounds. He makes signs we can understand like when the vicar comes. He'll watch my husband do things and copy them. He and Ian have a very good sign language, they can talk and chatter and laugh. He uses the motor mower and the strimmer. He's death to machinery with new blades and things but he loves machines and he can work with machines.

Neither Mr nor Mrs G were keen to talk about the economics of the situation but seemed pleased with the residents, both of whom could be left on their own to work without constant supervision when they were sure of the routines. They had used no special training techniques but merely worked alongside the residents until they were sure of the work. This was surprising, in that Mrs G was well aware of teaching pro- grammes that would break down the tasks but chose not to employ them. Mrs G often left Jill alone in the house for part of the day while she either worked outside or went out. Neither of them thought they were doing anything unusual in employing non-communicating adults with severe learning difficulties as they knew that other people in the area had previously employed Jill and Ian and that most of the residents worked in the community.

The Publicans

Mr and Mrs S had been senior social workers attached to London hospitals and had decided on a change of career seven years ago when they purchased the local pub which was the centre of village life in the parish. They arrived shortly after Greystones opened.

We were approached by Sister X who came to see us as she was looking for part-time jobs for some of the residents. They were fairly new to the whole thing. It just seemed to be an extension to the sort of work we'd done before so we said 'yes we'd take him on'. He works most days but it all came about in rather a confusing fashion. He likes to come so we said well if he wants to come more he can come more mornings if he wanted to.

Then they suddenly discovered last year he was doing an extra day. 'Oh dear' they said, 'why is he doing an extra day?' So I said 'well, if you remember he wanted to come'. No big deal about it. It seems they'd got their rotas mixed up and they looked for him on a Thursday and he wasn't at Greystones. They phoned and I said he's here, it's historic, he's been here on Thursdays for two years and presumably he wishes to continue.

They bring him every morning or occasionally he comes down on the bus. They collect him or we put him on the quarter to twelve bus, or very occasionally we give him a lift up. He comes at nine o'clock weekdays and ten o'clock on Saturday and Sunday. Sunday's his best day of the week – he likes Sunday best. It's our busiest morning. My husband deals with Barry mostly because he works for him. None of the other staff object to him at all.

Initially I think there was resistance to the home from the parish. I don't know the history but there were certain attitudes about it – as there always are when people have a home for the mentally handicapped in their midst. Initially there was a bit of suspicion and much looking at from the customers. When they saw him around the place in the morning they looked a bit askance but they didn't actually say anything to us. Surprisingly the people that you'd think would have no prejudice against it did and those you imagine would have – don't. Older lower-middle-class – white-collar workers did. Certain things were said – nothing particular but few remarks were made about one never knew what they were going to do next – you could never tell etc. There seemed to be the usual sort of suspicion and unease. We tried to educate them in a non-obvious way by showing them our own attitudes towards Barry.

They started coming as soon as we started here…we're weren't really objective about it. We were too busy and also we probably had an inherent belief that they had a right to be there and everybody else would have to accept it. I'm not sure we were very sharp about it…if we'd worried about the way the business was going! People just took their cue from us. Now they are all an accepted part of the customer group and they're all known by the different jobs they do. They say 'the one that works at'…if they don't know the name. They'll come into the pub as a group usually with somebody with them. Now people that know them often go and sit beside them, take their drinks over. Certain ones are quite fond of them and make a point of being very cheerful with them and friendly. Not for the whole evening but just to go and see them.

He had a form of training but we didn't set out to be formal. He comes in the morning and we're usually finishing off the residents' breakfasts so he clears the table, helps wash up, cleans the toilets, bottles up. Takes out the empty bottles from the night before and puts them in the cases. They've got to be sorted before they go back to the brewery. Some of them he can't sort – its something he doesn't seem to pick up. He can put all the large ones together but you find that unless you check from time to time to see how he's doing you can't be certain he does it. If you don't check things get mixed up. He does quite well but I think the sorting task could be beyond him...there's quite a mixture of bottles. But he's quite exceptional in his way picking up all the different jobs. I keep pointing out all the things he should be doing.

He understands what's going on here. He uses the word 'customer' repeatedly because when he first started I used tell him what do. 'We'll get the toilets really nice – or we'll do this really nice so it'll be nice for the customers when they come in they'll enjoy being in if it's nice and clean. ' He'll often say 'for the customers' when he works.

I wouldn't like to leave him in the building on his own as it might be unsafe but I can leave him to get on with his jobs so long as someone's around in the building. No-one would have to be near him. If you leave him too much you find the jobs are not very well done and if you ask him if they're done he always says they are – so you can't rely on him. I give him the money once week on a proper pay day. A Monday – he knows the day – he waits, and if it gets to the end of the morning and he thinks I might have forgotten and it gets a bit long he'll say 'it's Monday today Tom'. He has a bit of vocabulary. We don't expect very much from him. We tell him what to do and he knows what he wants straight away. We don't really present him with having to respond an awful lot. We talk to him in passing as we work – in a friendly manner, like 'have you been to the Black Bull last night'...and he sort of grins naughtily and nods his head if he's been. He thinks it great to go for a pint. They come up here about twice a week – according to if they've got any money.

We've always treated him normally, and not put too heavy stress on him. Whenever we've been away people tend to talk to him too much and he gets too excited. We have a bit of fun with him – but we tend not let him go far down that road. We tease him now and again and he responds quite nicely but we don't carry it on for too long as I don't think he can cope with it. When we first had a holiday for a fortnight I don't feel that the people that took over quite knew what was appropriate. They were friendly with him but there was too much banter – a bit at his expense. At times like that he'd do silly things. He'd go in the cellar as they'd been kidding him he was under manager – and he'd switch things off – things to do with the gas supply and things would go wrong and they'd suddenly realise that Barry has been interfering. But he never does that when we're here – and we don't sit here saying don't do this or don't do that. It was overstimulating for him.

With us he's treated as a member of the team. He's developed a lot in the three years. He was much more flat and not so happy. He's gone through stages where he's almost been challenging a bit...seeing how far he can go. There have been stages of change. He's quite different now and gives a bit of cheek to the staff. He knows when to say it and says it most appropriately to the bar maids and cleaners. One or two of the older women have a bit of fun with him – and his stock response is 'Yes grandma!' Bob is his hero...his first words when he comes in are 'Where's Bob?' and if he's out 'what's he gone for?'

Yet again the interview was nearly terminated when the question of pay was raised.

I wouldn't be prepared to pay him the going rate for doing work in the pub. Not the same as other people as I can't get the same from him. We're happy with him coming. Some of the tasks I have to go over and do myself. Some of the times I spend as much time making sure he's all right, checking...as he can be incredibly lazy at times. He works nicely in a limited way as long as you're quite happy to not expect too much. In a business situation where you've got to be careful how much money you use you couldn't afford him. We don't have high expectations but if it was going to cost too much it wouldn't pay me to have him at all. He loves the wage and he's keen on keeping hold of his money. One of the interesting things is that he always used to mop behind the bar – that was one of his jobs. And we recently had new flooring put down which is black and white and difficult to get looking nice. It became apparent that Barry couldn't quite manage to get this right. He was shown on various occasions by people how to do it with a cloth but he still didn't manage to do the corners. We decided we'd give him another job instead and let one of the other cleaners do the floor as you can't have people skating about on sticky beer. So without any prompting from us the cleaner said 'I'm going to do the floor from now because a more important job has been found for you'. She just said that off the top of her head as they're quite protective of him. They're all local people who are very kind people – good folk. In the mornings we're all doing too many jobs and there's not enough time – we're all pushed and there's quite a lot of times when it actually takes too much time supervising Barry. Most of the time he's well worth having. He particularly likes things to do with washing up. We believe that's what he did in the hospital – and because that side of things is more pushed he helps in that sort of thing without supervision. Often I say to Barry 'will you help clear the visitors rooms'. He brings the cups down and he loves to get in and clear the rubbish bins from the rooms. He's got a thing about the bins, he loves to discover rubbish. That's his obsession. He likes things to be orderly. He clears all the rubbish from the pub and puts it out in the bins. In fact at the social we went to at Greystones he couldn't really let himself go and enjoy himself – he was concerned about tidying up. You can't ever speak to him face to face. If you tried to engage him in conversation you'd get disappointed. You have to build up a system of communication with him. You sometimes conduct a sort of monologue when you're washing up. I'll say something like 'yes it was a very nice day yesterday' – and he'll join in. He adds a bit. Sometimes he just repeats but when he repeats I just ignore him and carry on to another bit. He keeps repeating 'are there any customers? But we say to people 'don't keep answering that question as he doesn't actually expect an answer'. We're always careful about the way we treat him and the way other people are treating him. If we think things are inappropriate we channel it off into something else.

We've seen them in training centres and going out. But for his level of intelligence he's got quite a good level of ability. Because it's informal and over a period we can give him time because everyone else is just doing practical tasks he's been able to respond better. He has to feel like the lynch pin, important. In a professional situation you have to plan programmes about what people are aiming to do, but here we've just a very informal practical orientation, just working with him, just caring over time.

Epilegomena

Why shouldest thou be as a stranger in the land? (Jeremiah 14. 8)

The reader who has stayed this far will have been subjected to a some-what fragmented whistle stop tour of England, Scotland and Wales. The various chapters have presented the author's research evidence on a variety of provisions for people with severe learning difficulties. They also include the opinions of people with severe learning disabilities, the professionals who care for them, and the ordinary citizens who (due to recent legislation) now find themselves living in rather closer proximity to such people than was ever envisaged. The professional reader may well be unused to such an eclectic juxtaposition in a single text. Inter-spersed throughout the book (contrasting with the necessary jargon) are the simple views of people responding to a new challenge in ways that seem to have no relevance to the customary professional presentations of relocation literature.

Johnson (1985), in a wide-ranging discussion on social policy and service development for people with mental handicap makes the point that normalisation is seen by professionals as a something that will enable mentally handicapped people to live an ordinary life. However, once the professionals have actually relocated people into the various types of community provisions, 'much of the success of the venture relies on the reception given to new residents by neighbours, local shop-keepers, publicans, cinemas and others'. Pointing out that little exists in print on this subject he suggests that the neglect of research into com-munity responses is a 'glaring omission'.

It has been usual to exclude such subjective views in the design, implementation and written evaluation of relocation projects. In some cases they are added in the final stages of an evaluation to indicate a successful aspect of the project. This may well be due to an assumption that the man in the street is not an expert in the field of learning disability and so has no skills to offer in implementing such a complex undertak-ing.

To counteract this assumption the author would like to draw the reader's attention to Greystones, where an entire village has absorbed 12 long-term institutionalised residents of the local subnormality hospi-tal – with no conventional professional intervention. Where profession-als in the village were competent to turn their nursing, teaching and social work skills to design learning strategies and programmes for work, they chose not to. It seemed that in every case they preferred to take a simple human approach. By working alongside their trainees on a one-to-one basis, respecting their individuality and limitations, they taught them by example in much the same way as they would have treated a more able apprentice. The location of Greystones has to remain anonymous as current legislation prohibits the residents (who set off so confidently to their daily work) from earning their wages. They could thus be debarred from such meaningful activities. None of the residents receive any special allowances such as mobility or attendance allowances and the consequent drop in their pensions would force the closure of the home. Greystones operates on a shoestring and has received no financial subsidies for the patients relocated from the hospital.

Examined from a sociological perspective, Greystones would appear to present an antidote to *micro-institutionalisation*. It may well be profitable to examine the evaluations of two other recent relocation projects, and other chapters in this book, in the light of this concept. The author has no intention of imposing on the reader the customary conclusions usually presented in these final pages. These were stated in the prologemenon. It is hoped that readers will have examined the evidence presented in the text and noted the various conclusions interspersed throughout. Multi-disciplinary readers can then draw those conclusions that are most helpful to their own particular practice. Readers wishing for a more conventional presentation may well prefer to stop reading at this point and possibly consult the full data, documentation and statistics supporting Chapters 4, 5 and 8 (Sinson 1990; 1992).

Booth *et al.* (1990) evaluated a joint planning initiative involving the social services, local health authorities and representatives of the voluntary sector. With no additional resources they pursued a programme of relocation within normal financial, political and administrative constraints. Forty-five people with learning difficulties were relocated in the wider community. Twenty-one people made the move from NHS hospital to hostel provision whilst 24 moved out of the hostels into various staffed and unstaffed flats in the community. The longitudinal research evaluation consisted of three sets of interviews with the two groups of 'movers', their relatives, their keyworkers or direct care staff. The first interviews took place before the move, the second after the move and the final interview was left for a further year to gauge the effectiveness of the new placement. The study effectively explored the hostel and hospital regimes of the movers, and compared the daily routine and care practice in the three different settings. The final report presented many challenging guidelines over a diversity of topics and many obvious success stories. The authors stated at the outset that 'it cannot be assumed that a move from hospital brings with it a less institutionalised pattern of living' and within the study there was considerable illustrative material to support the concept of *micro-institutionalisation*. With some ambivalence the authors concluded that 'hospital environments cannot be assumed to be more institutional than hostel environments and that 'deinstitutionalisation as opposed to merely relocation, calls for something more imaginative than simply substituting hostels for hospitals'.

The final interviews, after one year in the new placement, highlighted the community isolation of the hospital movers. Two out of three were said by staff and keyworkers to be bored due to lack of organised activity both during the day and weekend leisure time. They were few signs of any real gains in personal autonomy or self-determination on the part of the hospital movers, who were accompanied by hostel staff whenever they went out. There was no apparent increase in the numbers going to shops, pubs or cafés on their own. The authors make the point that 'Similarly in the hostels, as previously in hospitals, people's use of community facilities was mostly determined by staff who decided when and where they go'. The level of community participation in leisure activities was low among the hospital movers before relocation, and remained so afterwards. Although not stated in the text, it seems clear that none of the hospital movers had been educated to use their leisure time effectively and the hostel staff had no time to implement this sort of training. When people took part in leisure activities outside (whichever type of living unit they had been relocated to) it was in segregated settings such as Gateway and social education unit discos, or closed swimming sessions at the local baths. There was no recorded increase over the year in the use of public leisure facilities. The gains in experience of community leisure activities were scanty for both sets of movers, even for the hospital movers amongst whom it might have been thought the potential for change was greatest. A perceptive care worker summed up the prevalent hostel ethos.

> We only do basic care here. Looking to the future, if we cannot give her any more than she has here then all we've got is a mini-institution. If we don't keep her going forward she'll start to regress. Already the residents are in fixed routines. They all need more than we can give them. (Booth *et al* 1990, p.164)

The final results of the evaluation highlighted two main areas of concern. The issue of integration into the wider community and the lack of provisions for daytime activities for both sets of movers. The authors also concluded that the evidence of the study put into question whether these particular hostels should continue to feature in the long-term strategy. Sadly, the author's research study of ten similar geographically disparate group homes, indicates that the Kirklees hostels are representative of current practice in the field and in line with the government's plans for community care.

The private sector is well aware of this need to train people with learning disabilities to use their leisure time. In both Greystones and Wentwood the staffing and training emphasis is on the effective use of leisure time and community leisure facilities. These areas are programmed and recorded with meticulous documentation with a constant check on resident participation. Neither use segregated facilities for people with learning disabilities but ensure the residents have either staff or each other's company if they wish for companionship on a leisure outing.

The Andover project is a much longer running relocation project which has been extensively documented. It evolved from the Wessex experiment, a DHSS funded research and development project initiated in the 1960's. The lessons learned from this work indicated that community residential care in small houses was a realistic option for people with severe learning disabilities. Of particular interest is the Andover staffed community house opened in 1981 for eight residents, who were relocated from hospital and other sources. The evaluation of the first three years by Felce (1989) and Felce and Toogood (1988) looks at the policies behind this staffed housing development for adults with severe or profound learning disabilities, the lives of the residents, their families and careworkers. It also stresses the need for a variety of written operational policies and programmes to ensure that residents are kept as fully occupied as possible, both in the house and outside in their leisure time. Staff take infinite pains to ensure that residents have 'a high level of involvement in day-to-day activity' and provide 'each person living in the home with access to at least one activity at any time of the waking day'.

Yet, in the final evaluation of this successful and impeccable project, some of the same sad conclusions emerge.

> However, friendships outside family or staff remain limited and people's contact with the general public is almost entirely at a casual acquaintance level; a few fleeting interactions while shopping or the like. Staff have made efforts to encourage friendships but they are hard to achieve, certainly with that essential element of reciprocity of interest, power, and value which characterises true friendship. Achievement is not entirely absent but it is an area of limited success which may be more closely related to the nature of the service than to the staff's efforts within it. It is still a segregated service which provides for a relatively large group of people, spanning a considerable range of personal characteristics, competencies and aptitudes. These factors may constitute considerable barriers which limit the opportunity for the flower-

ing of close personal relationships; ones which add to the barriers
inherent in the real functional handicap of the people being served.
(Felce and Toogood 1988, p.189)

By this stage the reader may well begin to wonder whether the concept
of *community versus institution* could be a red herring. For the vast
majority of people with severe or profound learning disabilities, should
we instead be looking at the erstwhile *custodial institution* versus the
relocated *community institution*? There is clear evidence from the two
projects quoted that even small community houses, with their local
authority administration and staff shift system, function like small institutions. The North West Thames RHA register indicates that less than
3 per cent of people with severe or profound learning disabilities are
living in their own homes and so could be regarded as having been
discharged from custodial care. It is a mute point as to whether this
figure is arrived at by virtue of suitable people, or suitable accommodation, being available. Whichever, there is no reason to think this small
percentage of people able to function independently cannot be extrapolated to the country as a whole.

Examination of the independent sector indicates that exceptional
results are possible within an institutional framework. There is equally
clear evidence that in the public sector, given unsympathetic administration, the community group home merely becomes a breeding ground
for *micro-institutionalisation*.

When a more careful look is taken at the development of normalisation theories it is possible to see many ambiguities arising from them.
As Mesibov (1990) points out, most people seek out and spend time with
friends of similar interests. This enhances their self esteem because it
'implies we are desirable by suggesting we enjoy spending time with
similar others'. Misguided applications of normalisation theories dis-
courage people with severe or profound learning disabilities from similar pursuits with each other and encourage them to move into
community settings alongside their non-disabled peers. Advocates of
normalisation continuously emphasise that such 'peers are more desirable than themselves'. Almost certainly these desirable others do not
share the interests or limited skill levels of their neighbours with severe
or profound learning disabilities. Mesibov suggests that although, as yet,
these effects have not been fully explored, they almost certainly are
detrimental to the self-concepts of such people. Wolfensberger (1991),
the progenitor of such theories, now suggests that 'The kind of habilita-
tion and program-supported community living that some of us had
envisaged in the early days of the reform movement has been grossly
perverted and sabotaged'. Chapter 1 indicated some of the attitude

problems neighbours experienced when faced with community integration.

Several chapters indicate that it is not uncommon for relocated residents to refer with some nostalgia, to the busy social life they led in hospital. They often become sad when remembering the friends and staff they are no longer in contact with. As long ago as 1985 the Social Service Committee of the House of Commons (1985) grasped one of the ambiguities of their community care policy when looking at hospital closures. 'Discharge of patients to a "parish of origin"…is crude enough. When it leads to the separation of lifelong friendships and the fracture of local attachments, it really is inhumane'. There is no reason to believe that this same sentiment cannot be extrapolated to the wider community relocation of residents from group homes. The story of Mary in Chapter 7, who is 'in the community now', and feels segregated from her erstwhile group home friends, can be seen repeated in many parts of the country.

One of the most surprising facts to emerge during the investigation was ability of even the most disabled resident in the group homes to be aware of all the complexities of the staff duty rota. Sister X confirmed that during her 12 years on the wards of a large mental subnormality hospital, she too noticed a similar facility by even 'low grade' patients who in many cases showed little training ability or awareness of hospital life. The author established that many residents, who were unable to remember even one part of a three-part command, could recite the staff rota. They were also well aware of any changes due to the staff's family circumstances etc. A common thread running through relocated residents' memories of hospital life, was how good the staff were to them. When recalling their progress through the wards over the years they nearly always talked about significant members of staff and how good they were to them. Many of these memories went back well over ten or even twenty years.

The position was similar in the ten group homes, where staff often found it necessary to explain changes in the rota to the residents to account for their unexpected absences. There was no doubt that for the vast number of relocated residents their only 'significant others' were members of staff. These people had replaced their lost parents and siblings. This was especially true in the cases of individual community relocation where very often the only people to visit the 'movers' were their individual key workers.

Both Mrs F at the Ashes and Sister X at Greystones realised the importance of the staff as the only significant others many residents would ever have. Sister X went one step further. By drawing her staff from her own family members she created a large, well-contented, extended family. Although first names were used, Grandpa was related to by everybody as a father figure and residents also felt they had a stake in the next generation as the grandchildren grew up round them. Relationships between the residents flourished, they worked and played, struggled with a variety of household and structural problems, saved money for holidays and other luxuries just like the rest of us. In fact, they live an ordinary life. Somehow they seem to have achieved the blueprint by default!

Finally, the author would like to draw the reader's attention to your own particular personal circumstances. You belong to a generic group of responsible autonomous adults functioning in your own tiny microcosm surrounded by a variety of significant others. You will almost certainly have close family ties (which you may or may not choose to reject) parents, partners, siblings, children, colleagues and friends. You live in homes surrounded by neighbours of like abilities. No doubt you derive much satisfaction from the many and varied work and leisure interactions within this microcosm. It is possible that you would feel unhappy to be transplanted to a strange environment without this satisfactory network of significant others. It is probable you would feel somewhat alienated if, within this new environment, your mobility and communication skills were reduced.

Do we not want the same for all adults as we want for ourselves?

References

Alaszewski, A. and Ong, B.N.(1990) *Normalisation in Practice.* London: Routledge.

Audit Commission, (1989) *Developing Community Care for Adults with a Mental Handicap.* London: HMSO.

Booth, T., Simons, K. and Booth, W.(1990) *Outward Bound: relocation and community care for people with learning difficulties?* Buckingham: Open University Press.

Brechin, A. and Swain, J. (1988) 'Creating a "Working Alliance" with People with Learning Difficulties' in Brechin, A. and Walmsley, J. (eds) *Making Connections.* London: Hodder and Stoughton.

Brewer, G. O. and Kakilac, J. (1979) *Disabled Children.* New York: McGraw Hill.

British Psychological Society (1991) *A Search for Definitions.* Leicester: BPS.

Chamberlain, P. (1988) 'Moving into Ordinary Houses Supported by Staff – Key Factors for Success' in Horobin, G. and May, D. (eds) *Living With Mental Handicap.* London: Jessica Kingsley Publishers.

Clarke, A. D. B and Clarke, A. M. (1987) 'Research on Mental Handicap, 1957–87: a selective review'. *Journal of Mental Deficiency Research,* 31, 317–328.

Conroy, J. and Bradley, B. (1985) *Pennhurst Longtitudinal Study: A Report of Five Years of Research and Analysis.* Philadelphia: Temple University Developmental Disabilities Centre. Boston Human Services Research Institute.

DHSS (1971) *Better Services for the Mentally Handicapped.* Cmnd 4683, London, HMSO.

DHSS (1976) *Priorities for Health and Social Services in England: A Consultative Document.* London: HMSO.

DHSS (1980) *Mental Handicap: Progress, Problems and Priorities.* London: HMSO.

DHSS (1981a) *Report of a Study on Community Care.* London: Department of Health and Social Security.

DHSS (1981b) *Care in the Community: A Consultative Document of Moving Resources for Care in England.* London: Department of Health and Social Security.

DHSS (1983) *Health Services Development: Care in the Community and Joint Finance.* HC(83)S/LAC(83)S. London: Department of Health and Social Security.

DHSS (1984) *Health Service Management: Implementation of NHS Management Inquiry Report.* HC/34/1 London: Department of Health and Social Security.

DHSS (1984) *Helping Mentally Handicapped People with Special Problems.* London: HMSO.

DHSS (1987) *Homes and Hostels for Mentally Ill and Mentally Handicapped People at 31 March 1986.* (England),A/F86/11. London: Government Statistical Service.

Education (Disabled Children) Act 1970. London: HMSO.

Education Act 1944. London: HMSO.

Education Act 1970. London: HMSO.

Education Act 1981. London: HMSO.

Felce, D. (1989) *The Andover Project: Staffed housing for adults with severe or profound mental handicaps.* Kidderminster: BIMH Publications.

Felce, D. and Toogood, S. (1988) *Close to Home.* Kidderminster: BIMH Publications.

Garvey, K. and Kroese, B. S. (1991) Social Participation and Friendships of People with Learning Difficulties: A Review. *British Journal of Mental Subnormality, 37*, 2. 17–24.

Gunzburg, A. L. (1982) 'The Essential Environment' in Wynne Jones, A. (ed) *Residential Care for Mentally Handicapped People.* Taunton: SW MENCAP.

Gunzburg, H. C. (1968) *Social Competence and Mental Handicap.* London: Balliere, Tindall & Cassell.

Gunzburg, H. C. (1977) *P-A-C: Progress Assessment Chart of social and personal development. Manual (5th) edition.* Obtainable from MENCAP, London.

Gunzburg, H. C. (1990) Editorial. *British Journal of Mental Subnormality, 36*, 70, 1–3.

Gunzburg, H. C. and Gunzburg, A. L. (1987) *LOCO: Learning Opportunities Co-ordination. A Scale for Assessing Co-ordinated Learning Opportunities in Living Units for People with a Disability.* Obtainable from MENCAP, London.

Harre, R. and Lamb, R. (1983) *The Encycleapadic Dictionary of Psychology.* Oxford: Blackwell.

Health Services and Public Health Act 1968. London: HMSO.

Heber, R. (1959) A manual on terminology and classification in mental retardation. Monograph. *American Journal of Mental Deficiency,* 64.

House of Commons (1985) Second Report form the Social Services Committee, Session 1984–5. *Community Care with Special Reference to Adult Mentally and Mentally Handicapped People,* Vol 1. London: HMSO.

Independent Development Council (1984) *Next Steps.* London: IDC.

Itard, J. M. G. (1798) *The wild boy of Aveyron.* Trans by G. and M. Humphrey (1932) New York: The Century Co.

Jay Report. (1979) *Report of the Committee of Inquiry into Mental Handicap, Nursing and Care.* Cmnd 7468, London: HMSO.

Johnson, M. (1985) 'Social Policy and Service Development' in Craft, C. Bicknell J. and Hollins, S. (eds) *A Multi-Disciplinary Approach to Mental Handicap.* London: Bailliere Tindall.

King's Fund Centre (1980) *An Ordinary Life: Comprehensive Locally-based Residential Services for Mentally Handicapped People.* London: King's Fund Centre.

Lee, G. (1969) 'The Ely Scandal' *Parents Voice.* London: NSMHC.

Lewis, E. O. (1929) *Report on an investigation into the incidence of mental defect in six areas, 1925–27.* Report of the Mental Deficiency Committee, Part IV. London: HMSO.

McConkey, R. (1987) *Who Cares: Community Involvement with Disabled People.* London: Souvenir Press.

Mental Deficiency Act 1913. London: HMSO.

Mental Health (Amendment) Act 1982. London: HMSO.

Mental Health Act 1959. London: HMSO.

Mental Health Act 1983. London: HMSO.

Mesibov, G. B. (1990) 'Normalisation and its relevance today'. *Journal of Autism and Developmental Disorders, 20*, 3, 379–390.

National Health Service Act 1948. London: HMSO.

National Health Service Act 1977. London: HMSO.

National Health Service and Community Care Act 1990. London: HMSO.

NDG (1978) *Helping Mentally Handicapped People in Hospital.* London: National Development Group for Persons with Learning Disabilities.

Penrose, L. S. (1972) *The Biology of Mental Defect.* London: Sidwick and Jackson.

Perrin, B. and Nirje, B. (1989) 'Setting the record straight: a critique of some frequent misconceptions of the normalisation principle' in Brechin, A. and Walmsley J. (eds) *Making Connections: Reflecting on the Lives and Experiences of People with Learning Difficulties.* London: Hodder and Stoughton.

Renshaw, J., Hampson, R., Thomason, C., Darton, R., Judge, K. and Knapp, M. (1988) *Care in the Community: The First Steps.* University of Kent: PSSRU.

Report of the Mental Deficiency Committee (Wood Report) (1929) Parts I–IV. London: HMSO.

Report of the Royal Commission on the Care and Control of the Feeble-minded (1908) Vols I–VIII. London: HMSO.

Report of the Royal Commission on the Law Relating to Mental Illness and Mental Deficiency, 1954–57 (1957). London: HMSO.

Robinson, T. (1988) 'Normalisation: The Whole Answer?' in Brechin, A. and Walmsley, J. (eds) *Making Connections.* London: Hodder and Stoughton.

Rose-Ackerman, S. (1982) 'Mental retardation and society: the ethics and politics of normalisation' *Ethics.* 93, 81–101.

Roth, P. (1972) Village communities in Britain. *Cresset,* 18 (3) 41–5.

Seltzer, M. (1984) 'Correlates of community opposition to community residences for mentally retarded persons'. *American Journal of Mental Deficiency,* 89, 1–8.

Shearer, A. (1986) '*Building Community With People With Mental Handicaps. Their Families and Friends'.* Campaign for People with Mental Handicaps and the King Edward's Hospital Fund.

Sinson, J. (1973) Assessment and social education of SSN children in a pre-school unit. *British Journal of Subnormality,* 17.

Sinson, J. (1975) Downs Infants: an interdisciplinary approach involving parents. *International Journal of Rehabiliation Research.* 1, 59–69.

Sinson, J. (1985) *Attitudes to Downs Syndrome.* London: Mental Health Foundation.

Sinson, J. (1985) *Integrating Young Downs Children.* Videotape.

Sinson, J. (1986) *Integrating Young Downs Children in England, France and Italy.* Videotape.

Sinson, J. (1988) 'The behaviour of Downs, Chinese and non-handicapped children during a first encounter'. *British Journal of Mental Subnormality,* 34, Part 2, 67, 97–104.

Sinson, J. C. (1990) Micro-instutionalisation? Environmental and managerial influences in ten living units for people with mental handicap. *The British Journal of Mental Subnormality,* 36, part 2, no 71, 77–86.

Sinson, J. (1992) 'A Sixth Form College for Mentally Handicapped Adolescents: Wentwood Education' in Gunzburg, H. C. (ed) 'Despite Mental Handicap'. Monograph. *British Journal of Mental Subnormality.*

Sinson, J. C. and Stainton, C. L. S. (1990) An investigation into attitudes (and attitude change) towards mental handicap. *British Journal of Mental Subnormality,* 36, Part I, 70, 53–64.

Sinson, J. and Wetherick, N. E. (1981a) 'The behaviour of children with Down's syndrome in normal playgroups'. *Journal of Mental Deficiency Research,* 25, 113–20.

Sinson, J. and Wetherick, N. E. (1980) *Katy Goes to Playschool.* Videotape.

Sinson, J. and Wetherick, N. E. (1981b) *What Katy (and Anna, Rachel, David etc.) Did Next.* Videotape.

Sinson, J. and Wetherick, N. E. (1982) 'Mutual gaze in pre-school Down and normal children'. *Journal of Mental Deficiency Research,* 26, 123–29.

Sinson, J. and Wetherick, N. E. (1986) Integrating Young Down's Children. Gaze, Play and Vocalisation in the Initial Encounter. *British Journal of Mental Subnormality,* 32, 63, 93–101.

Stockdale, J. E. and Farr, R. M. (1987) *Social Representation of Handicap in Poster Campaign.* Paper presented at the London Conference of the British Psychological Society.

Wagner, G. (1988) *Residential Care: A Positive Choice. and Residential Care: The Research Reviewed.* London: HMSO.

Warnock, M. (1978) *Special Educational Needs. Report of the Warnock Committee of Inquiry into the Education of Handicapped Children and Young People.* Cmnd. 7212. London: HMSO.

Williams, F. (1988) 'Mental Handicap and Oppression in Brechin, A. and Walmsley, J. (eds) *Making Connections.* London: Hodder and Stoughton.

Williams, P. (1986) 'Evaluating services from the comsumers point of view' in Beswick, J., Zadik, Z., and Felce, D. (eds) *Evaluating Quality of Care.* Kidderminster: BIMH Conference Series.

Wolfensberger, W. (1972) *The Principle of Normalisation in Human Services.* Toronto: National Institute on Mental Retardation.

Wolfensberger, W. (1976) 'The Origin and Nature of our Institutional Models' in Kugel, R. and Shearer, N. (Ed.) *Changing Patterns in Residential Services for the Mentally Retarded.* pp.35–82 revised edition. President's Committee on Mental Retardation.

Wolfensberger, W. (1983) Social Role Valorisation: a proposed new term for the principle of normalisation. *Mental Retardation,* 21, 6, 234–9.

Wolfensberger, W. (1991) Reflections on a Lifetime in Human Services and Mental Retardation. *Mental Retardation,* 29, 1, 1–15.

Wolfensberger, W. and Glenn, L. (1973) *PASS: a method of the quantative evaluation of human services.* Toronto: National Institute on Mental Retardation.

Wolfensberger, W. and Tullman, S. (1989) 'A brief outline of the principle of normalisation' in Brechin, A., and Walmsley, J. (eds) *Making Connections:* London: Hodder and Stoughton.

Woodward, M. (1961) 'The Application of Piaget's Theory to the Training of the Subnormal'. *British Journal of Mental Subnormality,* 8, 17–25.

Index